Course   Annual Editions
         Homeland Security, 3/e
         By Thomas J. Badey

http://create.mheducation.com

This McGraw-Hill Create text may include materials submitted to
McGraw-Hill for publication by the instructor of this course.
The instructor is solely responsible for the editorial content of such
materials. Instructors retain copyright of these additional materials.

ISBN-10: 1121670911   ISBN-13: 9781121670914

Contents

Credits

Unit X 161

Preface

On November 25, 2002, 14 months after the attacks on September 11, President Bush signed into law the Homeland Security Act of 2002. In what some have described as the most significant restructuring of the federal government since the National Security Act of 1947, a new Department of Homeland Security (DHS) was created combining 22 federal agencies, over 170,000 employees, and a budget of over $40 billion. With the appointment of Tom Ridge, who championed its creation, as its first Secretary on January 24, 2003, the Department of Homeland Security began the monumental tasks of restructuring major elements of the federal government, while attempting to improve domestic security and prevent another 9/11. A decade later, much of this process has been completed. Yet questions about the effectiveness of the organization remain. As natural disasters and terrorist threats have tested the capabilities of this governmental department, the reviews have been mixed. Those critical of the lack of cooperation between government agencies prior to 9/11 are doubtful that adding another mammoth government bureaucracy has made America safer. Others remain convinced that only massive efforts by the federal government can prepare America for the inevitable biological, chemical, or radiological attacks from rogue states or international terrorist networks dedicated to our destruction. This anthology attempts to highlight the complex challenges and the potential pitfalls of contemporary homeland security policy.

The selections in this *Annual Editions: Homeland Security* were chosen to provide a broad overview and reflect a diversity of viewpoints and perspectives. This anthology is a complete revision of the previous edition. As homeland security continues to evolve, the selection of current articles on the topic of homeland security continues to present a particular challenge. Articles in this introductory reader were chosen from a variety of sources and thus reflect different writing styles. Elements such as the timeliness and readability of the articles were important criteria used in their selection. It is our hope that this broad selection will provide easy access at various levels and will thus stimulate student interest and discussion.

This anthology is divided into several units. The unit **What Is Homeland Security?** addresses the fundamental question: What is homeland security? It highlights not only the evolution of a homeland security strategy but it also provides an overview of the functions and priorities of this ever-changing organization under the leadership of its current secretary Janet Napolitano. In addition, it provides insights into the challenges facing the growing academic and professional discipline that has emerged in its wake. **Threats to Homeland Security** focuses on some of the new threats facing the Department of Homeland Security. From home-grown terrorism to nightmare scenarios, it identifies some of the critical challenges the DHS faces in fulfilling its complex mission. The unit **Vulnerabilities** identifies some of the major weaknesses that exist in many areas of our daily lives. It highlights the diversity and complexity of the challenges that the DHS has to face on a daily basis. **The Federal Government and Homeland Security** examines the role of the federal government in homeland security. Issues such as the operation of fusion centers, federal government spending, and cargo and passenger screening have drawn public criticism and highlight the complexity involved in the efficient and effective implementation of policy. The unit **State and Local Governments and Homeland Security** offers some insight into the complex political problems that affect the implementation of homeland security initiatives at the state and local levels. It seeks to highlight the tension between the real need for security and political gamesmanship. **Emergency Management and Response** is the next unit. While the national debate about homeland security often centers on the role of the federal government, recent disasters continue to underscore the importance of adequate training and preparation for first responders. Specialized training programs and techniques that apply lessons learned from previous disasters and good emergency planning at the local level are keys to an effective disaster response. The unit **New Technologies in Homeland Security** identifies some of the new tools that may improve passenger, cargo, and border security in the future. The intelligence community plays a vital role in protecting the United States from future threats. **Intelligence and Homeland Security** explores some of the problems associated with obtaining accurate and timely intelligence. **Homeland Security and Civil Liberties** examines the potential impact of efforts to improve homeland security on civil liberties. It highlights the effect that efforts to increase security can have on the daily lives of individuals. Finally, the unit **The Future of Homeland Security** identifies some of the challenges the future of homeland security faces, and offers some recommendations on how homeland security can be improved.

Annual Editions: Homeland Security provides a broad overview of the major issues associated with homeland security. It is our hope that this anthology will provide students with an introduction to the issues related to homeland security and serve as a stimulus for further in-depth exploration of this vital topic.

I would like to thank the individuals who have kindly agreed to serve as members of the advisory board for this anthology. I look forward to your comments and suggestions so that we can continue to improve the selections and materials in this anthology. I am also grateful to two of my undergraduate students who volunteered their time to help in the revision of this collection of writings. I would particularly like to thank Mikhaila Calice and Jonathan Harman for their help in sorting through and reviewing the numerous articles that were submitted for consideration. These students provided valuable insights and above all a critical students' perspective, which made my job much easier.

Editor

Thomas J. Badey
Randolph-Macon College

Thomas J. Badey is a professor of political science and the director of the International Studies Program at Randolph-Macon College in Ashland, Virginia. He received a BS in sociology from the University of Maryland (University College) in 1986 and an MA in political science from the University of South Florida in 1987. In 1993, he earned his PhD in political science from the *Institut für Politische Wissenschaft* of the *Ruprecht-Karls Universität* in Heidelberg, Germany. From 1979 to 1988, Dr. Badey served as a security policeman in the United States Air Force and was stationed in the United States, Asia, and the Middle East. Currently he teaches courses on International Terrorism and on Terrorism and Homeland Security and has written a number of articles on the subject. He is also the editor of the McGraw-Hill Contemporary Learning Series *Annual Editions: Violence and Terrorism.*

Academic Advisory Board

Members of the Academic Advisory Board are instrumental in the final selection of articles for *Annual Editions* ExpressBooks. Their review of the articles for content, level, and appropriateness provides critical direction to the editor(s) and staff. We think that you will find their careful consideration reflected in this ExpressBook.

Cynthia Brown
Western Carolina University

Ralph G. Carter
Texas Christian University

Paul B. Davis
Truckee Meadows Community College

Dick De Lung
Wayland Baptist University

David Gray
Fayetteville State University

Michael A. Langer
Loyola University–Chicago

Charles Loftus
Arizona State University

Robert J. Louden
John Jay College–CUNY

Ruben Martinez
University of Texas–San Antonio Downtown

David McEntire
University of North Texas

Randall K. Nichols
Utica College

William H. Parrish
Virginia Commonwealth University

Richard Pearlstein
Southeastern Oklahoma State University

Gary R. Perlstein
Portland State University

Richard Perlstein
Southeastern Oklahoma State University

Peter Phipps
Dutchess Community College

Chester L. Quarles
University of Mississippi

Marco Rimanelli
Saint Leo College

William L. Waugh
Georgia State University

Jason Weber
Rasmussen College, Bloomington

Leonard Weinberg
University of Nevada, Reno

Darren Wheeler
Ball State University

Prepared by: Thomas J. Badey, *Randolph-Macon College*

Correlation Guide

The *Annual Editions* series provides students with convenient, inexpensive access to current, carefully selected articles from the public press. **Annual Editions: Homeland Security, 3/e** is an easy-to-use reader that presents articles on important topics such as *areas of vulnerabilities, civil liberties, the future of homeland security,* and many more. For more information on other McGraw-Hill Create™ titles and collections, visit www. mcgrawhillcreate.com.

This convenient guide matches the units in **Annual Editions: Homeland Security, 3/e** with the corresponding chapters in one of our best-selling McGraw-Hill Homeland Security textbooks by Forest et al.

Annual Editions: Homeland Security, 3/e	**Homeland Security and Terrorism: Readings and Interpretations, 2/e by Forest et al.**
Unit: What is Homeland Security?	**Section 1.1:** Defining Homeland Security
Unit: Threats to Homeland Security	**Section 1.2:** Defining the Threat
Unit: Vulnerabilities	**Section 1.3:** Specific Areas of Vulnerability
Unit: The Federal Government and Homeland Security	**Section 2.1:** National Response
Unit: State and Local Governments and Homeland Security	**Section 2.2:** State and Local Response
Unit: Emergency Management and Response	**Section 2.2:** State and Local Response **Section 2.3:** Fostering Resiliency
Unit: New Technologies in Homeland Security	**Section 1.3:** Specific Areas of Vulnerability **Section 2.2:** State and Local Response **Section 2.3:** Fostering Resiliency
Unit: Intelligence and Homeland Security	**Section 2.2:** State and Local Response **Section 3.1:** Legal and Ethical Controversies in Securing the Homeland **Section 3.2:** Competing Perspectives on the USA PATRIOT Act
Unit: Homeland Security and Civil Liberties	**Section 3.2:** Competing Perspectives on the USA PATRIOT Act
Unit: The Future of Homeland Security	**Section 3.1:** Legal and Ethical Controversies in Securing the Homeland **Unit 4:** Alternatives to Explore

Prepared by: Thomas J. Badey, *Randolph-Macon College*

Topic Guide

Unit I

UNIT

Prepared by: Thomas J. Badey, *Randolph-Macon College*

What Is Homeland Security?

The events of September 11, 2001, have left deep scars on the American psyche. It is almost inconceivable that the actions of so few could change the lives of so many. Fourteen months after 9/11, on November 25, 2002, President George Bush signed into law the Homeland Security Act of 2002. In the most comprehensive reorganization of the nation's security apparatus since the passage of the National Security Act of 1947, a new Department of Homeland Security (DHS) was created. The change encompassed 22 existing federal agencies and impacted over 170,000 employees. In its efforts to consolidate the nation's response capabilities to disasters and emergencies, natural or human-made, the Bush Administration created a new super-bureaucracy eclipsed only by the existing Department of Defense.

As the primary legislative response to the attacks on September 11, the DHS is in the unenviable position of having to be everything to everyone. At first glance, the mission of the DHS appears simple—to make Americans safer. Accomplishing this mission, however, has been difficult. The department's slow response to natural disasters, continuing gaps in airport security, the lack of effective border security, and the never-ending burden-sharing battles with states and localities have led to public criticism. These problems have cast doubt on the ability of the DHS to complete its assigned mission.

The long-term success of the DHS, however, depends as much on its own ability to meet the complex challenges of the twenty-first century security environment as on the actions of others. The DHS is heavily dependent on the support from the president, Congress, the intelligence community, and local law-enforcement agencies.

In 2002, President Bush championed the creation of the DHS and was one of the strongest supporters of the new agency. When President Obama inherited the agency in 2009, it was already well established. Despite U.S. involvement in Iraq and Afghanistan and increasingly strained resources, the department has survived the inevitable interagency budget rivalries and has continued to grow. As political leadership changes and as national priorities shift, continued executive support is critical for the long-term success of the DHS.

Congressional support is equally important. Although the Department of Homeland Security was built on promises that it would cost no more than the operation of the already existing agencies, the reality is that even beyond so-called "transitional costs" the DHS has required significant increases in funding and its budget continues to grow. A record national debt, increasing deficits, escalating defense costs, and an uncertain economic future will continue to test congressional resolve in funding this department.

Partly to allay the fears of the intelligence community that portions of its $50 billion budget could be usurped by the creation of a new department, the DHS was left with limited intelligence collection and analytical capability. Thus, the DHS remains heavily dependent on the analytical capabilities and the resources of an intelligence community known for its reluctance to share information with others. Although directors of the CIA and the FBI have pledged their support for the DHS, it remains to be seen how bureaucratic hurdles, interagency rivalries, and future turf wars may affect this commitment in the future.

The Department of Homeland Security is also dependent on the cooperation of first responders and local law-enforcement agencies. Many agree that local law-enforcement agencies may be the key to the success of DHS, but beyond promises of additional federal funds and some joint disaster exercises, there has been only a limited effort to actively incorporate these agencies into the day-to-day activities of the DHS. Amidst rising criticism from state and local government officials of inadequate or inequitable distribution of federal counter-terrorism funds, the DHS continues to face an uphill battle as it tries to pacify the economic concerns of local law-enforcement agencies and first responders, while eliciting their cooperation and support for national security priorities and policies.

As the Department of Homeland Security continues to negotiate its role in national security, the debate about what exactly that role should be continues. The articles in this unit focus on the question: What Is Homeland Security? They explore the strategic goals, institutional structures, and budget priorities of the DHS. The readings also examine the role that the evolving academic discipline of homeland security may play in the continued evolution of homeland security.

Article

Prepared by: Thomas J. Badey, *Randolph-Macon College*

Homeland Security: Advancing the National Strategic Position

Sharon Caudle

Learning Outcomes

After reading this article, you will be able to:

- Identify four policy concerns which should be considered in advancing the U.S. National Preparedness Strategy.

- Explain the purpose of National Strategy for Homeland Security issued in July of 2002.

- Describe the goals of Presidential Policy Directive 8.

Introduction

In March 2011, President Obama issued *Presidential Policy Directive 8: National Preparedness*. Its issuance and resulting implementation documents affirmed existing policy crafted under President George W. Bush, but the directive began a new chapter in the intent and scope of preparedness. Preparedness goals, risk assessment, tools, programs, and results expected from them experienced, to a greater or lesser extent, major refinements. To better understand the current policy, this article first chronicles the decade of refinement in the definition of national preparedness, its doctrines, and guidance from early framing under President Bush to the modifications made under President Obama.

Building on this history, the article describes a number of emerging policy themes and identifies policy concerns for federal policymakers to consider as the national preparedness strategic direction continues to advance. These concerns are (1) the operational approach to meeting a national preparedness goal; (2) implementation of capabilities by the "whole community"—from the federal government to individual citizens—to address the "maximum of maximums" threats; (3) the inclusion of slowly emerging threats as priorities for action in near-term preparedness strategies; and (4) federal control over other governmental levels in the national interest. At bottom, these policy concerns have a common root: whether the resources spent on the readiness efforts were worthwhile. Going forward, more realistic assessment of threats and preparedness capabilities and the identification of a proper balance

of responsibility sharing seem in order. In addition, appropriate measurement approaches may well be found in management system standards already in existence.

President Bush and the Formative Years

After the September 2001 terrorist attacks, the federal government raised terrorism as the primary domestic threat. Major policy developments, the creation of a new domestic security department, and the issuance of a specific national homeland security strategy reflected the criticality of the threat. In June 2002, President Bush released *Securing the Homeland: Strengthening the Nation*.[1] The president called the terrorist threat a permanent national condition and homeland security a new national calling. The document previewed the first homeland security national strategy, intended to be the national blueprint for confronting terrorism and that called for the federal government to partner with other levels of government, the private sector, and citizens. In another document, the president presented the organizational structure at the federal level considered best suited to meet the terrorism threat: the Department of Homeland Security (DHS).[2] The Homeland Security Act of 2002 (P.L. 107–296) subsequently authorized the new department.

In July 2002, the Office of Homeland Security issued the first *National Strategy for Homeland Security*.[3] The *Strategy* defined homeland security as "a concerted national effort to prevent terrorist attacks within the United States, reduce America's vulnerability to terrorism, and minimize the damage and recover from attacks that do occur."[4] Terrorism prevention, vulnerability reduction, and minimizing damage and recovery were set as homeland security's strategic objectives. This initial definition of preparedness carried over during the subsequent decade. Prevention meant action at home and abroad to deter, prevent, and eliminate terrorism. Reducing vulnerability meant identifying and protecting critical infrastructure and key assets, and detecting terrorist threats and augmenting defenses, while balancing the benefits of mitigating risk against economic costs and infringements on individual liberty. Response and recovery focused on managing the consequences of attacks and building and maintaining the financial, legal, and social systems to recover.

The Overarching Goal and Policy and Operational System

Starting in early 2003, the Bush Administration began issuing a number of directives and guidance, thereby accelerating the formation of a national preparedness goal and supporting policy and operational system. In February 2003, the president issued *Homeland Security Presidential Directive 5* requiring a National Incident Management System (NIMS) and a National Response Plan.[5] The Homeland Security Act of 2002 also required the consolidation of existing federal government emergency response plans into a single national response plan. DHS issued the *National Response Plan* in December 2004,[6] which was subsequently replaced by the *National Response Framework* in January 2008.[7]

President Bush's December 2003 issuance of *Homeland Security Presidential Directive 8* (HSPD-8) emerged as the major policy development for national preparedness.[8] HSPD-8 crafted homeland security's strategic position as national preparedness for all major events—terrorism, major disasters, and other domestic emergencies. It defined preparedness in terms of planning, operations, and equipment at all levels of government to prevent, respond to, and recover from major events. The directive mandated a national domestic all-hazards preparedness goal, established mechanisms to advance federal delivery of preparedness assistance to other governments, and described actions to further improve federal, state, and local entity preparedness.

The national preparedness goal was the critical policy requirement in HSPD-8. The goal was to establish measurable readiness priorities and targets, with the caveat that they balance the potential threat and emergency events with resources. Readiness metrics, standards, and a system to assess the nation's overall preparedness to respond to major events emphasized actual results. There was an emphasis on assessing response in comparison to the objectives of prevention and recovery. The fiscal year 2005 DHS appropriations legislation (P.L. 108-234) established a statutory requirement for implementing HSPD-8. The legislation called for nationally accepted first responder preparedness levels by January 31, 2005, state and local adoption of national preparedness standards in fiscal year 2005 as part of federal grant guidance guidelines, and issuance of national preparedness goal final guidance by March 31, 2005.

DHS met the March 2005 deadline with the *Interim National Preparedness Goal.*[9] DHS stated the *Interim Goal* enabled the nation to answer: "How prepared do we need to be?" "How prepared are we?" and "How do we prioritize efforts to close the gap?" The *Interim Goal* identified fifteen national planning scenarios and a target capabilities list (to accomplish necessary preparedness tasks in a universal task list) as two planning tools. The scenarios, issued earlier in 2004 by the Homeland Security Council, described plausible terrorist attacks and natural disasters intended to stretch the nation's prevention and response capabilities for events such as a nuclear detonation, pandemics, chemical and biological attacks, a major hurricane or earthquake, and a cyber attack. Collectively, the scenarios identified a complete array of preparedness needs.[10]

The target capabilities list identified what was necessary to carry out critical operations and tasks in response to a major disaster or catastrophe based on the combined planning scenarios. It was derived from a universal task list intended to respond to the planning scenario events. For example, an incident management task included the coordination of transportation operations. The *Interim Goal* stated that such a capability was to provide the means to accomplish one or more tasks under specific conditions and to specific performance standards. It also reflected national preparedness as a continuous cycle of activity to develop the necessary elements, such as plans, policies, and equipment, vital to maximize capabilities. The target capabilities list set forth a set of essential capabilities, stated as necessary in whole or in part by various levels of government to carry out certain tasks to prevent, protect against, respond to, and recover from terrorist attacks and major disasters. Further, the *Interim Goal* included a number of national priorities, such as implementing NIMS and the *National Response Plan.*

The *Interim Goal* results were intended to be national, not purely federal products, but clearly governmental. However, efforts would be needed by all levels of government and between government and private-sector and nongovernmental organizations to identify threats, determine vulnerabilities, and identify required resources, all part of capabilities-based planning and operations.

Implementing the Preparedness Goal and Further Goal Updates

With the issuance of the *Interim Goal,* implementing guidance took center stage, expected to solidify the use of capabilities-based planning and related tools. Initial guidance was included in fiscal year 2005 homeland security grant program guidance.[11] In April 2005, the DHS issued the *National Preparedness Guidance.*[12] This document provided a more detailed explanation of the content and use of capabilities-based planning that was to support achievement of the interim goal, including the national planning scenarios, the universal task list, and the target capabilities list. It also expanded on the national priorities, standards and strategies for preparedness assessments of capabilities, and included a timeline for HSPD-8 implementation. Hurricane Katrina exposed a number of preparedness gaps, so Subtitle C of the Post-Katrina Emergency Reform Act of 2006 (P.L. 109-295) continued the call for immediate implementation of the HSPD-8 requirements, adding to the institutionalization of capabilities development because of legislative mandates.

Fiscal year 2006 appropriations legislation (P.L. 109-90) called for DHS to issue a final national preparedness goal by the end of December 2005. That month, DHS issued a new draft of the *National Preparedness Goal.*[13] This draft *Goal* presented the achievement of capabilities as the central feature in the road from prevention to recovery from domestic incidents. The draft expanded attention on minimizing the impact of major events such as was experienced during the major hurricanes of 2005. The DHS defined the goal as "to achieve and sustain risk-based target levels of capability to prevent, protect against, respond to, and recover from major events, and to minimize their impact on lives, property, and the economy, through systematic and prioritized efforts by federal, state, local and tribal entities, their private and non-governmental partners, and the general public."[14] As was the case with the use of target levels of capability in the definition of the goal, the definition of preparedness was stated as "the range of deliberate, critical tasks and activities necessary to build, sustain, and improve the operational capability to prevent, protect against, respond to, and recover from domestic incidents."[15] The draft called again for the collective efforts at all levels of government and between government and private sector and nongovernmental organizations in a collective effort.

The December 2005 draft *Goal* further delved into the specifics of preparedness. Operationally, for example, it meant establishing guidelines, protocols, and standards for planning, training and exercises, personnel qualification and certification, equipment certification, and publication management. The draft *Goal* reiterated previous policy and guidance that the target capabilities list would be the primary source of readiness metrics. Standards to assess national preparedness collectively would be found in the goal and the capabilities-based planning tools, such as the national planning scenarios and the target capabilities list.

In September 2007, DHS updated the national preparedness goal and its guidance in the *National Preparedness Guidelines*.[16] The *Guidelines* contained four critical elements. One was the national preparedness vision, which the *Guidelines* called a concise statement of the nation's core preparedness goal for the nation: "a nation prepared with coordinated capabilities to prevent, protect against, respond to, and recover from all hazards in a way that balances risk with resources and need."[17] Other elements were the national planning scenarios; the universal task list of some 1,600 unique tasks to prevent, protect against, respond to, and recover from the major events represented by the national planning scenarios; and the target capabilities list containing thirty-seven specific capabilities that communities, the private sector, and the levels of government should collectively have for effective disaster response.

The DHS stated that the publication of the *Guidelines* actually finalized the national goal and its related preparedness tools. The new *Guidelines* retained a capabilities-based approach to organize and synchronize national efforts in and investments for prevention, protection, response and recovery. The *Guidelines* also incorporated lessons learned from Hurricane Katrina and a 2006 review of states' and major cities' emergency operations and evacuation plans. Readiness metrics remained a feature of the national goal, although specific metrics and standards remained under development.

A New National Strategy for Homeland Security

In October 2007, the Homeland Security Council issued a new *National Strategy for Homeland Security*.[18] While the first strategy identified terrorism as the central threat, the 2007 Strategy reflected better understanding of terrorist threats and additional risks, what it called the full range of potential catastrophic events, including natural disasters, infectious diseases, and man-made accidents. While the *Strategy* said that effective preparation for catastrophic natural disasters and man-made disasters was not homeland security per se,[19] such preparation could increase homeland security.

Consistent with earlier policy documents, the *Strategy* presented the bedrock principle of a culture of preparedness and partnership that would share responsibility for homeland security across the entire nation—local, tribal, state, and federal governments, faith-based and community organizations, and businesses. Further, its four objectives remained consistent with earlier policies: (1) prevent and disrupt terrorist attacks; (2) protect the American people, critical infrastructure, and key resources; (3) respond to and recover from incidents that do occur; and (4) continue to strengthen the foundation to ensure long-term success. The fourth objective was targeted directly at homeland security management. The *Strategy* consistently stated the importance of capabilities to anticipate and handle incidents and the need to create and institutionalize a comprehensive homeland security management system incorporating all stakeholders.

The new *Strategy* directly discussed the establishment and institutionalization of a comprehensive Homeland Security Management System that would build on the planning and operations detailed in the National Preparedness Guidelines. The System was to have activity in the four phases of (1) guidance (presidential directives and other key policies); (2) planning (family of strategic, operational and tactical plans); (3) execution of operational and tactical level plans; and (4) assessment and evaluation of both operations and exercises.

In sum, under President Bush, combating terrorism within the United States was seen as a truly national, not a federal, responsibility, although the federal government assumed control of policy and strategy development, buttressed with federal grants to states and localities. In line with a managing for results philosophy, homeland security was to have specific goals, performance targets, and performance measures. The emergency management structure would continue its traditional role of anticipating the aftermath of any attack or emergency.

President Obama and Strategic Adjustments

The change of administrations after the 2008 national election marked a confirmation of but continued refinements in national homeland security policies and strategies. Shortly after taking office, President Obama initiated a study to examine the organization of the White House to deal with homeland security and counterterrorism. He stated "Homeland Security is indistinguishable from National Security—conceptually and functionally, they should be thought of together rather than separately."[20] The result was a new national security staff no longer divided between national security and homeland security.[21] In February 2010, DHS released the legislatively required *Quadrennial*

Homeland Security Review Report.[22] As was the case with earlier policies, the *Report* called for a national framework of collective efforts and shared responsibilities to build and sustain critical homeland security capabilities. The grave security environment (beyond terrorism) identified in the *Report* clearly supported a broader security stance: it was expected that violent extremist groups would use terrorism to attack United States targets, social and/or political instability would continue, health threats would be more difficult to prevent, technological developments and cyber threats would pose threats, climate change would increase weather-related hazards, multiple simultaneous crises were likely, and complacency would be a danger as major crises receded from memory.

President Obama released a new *National Security Strategy* that reflected the homeland security policies and concepts identified in the *Quadrennial Review Report.*[23] The *Strategy* emphasized that the traditional distinctions between homeland and national security was no longer appropriate. The *Strategy* reaffirmed the "whole of government" approach, which is the need for all levels of government, if not the entire country, to strengthen national preparedness. The *Strategy* retained the earlier policy notions of a homeland security enterprise (federal, state, local, tribal, territorial, nongovernmental, and private-sector entities, as well as individuals, families and communities sharing a common national interest in American safety and security) and a culture of preparedness.

Presidential Policy Directive 8

The 2010 *Quadrennial Review Report* and the newer *National Security Strategy* set the stage for a restatement and revitalization of the presidential direction for national preparedness. President Bush's 2003 HSPD-8, which had been codified by Congress, was replaced by President Obama's March 2011 *Presidential Policy Directive 8 National Preparedness* (PPD-8).[24] The new directive reaffirmed past policies and direction. PPD-8 stressed the need for systematic preparation for the greatest risk, the shared preparedness responsibility from government to the citizen ("all-of-Nation"), and a capabilities-based approach to preparedness. The directive stipulated the development of (1) a national preparedness goal identifying the core capabilities necessary for preparedness and (2) a national preparedness system guiding activities enabling the nation to achieve the goal. National preparedness was defined as actions taken to plan, organize, equip, train, and exercise to build and sustain the capabilities necessary to prevent, protect against, mitigate the effects of, respond to, and recover from the threats posing the greatest risk to the nation's security.

PPD-8 required that a new national preparedness goal address specific threats and vulnerabilities. This overtly reduced reliance on national planning scenarios issued several years earlier as yardsticks to measure preparedness capabilities. The goal was to define the core capabilities necessary to prepare for incidents posing the greatest risk to the nation's security. This made concrete the new policy emphasis on maximum capacity for any major disaster or catastrophe that would emerge in implementation efforts.

The directive also mandated a new piece to the national preparedness system—planning frameworks for each of the five preparedness objectives—from prevention to recovery. It was envisioned that each planning framework would include a basic plan to address all-hazards. There would be roles and responsibilities at the federal level, but annexes would address unique requirements for particular threats or scenarios. The directive also required a "campaign" to build and sustain preparedness. This would integrate community-based, nonprofit, and private sector preparedness programs, research and development activities, and preparedness assistance.

The Implementation of PPD-8

The DHS has issued a flurry of documents in response to PPD-8's mandates. In May 2011, DHS issued the *Implementation Plan for Presidential Policy Directive 8: National Preparedness.*[25] The *Implementation Plan* clarified that PPD-8's reference to "all-of-Nation" was the same as "whole community," or the participation of the private and nonprofit sectors, including nongovernmental organizations, and the general public. The DHS was to perform a strategic, national-level risk assessment applicable to national, regional, and local levels. The assessment would help identify where core capabilities and associated performance objectives for the entire homeland security community should be placed, building the maximum preparedness capacity needed to respond to a catastrophic event.

Thus, the whole community is to develop core capabilities for incidents posing the greatest risk to the nation's security. FEMA (Federal Emergency Management Agency) administrator Craig Fugate described the change as planning for a "meta-scenario" (or "maximum of maximums") disaster. This was a worst-case scenario based on different hazards that challenges preparedness and overwhelms the response capabilities of every governmental level.[26] The scenario, a no-notice event, contemplated the impact area of at least 7 million population and 25,000 square·miles, and involving several states and FEMA regions. It results in 190,000 fatalities in its initial hours, with 265,000 citizens requiring emergency medical attention. There is severe damage to critical infrastructure and key resources, including transportation. The fiscal year 2011 Regional Catastrophic Grant Program guidance used the meta-scenario to promote preparing for a catastrophe where extraordinary levels of mass casualties, damage, and disruption overwhelm traditional and well-established government response and recovery plans and procedures.

In September 2011, DHS issued the *National Preparedness Goal First Edition.*[27] The new *Goal* included detailed tables with core capabilities for prevention through recovery (called mission areas) and their preliminary targets. For example, prevention capabilities included planning, public information and warning, operational coordination, forensics and attribution, intelligence and information sharing, interdiction and disruption, and screening, search, and detection. Each capability was described; to illustrate, interdiction and disruption is to delay, divert, intercept, halt apprehend, or secure threats and/or hazards.

The document made clear that these core capabilities presented an evolution from the voluminous target capabilities list developed in response to HSPD-8. The core capability targets would be the performance thresholds for each core capability and the basis to develop performance measures to evaluate progress in meeting the targets. The description of the core capabilities and their preliminary targets were significantly streamlined from the task and capability lists issued in response to HSPD-8 and subsequently tied to federal homeland security funding. While still prescriptive, it appears the notion was that streamlining should create more room for members of the homeland security community to craft capabilities tailored to local and regional considerations, as well as the national interest.

The *Goal* stated that a strategic national risk assessment should confirm the need for an all-hazards, capability-based approach to preparedness planning. The DHS December 2011 unclassified *Strategic National Risk Assessment* grouped threats and hazards into national-level events to test the nation's preparedness.[28] These included natural, technological/accidental, and adversarial/human caused threat and hazard groups:

Natural	Animal disease outbreak, earthquake, flood, human pandemic outbreak, hurricane, space weather, tsunami, volcanic eruption, wildfire.
Technological or Accidental	Biological food contamination, chemical substance spill or release, dam failure, radiological substance release.
Adversarial or Human-Caused	Aircraft as a weapon, armed assault, biological terrorism attack (non-food), chemical/biological food contamination terrorism attack, chemical terrorism attack (non-food), cyber attack against data, cyber attack against physical infrastructure, explosives terrorism attack, nuclear terrorism attack, radiological terrorism attack.

The *Goal* did not address slowly emerging threats or drivers of threats such as climate change identified in the *Quadrennial Homeland Security Review Report.* This was purposeful. The unclassified *Strategic National Risk Assessment* said it evaluated the risk from known threats and hazards. Those events, it noted, had a distinct beginning and end and were clearly linked to homeland security missions. Thus, political, economic, environmental, and societal trends possibly contributing to a risk environment but not national events for homeland security were excluded from the assessment. Nevertheless, the document said non-national-level threats, such as droughts and heat waves, could pose risks to jurisdictions and should be considered in preparedness planning.

In November 2011, DHS released a brief description of a new *National Preparedness System.*[29] Its components included (1) identifying and assessing risk, (2) estimating capability requirements, (3) building and sustaining capabilities, (4) planning to deliver capabilities, (5) validating capabilities, and (6) reviewing and updating. To identify and assess risk, the *System* document stated that the *Strategic National Risk Assessment* would analyze the greatest risks to the nation. The *Threat*

and Hazard Identification and Risk Assessment guidance under development at that time would provide a common, consistent approach to identify and assess risks and associated impacts.

Measuring progress toward achieving the National Preparedness Goal could be done through tools such as exercises, remedial action management programs, and assessments. The National Exercise Program was deemed the principal mechanism to measure readiness, supplemented by exercises done by individual organizations. Training and performance during actual events would test and validate achievement of desired capabilities. Ongoing sharing of lessons learned and monitoring also would occur through a remedial action management program and a comprehensive assessment system of the whole community. A *National Preparedness Report* was targeted for November 2012.

On March 6, 2012, the Federal Emergency Management Agency (FEMA) released draft national framework documents for comment. The working drafts included the *National Prevention Framework,* the *National Protection Framework,* the *National Mitigation Framework,* and the *National Response Framework.* These documents briefly described factors such as stakeholder roles and responsibilities and coordinating structures to deliver core capabilities. The January 2008 *National Response Framework* will be superseded once the new framework is finalized. Comments on the drafts were due to FEMA no later than April 2, 2012. FEMA had already released the *National Disaster Recovery Framework* in September 2011. This framework replaced the existing National Response Framework's Emergency Support Function #14—Long Term Community Recovery.[30] FEMA also released a draft of the *Recovery Interagency Operational Plan* intended to implement the already published *National Disaster Recovery Framework.* The detailed draft specifically covered items such as the concept of operations for federal recovery support to stakeholders and maintaining readiness.

Concerns in Strategy and Implementation

In sum, national preparedness has been the subject of a significant amount of Presidential and Congressional attention and direction since September 2001. Perhaps lost in the detail is a number of broad policy themes running through the refinement in the national preparedness strategic direction to this point in time. These include:

- Homeland security—previously a domestic focus—is placed within national security. The federal government, particularly the Federal Emergency Management Agency, is established as the lead for national preparedness policy and guidance.

- Preparedness is defined with the full coverage of objectives: prevention, protection, mitigation, response, and recovery, with response and recovery no longer the centerpieces of preparedness.

- The full range of potential catastrophic events, including natural disasters, infectious diseases, and man-made accidents join terrorism as the focus for homeland security. Known threats with a distinct beginning and end are central to homeland security risk management and preparedness. Slowly emerging threats are not an initial emphasis.

- Maximum capacity for a catastrophic event (a meta-scenario) is set as the benchmark for preparedness, replacing a more generic "major disaster" on a local or regional level.

- The whole homeland security community has the responsibility to protect national interests and way of life, anticipating that all levels of government will be initially overwhelmed. Core capabilities and targets for a national effort update past prescriptive, detailed individual tasks and target capabilities.

- A homeland security management system detailed to accomplish homeland security and crafted with planning frameworks, performance expectations, and assessment and adjustment requirements. Measurable readiness priorities and targets to be developed and assessed, primarily through exercises and actual events.

National preparedness policy certainly is not static: refinements will continue as the newer national preparedness directives and operational guidance are implemented and others are issued. There are three concerns that federal policymakers might consider as the national preparedness strategic direction continues to advance. These are (1) the operational approach to meeting a national preparedness goal; (2) implementation of capabilities by the "whole community"—from the federal government to individual citizens—to address the "maximum of maximums" threats; and (3) the inclusion of slowly emerging threats as priorities for action in near-term preparedness strategies.

Alternative to the Current Capabilities Development Approach

The current and earlier national preparedness goals and their implementing documents, as well as federal legislation, have identified the need to build and sustain specific preparedness capabilities for the entire homeland security community. Federal, state, and local governments, nongovernmental organizations, private organizations, and the general public are that community. National preparedness comes from capabilities across this whole community. The DHS in large part adopted the capabilities approach (used by the defense community in many countries) from the Department of Defense.[31] HSPD-8 required a national preparedness goal to define measurable readiness (preparedness) priorities and targets, but also with a caveat about the resource investments. PPD-8 called for actions to achieve a preparedness approach to optimize the use of available resources.

Developing capabilities may have been the optimal route at that time toward achieving preparedness, but whether other alternatives that were better investments were considered was not made explicit—if, in fact, they were even considered. The DHS has provided billions in preparedness grants intended to aid states, urban areas, tribal governments, and nonprofit organizations, supposedly to strengthen their capabilities to meet threats associated with potential terrorist attacks and other hazards. Over time, the department has attempted to link dollars spent with the development of capabilities.[32]

However, whether this approach has been or will be successful is unclear, as assessing preparedness based on national preparedness capabilities remains very elusive. Summing the difficulties, the Government Accountability Office (GAO) found that evaluation efforts that collected data on national preparedness capabilities faced limitations such as data reliability and the lack of standardized data collection.[33] According to GAO, FEMA had problems in completing a comprehensive assessment system and developing national preparedness capability requirements based on established metrics. The GAO continues to cite these operational and implementation weaknesses, even though the assessment of capabilities and evaluation of preparedness is a legislative requirement.[34] Concerns have also surfaced in the defense community regarding measuring capabilities and their results. For example, an article in 2007 described significant ambiguity in the definition of capability and its use.[35] In a similar vein, another report in 2011 stated that no one had been able to adequately create analytical tools to quantify capability to compare effectiveness with "units of capability."[36]

In addition, GAO specifically found problems with at least one tool mentioned by the new *National Preparedness Goal* as central to measuring progress—the National Exercise Program.[37] The FEMA implementation of the national program has run consistently into problems, such as ensuring that federal and state governments addressed deficiencies identified by the exercises. In March 2011, FEMA developed a new *National Exercise Program Base Plan* that extensively revised the program, with major changes in requirements and leadership.[38] The verdict is still out whether the past history of the DHS in failing to adequately measure progress will be reversed.

Thus, still left unanswered is the most significant question: What preparedness did the billions of dollars buy? With federal funding constraints and similar challenges for other levels of government and other members of the homeland security community for the foreseeable future, this is an opportune time to consider if other policy options might be more cost effective or, at a minimum, justify the current policy of capabilities development and sustainability.

The capabilities approach is not etched in stone. There is at least one policy option the federal policymakers might consider to contrast with the capabilities approach. This option is grounded already in Congressional legislation and administration policies. Simply, it is the application of national and/or international management system preparedness standards useful for all organizations. This approach has been advocated in the past.[39]

Two national voluntary programs use management system preparedness standards, not elusive core capabilities, as the benchmark for preparedness requirements. Legislation implementing many of the 9/11 Commission's recommendations (Section 524 of the August 2007 P.L. 110-53) called for DHS to create a voluntary private sector preparedness program with standards, including accreditation and certification processes. In June 2010, DHS produced the Private Sector Preparedness

Accreditation and Certification Program (PS-Prep). Three management system standards were approved for adoption in the program: ASIS SPC.1-2009 *Organizational Resilience: Security Preparedness, and Continuity Management System;* British Standard 25999-2:2007 *Business Continuity Management;* and National Fire Protection Association 1600: 2007/2010 *Standard on Disaster/Emergency Management and Business Continuity Programs.* At the end of September 2010, DHS announced a certification program tailored to the needs of small business.

The other national effort using management system standards is the current Emergency Management Accreditation Program (EMAP), a voluntary review process for state and local emergency management programs. EMAP certifies government programs against standards directly based on NFPA 1600. State and local entities can use federal homeland security grant funding to pay for EMAP activities. Interestingly, at one time, FEMA used the EMAP standards to administer its National Emergency Baseline Capability Assurance Program. If there truly were to be a "whole of community" effort, it would seem to be a necessary condition to have a compatible approach for all the entities involved.

Still to be resolved would be whether adoption of the management system preparedness standards should be mandated, perhaps tied to federal funding or regulations, and how certification or accreditation against the standards would be conducted. Normally, management system standards such as those under the PS-Prep program or EMAP are voluntary, although compliance with such standards may be seen as part of a legal standard of care across an industry.

Government agencies such as DHS could implicitly mandate standards by using them as guidelines for complying with regulatory requirements. Or the agencies may forego a mandatory regulation if they view voluntary compliance as meeting policy goals. This seems to be the legislative and executive branch approach taken with the PS-Prep voluntary standards for the private sector. Established provisions can be invoked for mandatory adoption as part of national regulatory frameworks or legislation. The National Technology Transfer and Advancement Act of 1995 and resulting Office of Management and Budget (OMB) Circular A-119 (revised in 1998) mandated that federal agencies use management system standards developed by either domestic or international standards bodies instead of federal government-unique standards (e.g., the National Preparedness Goal) in their regulatory or procurement activities.

To date, DHS has not publicly addressed how the management system standard voluntary program is to be reconciled, if at all, with building and sustaining core capabilities. At a minimum, metrics identified as part of implementing the National Preparedness Goal should be compared to those in PSPrep and the EMAP standards.

Implementing Whole Community Efforts for the Maximum of Maximums

A second concern is realistically implementing a whole community effort in anticipation of a maximum of maximums effort. In June 2011 testimony, FEMA Administrator Fugate stated that emergency management historically planned for scenarios to which government could respond and recover from.[40] He testified that modern disaster planning should be for a "meta-scenario" (or "maximum of maximums" event) destined to overwhelm all levels of government. Such worst-case planning would require the efforts of a whole community approach intended to leverage the expertise and resources of governmental and non-governmental stakeholders—the entire emergency management community from the federal government to individuals, families, and communities. This philosophy was further defined in FEMA's *A Whole Community Approach to Emergency Management: Principles, Themes, and Pathways for Action.*[41]

The emphasis on shared responsibility and coordination in the whole community concept reaffirms past policies. President Bush's June 2002 proposal to create DHS expressed hope that the agency would make state, local, and private sector coordination one of its "key components."[42] The 2002 *National Strategy for Homeland Security* viewed homeland security as a concerted national effort. The approach was based on shared responsibility and partnership involving the Congress, state and local governments, the private sector, and the American people in a concerted national effort to prevent attacks.[43]

The draft national planning frameworks are very general in their discussion of the roles and interactions of the whole community to achieve capability targets and what scarce resources practically can be expected for investment. Presumably, explicit guidance will await finalization of the National Preparedness System and the planning frameworks and their implementation plans. For example, the National Disaster Recovery Framework and the draft *Recovery Interagency Operational Plan* are explicit in terms of requirements and hierarchy, but not the practical issue of funding and the sharing of resources within and across stakeholders from the government to the individual citizen.

However, is it realistic to root whole community preparedness in anticipation of a truly mega-disaster scenario? A mega-disaster is a very high bar for the initial and ongoing investment in preparedness core capabilities defined in the *National Preparedness Goal* and draft national planning frameworks. All homeland security actors must anticipate and be ready for a "no-notice" catastrophe much more severe than virtually all past major disasters in the United States, including Hurricane Katrina, the 1964 Alaska earthquake and tsunami, or the 1993 eastern and central superstorm. A mega-disaster, under FEMA's criteria, would be akin to "no notice" devastating earthquakes, tsunamis, and volcanic eruptions that killed or injured hundreds of thousands and leveled cities. A nuclear event in a major urban area or a fast-moving worldwide pandemic also would overwhelm immediate response and recovery for a good length of time.

It is not clear how the federal government can direct and pragmatically facilitate the crafting and sustaining of capabilities across the whole community necessary for a mega-disaster with these levels of devastation going forward. Preparing for a mega-disaster appears to run counter to the professed emphasis on risk management and setting priorities for preparedness, not a worst-case scenario for the entire nation to anticipate. It well may be that emergency managers will actually scale the requirements to a more convincing expectation. For example, Northeast emergency managers have posited the following possible mega-disasters:[44]

- A 6.5 earthquake striking a heavily populated urban area causing billions of dollars in damage and killing hundreds.
- A category 3 hurricane making landfall over Long Island, NY and tracking up through New England killing hundreds and causing billions of dollars in damage.
- An F5 tornado striking a heavily populated area killing a thousand people and causing hundreds of millions in damage.
- A major blizzard hitting the Northeast during a heavy rush hour commute with over fifty inches of snow and hurricane force winds causing billions of dollars in damage along the coast, widespread extended power outages and stranding thousands.

Emerging Threat Priorities

A third concern in the strategic direction is addressing threats that are slowly emerging as a direct threat to national security. Among other things, the September 2010 Local, State, Tribal, and Federal Preparedness Task Force report to Congress called for (1) improving the ability to strategically forecast emerging preparedness requirements and associated policies and/or capabilities and (2) develop a strategic policy planning process that prepares for future challenges by performing long-range assessments.[45] The Task Force said that the complexity of the envisioned homeland security and emergency management enterprise, especially in terms of non-governmental roles, means that desired preparedness outcomes often may take years to achieve. In their view, a range of dynamic issues—such as the environment, demographics, economics, and health trends—are likely to play increasingly important roles. Preparedness policies, therefore, should be anticipatory, not reactionary, enabling anticipatory investments in key areas.

As mentioned earlier, the hazards listed in the *National Preparedness Goal* reference well-known, specific event hazards and attacks determined by the current *Strategic National Risk Assessment*. However, the current *National Security Strategy* and *Quadrennial Homeland Security Review Report* explicitly define a strategic threat environment and global trends that appear to have national preparedness implications, although they are not described as imminent. These include the gradual emergencies and disasters that result from dependence upon fossil fuels, global climate change, fragile and failing states, and global illicit trafficking and related transnational crime, and economic and financial instability.

A 2009 article on national security strategies presented drivers of changes in security on a national and global scale, such as pandemics, population changes, and economic stress.[46] These drivers translate into threats to security, whether individually or collectively, which countries have incorporated into their strategies. In other countries, the security environment includes these longer-term threats. In general, their national security strategies (including those covering homeland security or domestic security) incorporate them into the strategies and follow-on policy and operational requirements and guidance. For example, climate change or environmental change pose dangers that may occur on a national or global scale, such as more frequent heat waves, droughts, flooding, reduced crop yields, and wildfires.[47]

The *National Preparedness Goal* and supporting documents target building and sustaining capabilities narrowly for the near term threat of a meta-scenario. It is not clear how these capabilities will prepare the country for the challenges of the longer-term, slowly emerging threats. Certainly past history is informative: flooding and famines because of drought and crop failure have killed millions worldwide.

There have been a multitude of studies on these drivers or changes with recommendations for immediate action. The Organization for Economic Co-Operation and Development (OECD) presented an analysis of "global shocks"—cascading risks that become active threats as they spread across global systems.[48] These included pandemics, financial crises, critical infrastructure disruption, cyber risks, geomagnetic storms, and social unrest. As the OECD study pointed out, surveillance is central to risk assessment and management. In addition, security agencies, working with regulatory agencies, should use, adapt, and implement risk-assessment tools to design more resilient national and international systems. Emergency management of future global shocks, OECD said, called for policy options such as (1) surveillance and early warning systems, (2) strategic reserves and stockpiles of critical resources, (3) addressing where countermeasures to systemic threats have been weak, and (4) monitoring of future developments that could pose potential risks. OECD cited challenges such as insufficient skills and knowledge to manage global shocks and obstacles to international cooperation and coordination.

The DHS certainly understands the need for action anticipating these global shocks. The FEMA Strategic Foresight Initiative, initiated in 2010, emphasizes the importance of understanding and addressing the drivers of future change.[49] The FEMA urges the emergency management community to establish a foresight capability—identifying key future issues, trends, and other factors with an eye to executing an agenda for action over the next twenty years. Not surprisingly, FEMA identifies well-known drivers—universal access to and use of information, technological innovation and dependency, shifting US demographics, climate change, global interdependencies and globalization, government budget constraints, critical infrastructure deterioration, and the evolving terrorist threat. The FEMA study says that through the foresight process, over the next few decades, very rapid change and complexity will define the emergency management environment. FEMA says that even slow-moving and predictable trends such as demographic changes could be radically changed because of drivers such as climate change or pandemics.

FEMA sees a number of emergency management capabilities as needed as part of strategic foresight that could be included in preparedness efforts. For example, these include addressing dynamic and unprecedented shifts in local and regional population characteristics and migratory flows; anticipating emerging challenges and developing appropriate plans and contingencies; employing alternative surge models to meet the challenging confluences of social, technological, environmental, economic, and political factors and conditions; and remediating hidden vulnerabilities in critical supplies from water to energy to medical products to offset threats to the full scope of emergency management activities.

Federal Control Over Other Governmental Levels for the National Interest

A fourth area of concern that overarches the other three is the stated importance and needed leadership of the whole homeland security community and the actual federal control over other levels of government. An article discussing federalism and homeland security noted that the September 2001 terrorist attacks created a high demand for national homeland security policy and action.[50] The many federal homeland security directives, mandates, and grant compliance requirements have framed and centralized control of the national homeland security agenda, even if there was collaboration in the development with selected state and local officials. Hurricane Katrina presented another opportunity for an expanded federal government role in disasters because of the failures of individual agencies and weak intergovernmental collaboration.

As a result, it is difficult to find the appropriate balance between federal control over the national interest and its objectives and local flexibility and discretion under federalism. The homeland security links between the broadened national security strategy and national preparedness goal and then state and local support depend on state and local implementation of the national direction. At present, the *National Preparedness Goal* and its supporting documents have limited language about state and local flexibility and the meeting of specific and direct state and local interests. The streamlining of lists of core capabilities and their preliminary targets is encouraging, but federal approval of state and local implementation will be the proof if state and local jurisdictions can craft capabilities responsive to their needs as well as what is seen as the national interest. This will be a continuing concern as budget decisions consider fiscal austerity and the funding needed to build and sustain preparedness capabilities for a mega-disaster.

Conclusion

The September 2010 Local, State, Tribal, and Federal Preparedness Task Force report commissioned by Congress underscored the importance of preparedness as a major policy agenda, but also warned of the central difficulty. The Task Force determined,

> The basic tenets of preparedness...are relatively uncontroversial within both the emergency management discipline and homeland security policy. What has changed is the realization that preparedness can be only as effective as the goals and priorities for readiness. The challenge

is determining what our readiness goals and priorities should be, from which preparedness activities are subsequently derived and then measured against.[51]

Over the past decade, the federal government has done much to determine national preparedness or readiness goals and priorities. In the next decade of homeland security as part of national security, the threat environment—the security environment—is somewhat known, but also uncertain. New threats may emerge and others wane. The larger social and economic environment, such as fiscal austerity and demographic changes create instability in what can, and should be done.

PPD-8 emphasizes the vital role of preparedness in protecting the nation, its people, its vital interests, and its way of life. Preparedness on the part of all members of the homeland security community in this national endeavor should be done in ways that emphasize the principles of clarity, sustainability, integration, balance, and accountability. This article suggests that federal policymakers, in concert with others with preparedness responsibilities, should consider refinements in a number of fundamental policy areas that are in line with these principles.

Preparedness expectations to meet all threats—whether imminent or slowly emerging—should be clear. Common sense should reign. Expectations about sustainability of funding to meet whole of community preparedness for a mega-disaster must consider and then reflect the reality of funding—whether from governmental or other sources. Even apart from funding, preparedness principles and activities should be seamlessly integrated into ongoing programs and business processes, such as the adoption of management system standards. Balance should be applied in assessing the costs and benefits of preparedness and required capabilities and their impact on non-preparedness goals. Lastly, accountability calls for identifying preparedness accountability points, performance goals, and measures reflective of the national interest, yet also local flexibility and discretion within our federalist system.

Notes

1. George W. Bush, *Securing the Homeland: Strengthening the Nation* (Washington, DC: The White House, June 17, 2002).

2. George W. Bush, *The Department of Homeland Security* (Washington, DC: The White House, June 2002).

3. Office of Homeland Security, *National Strategy for Homeland Security* (Washington, DC: The White House, July 2002).

4. Ibid., 2.

5. George W. Bush, *Homeland Security Presidential Directive/ HSPD-5 Management of Domestic Incidents* (Washington, DC: The White House, February 28, 2003).

6. US Department of Homeland Security (DHS), *National Response Plan* (Washington, DC: Department of Homeland Security, December 2004).

7. DHS *National Response Framework* (Washington, DC: Department of Homeland Security, January 2008).

8. George W. Bush, *Homeland Security Presidential Directive/ HSPD-8 National Preparedness* (Washington, DC: The White House, December 17, 2003).

9. DHS, *Interim National Preparedness Goal* (Washington, DC: Department of Homeland Security, March 31, 2005).

10. Homeland Security Council, *National Planning Scenarios* (Washington, DC: The White House, 2005).

11. DHS, *Fiscal Year 2005 Homeland Security Grant Program, Program Guidelines and Application Kit.* (Washington, DC: Department of Homeland Security, 2005).

12. DHS, *National Preparedness Guidance* (Washington, DC: Department of Homeland Security, April 27, 2005).

13. DHS, *National Preparedness Goal* (Washington, DC: Department of Homeland Security [draft], December 2005).

14. Ibid., 1.

15. Ibid., A-2.

16. DHS, *National Preparedness Guidelines* (Washington, DC: Department of Homeland Security, September 2007).

17. Ibid., 1.

18. Homeland Security Council, *National Strategy for Homeland Security* (Washington, DC: The White House, October 2007).

19. Ibid., 3.

20. Barack Obama, *Presidential Study Directive* (Washington, DC: The White House, February 23, 2009).

21. The White House, *Statement by the President on the White House Organization for Homeland Security and Counterterrorism* (Washington, DC: The White House, May 26, 2009).

22. DHS, *Quadrennial Homeland Security Review Report: A Strategic Framework for a Secure Homeland* (Washington, DC: Department of Homeland Security, February 2010).

23. Barack Obama, *National Security Strategy* (Washington, DC: The White House, May 2010).

24. Barack Obama, Barack, *Presidential Policy Directive/PPD-8* (Washington, DC: The White House, March 30, 2011).

25. DHS, *Implementation Plan for Presidential Policy Directive 8: National Preparedness* (Washington, DC: Department of Homeland Security, May 2011).

26. Craig Fugate, "Evolution of Emergency Management and Communication," statement before the US Senate Committee on Appropriations, Subcommittee on Homeland Security (June 8, 2011).

27. DHS, *National Preparedness Goal First Edition* (Washington, DC: Department of Homeland Security, September 2011).

28. DHS, *The Strategic National Risk Assessment in Support of PPD 8: A Comprehensive Risk-Based Approach toward a Secure and Resilient Nation* (December 2011).

29. DHS, *National Preparedness System* (November 2011).

30. US Federal Emergency Management Agency (FEMA), *National Disaster Recovery Framework* (September 2011).

31. Sharon L. Caudle, "Homeland Security Capabilities-based Planning: Lessons from the Defense Community," *Homeland Security Affairs* I, no. 2 (Fall 2005), www.hsaj .org/?article=1.2.2.

32. See, for example, Local, State, Tribal, and Federal Preparedness Task Force, *Perspective on Preparedness: Taking Stock Since 9/11* (Report to Congress, September 2010).

33. William O. Jenkins, "FEMA Has Made Limited Progress in Efforts to Develop and Implement a System to Assess National Preparedness Capabilities," Letter to Subcommittee on Homeland Security Committee on Appropriations (October 29, 2010).

34. William O. Jenkins, "Managing Preparedness Grants and Assessing National Capabilities: Continuing Challenges Impede FEMA's Progress," testimony before the House Subcommittee on Emergency Preparedness, Response, and Communications (GAO-12-526T, March 20, 2012).

35. Michael Fitzsimmons, *Whither Capabilities-based Planning?* (Washington, D.C.: National Defense University Institute for National Strategic Studies, 2007), 102, www.dtic.mil/cgi-bin/GetTRDoc?AD=ada517897.pdf& Location=U2&doc=GetTRDoc.pdf.

36. Michael F. Cochrane, "Capability Disillusionment," *Defense AT&L* (July–August 2011), www.dau.mil/pubscats/ATL%20 Docs/July-Aug11/DATL%20July-Aug11.pdf.

37. US Government Accountability Office, *National Preparedness: FEMA Has Made Progress, but Needs to Complete and Integrate Planning, Exercise, and Assessment Efforts* (GAO-09-369, April 2009).

38. FEMA, *National Exercise Program* (March 18, 2011).

39. Sharon L. Caudle, "National Preparedness Requirements: Harnessing Management System Standards," *Homeland Security Affairs* 7, article 14 (June 2011) www.hsaj .org/?article=7.1.14.

40. Craig Fugate, "Evolution of Emergency Management and Communication," written statement before the US Senate Committee on Homeland Security (June 8, 2011).

41. FEMA, *A Whole Community Approach to Emergency Management: Principles, Themes, and Pathways for Action* (FDOC 104-008-1, December, 2011).

42. The White House. *The Department of Homeland Security* (June 2002), 3.

43. Office of Homeland Security. *National Strategy for Homeland Security* (July 2002), 2.

44. "Northeast Planning for the 'Maximum of Maximums," *NESEC News* 13, no. 4 (Winter 2010), www.nesec.org.

45. Local, State, Tribal and Federal Preparedness Task Force, *Perspective on Preparedness.*

46. Sharon Caudle, "National Security Strategies: Security from What, for Whom, and by What Means," *Journal of Homeland Security and Emergency Management* 6, article 22 (2009).

47. Peter Hough, *Understanding Global Security,* 2nd ed. (London: Routledge, 2008).

48. Organization for Economic Cooperation and Development (OECD), *Future Global Shocks: Improving Risk Governance.* (OECD Reviews of Risk Management Policies, OECD Publishing, 2011).

49. FEMA, *Crisis Response and Disaster Resilience 2020: Forging Strategic Action in an Age of Uncertainty* (Washington, DC: FEMA Office of Policy and Program Analysis, January 2012).

50. Sharon L. Caudle, "Centralization and Decentralization of Policy: The National Interest of Homeland Security," Journal of Homeland Security and Emergency Management 8, article 56 (2011), www.bepress.com/jhsem/vol8/iss1/56.

51. Local, State, Tribal and Federal Preparedness Task Force. *Perspective on Preparedness*, 6.

Critical Thinking

1. How has national strategy evolved since 9/11?
2. What are the main concerns in implementation of a National Homeland Security Strategy?
3. What are the threat priorities?
4. What should the threat priorities be?

Create Central

www.mhhe.com/createcentral

Internet References

Department of Homeland Security

www.dhs.gov/national-strategy-homeland-security-october-2007

Whitehouse Archives

http://georgewbush-whitehouse.archives.gov/infocus/homeland/nshs/2007/index.html

Presidential Policy Directive 8

www.dhs.gov/presidential-policy-directive-8-national-preparedness

DR. SHARON CAUDLE is a graduate faculty member at the Bush School of Government and Public Service, Texas A&M University. Before joining the School, she was with the US Government Accountability Office's Homeland Security and Justice Team in Washington, DC. She is a senior fellow of The George Washington University's Homeland Security Policy Institute and has authored numerous articles and book chapters on topics ranging from public performance management to homeland/national security issues. She earned her master's and doctorate in public administration from The George Washington University in Washington, DC, and a master's in national security, homeland security and defense from the Naval Postgraduate School's Center for Homeland Security and Defense in Monterey, CA.

Article   Prepared by: Thomas J. Badey, *Randolph-Macon College*

Secretary Napolitano Announces Fiscal Year 2013 Budget Request

Office of the Press Secretary

Learning Outcomes

After reading this article, you will be able to:

- Identify the Homeland Security budget priorities for FY 2013.

- Discuss the challenges the DHS faces in the allocation of resources.

- Identify the agencies within DHS that appear to be the primary beneficiaries of the FY2013 budget.

W ashington—Secretary of Homeland Security Janet Napolitano today unveiled the Department of Homeland Security's (DHS) fiscal year (FY) 2013 budget request of $39.5 billion in net discretionary funding. An additional $5.5 billion for the Disaster Relief Fund (DRF) is provided separately, pursuant to the Budget Control Act of 2011 (BCA). Recognizing the current fiscal environment, the Department's net discretionary amount is 0.5 percent below the FY 2012 enacted level.

"Ten years after the September 11th attacks, America is stronger and more secure today, thanks to the strong support of Congress; the tremendous work of the men and women of DHS and our local, state and federal partners across the homeland security enterprise," said Secretary Napolitano. "The Department's FY 2013 budget request preserves core frontline priorities by cutting costs, sharing resources across components, and streamlining operations wherever possible."

The FY 2013 budget request redirects over $850 million in base resources from administrative and mission support areas, including contracts, personnel (through attrition), information technology, travel, personnel moves, overtime, directed purchasing, professional services, and vehicle management to frontline operations. Through the Department-wide Efficiency Review, which began in 2009, as well as other cost-saving initiatives, DHS has identified over $3 billion in cost avoidances and reductions, and redeployed those funds to mission-critical initiatives across the Department.

The FY 2013 budget request prioritizes the mission areas outlined in the Department's 2010 Quadrennial Homeland Security Review and the 2010 Bottom-Up Review, the first complete effort undertaken by the Department to align its resources with a comprehensive strategy to meet the nation's homeland security needs.

The budget builds on the progress the Department has made in each of its mission areas while providing essential support to national and economic security.

FY 2013 Budget Priorities
Preventing Terrorism and Enhancing Security

Guarding against terrorism was the founding mission of DHS and remains the Department's top priority. The FY 2013 budget safeguards the nation's transportation systems through a layered detection system focusing on risk-based screening, enhanced targeting and information sharing efforts to interdict threats and dangerous people at the earliest point possible. The budget supports the administration's Global Supply Chain Security Strategy across air, land, and sea modes of transportation by strengthening efforts to prescreen and evaluate high-risk containers before they are shipped to the U.S. and annualizing positions that provide the capacity to address security vulnerabilities overseas. Funding is included for Securing the Cities to protect our highest risk cities from radiological or nuclear attack and national bio preparedness and response efforts. The budget also continues strong support for State and local partners through a new consolidated grant program, training, fusion centers, and intelligence analysis and information sharing on a wide range of critical homeland security issues.

Securing and Managing Our Borders

Protecting the nation's borders—land, air, and sea—from the illegal entry of people, weapons, drugs, and contraband is vital to homeland security, as well as economic prosperity. Over the past several years, DHS has deployed unprecedented levels of personnel, technology, and resources to the Southwest Border. At the same time, DHS has made critical security improvements along the Northern Border while strengthening efforts to increase the security of the nation's maritime borders. The FY 2013 budget continues the Administration's unprecedented focus on border security, travel and trade by supporting 21,370

Border Patrol agents and 21,186 CBP Officers at our ports of entry as well the continued deployment of proven, effective surveillance technology along the highest trafficked areas of the Southwest Border. To secure the nation's maritime borders, the budget invests in recapitalization of Coast Guard assets including the sixth National Security Cutter, Fast Response Cutters as well as the renovation and restoration of shore facilities. The budget also includes resources to ensure that the Coast Guard's aviation fleet is mission-ready and provides operational funding for new assets coming on line.

Enforcing and Administering Our Immigration Laws

DHS is focused on smart and effective enforcement of U.S. immigration laws while streamlining and facilitating the legal immigration process. Supporting the establishment of clear enforcement priorities, recent policy directives and additional training for the field, the budget continues the Department's efforts to prioritize the identification and removal of criminal aliens and repeat immigration law violators, recent border entrants and immigration fugitives. Nationwide implementation of Secure Communities and other enforcement initiatives, coupled with continued collaboration with DOJ to focus resources on the detained docket and priority cases on the non-detained docket, is expected to continue to increase the number of criminal aliens and other priority individuals who are identified and removed. The budget provides the resources needed to address this changing population, while continuing to support Alternatives to Detention, detention reform, and immigrant integration efforts. The budget also focuses on monitoring and compliance, promoting adherence to worksite-related laws through criminal prosecutions of egregious employers, Form I-9 inspections, and expansion of E-Verify.

Safeguarding and Securing Cyberspace

DHS leads the federal government's efforts to secure civilian government computer systems and works with industry and state, local, tribal and territorial governments to secure critical infrastructure and information systems. The FY 2013 budget makes significant investments in cybersecurity to expedite the deployment of EINSTEIN 3 to prevent and detect intrusions on government computer systems; increases federal network security of large and small agencies; and continues to develop a robust cybersecurity workforce to protect against and respond to national cybersecurity threats and hazards. The budget also focuses on combating cyber crimes, targeting large-scale producers and distributors of child pornography and preventing attacks against U.S. critical infrastructure through Financial Crimes Task Forces.

Ensuring Resilience to Disasters

The Department's efforts to build a ready and resilient nation focus on a whole community approach to emergency management by engaging partners at all levels to ensure that we work together to build, sustain, and improve our capability to prepare for, protect against, respond to, recover from, and mitigate all hazards. In the event of a terrorist attack, natural disaster or other large-scale emergency DHS provides the coordinated, comprehensive federal response while working with federal, state, local, and private sector partners to ensure a swift and effective recovery effort. To ensure that FEMA is able to support these efforts, the DRF, which provides a significant portion of the total federal response to victims in presidentially declared disasters or emergencies, is funded largely through authority provided under the BCA. To support the objectives of the National Preparedness Goal, the administration proposes a new homeland security grants program in FY 2013 to create a robust national response capacity based on cross-jurisdictional and readily deployable state and local assets. The FY 2013 budget also funds FEMA's continued development of catastrophic plans, which include regional plans for response to biological events and earthquakes.

Providing Essential Support to National and Economic Security

DHS provides essential support to many areas of national and economic security. In addition to supporting Coast Guard's current operations in the Polar Regions, the budget initiates acquisition of a new polar icebreaker to address Coast Guard emerging missions in the Arctic. The budget also continues to support ICE's and CBP's enforcement and investigative efforts to protect U.S. intellectual property rights and collect customs revenue.

Critical Thinking

1. What are the FY 2013 Homeland Security budget priorities?
2. What should the Homeland Security budget priorities be?
3. Should the Homeland Security budget be increased?

Create Central

www.mhhe.com/createcentral

Internet References

Department of Homeland Security Budget
    www.dhs.gov/dhs-budget
Congressional Budget Office
    www.cbo.gov/publication/43520
Government Computer News
    http://gcn.com/articles/2012/03/23/dhs-2013-budget-cyber-threat-senate
    -hearing.aspx

From Office of Press Secretary, February 2012.

Article   Prepared by: Thomas J. Badey, *Randolph-Macon College*

Homeland Security in America

Past, Present, and Future

Roger L. Kemp

Learning Outcomes

After reading this article, you will be able to:

- Describe how and why the department of Homeland Security was formed.

- Discuss the intent of the color-coded Homeland Security Advisory System.

- Understand the role Citizen Assistance and Support Groups in Homeland Security.

- Explain how the Homeland Security has evolved since 9/11.

Eleven days after the September 11, 2001, terrorist attacks, then-President Bush appointed the first-ever director of the nascent Office of Homeland Security. This new office, located in the White House, was to oversee and coordinate a comprehensive national strategy to safeguard the United States against terrorism and to respond to any future attacks. A year later, with the passage of the Homeland Security Act by Congress in November 2002, the Department of Homeland Security (DHS) formally came into being as a stand-alone, Cabinet-level, department to further coordinate and unify national homeland security efforts, opening its doors on March 1, 2003. This new department integrated all or part of 22 different Federal departments and agencies into a single unified entity.

Since this time, only a little more than a decade ago, our nation has seen the initiation and implementation of two national warning systems, the most recent of which was launched in April of 2011. We've also seen the emergence of several emergency- and disaster-related citizen support groups, designed to serve law-enforcement agencies and first responders at all levels of government—city, county, state, and federal. Furthermore, we've seen critical information being placed on government websites for public officials, first responders, and citizens in general. This information has become more sophisticated in recent years and continues to be improved. Federal government agencies are even entering the world of social media to further help inform citizens of all ages how to prepare for and respond to disasters and emergencies of all kinds.

These events, which continue to unfold in the dynamic and evolving field of homeland security, are highlighted below. To provide proper coverage, the information is presented under the headings: National Warning Systems; Citizen Assistance and Support Groups; and Homeland Security and the Future. This paper describes state-of-the-art trends in this field to help public officials and first responders become educated to better serve the public. The goal of all government officials during emergencies and disasters has always been to reduce loss of life and property. While this is still the goal, the processes and mechanisms for achieving it have become increasingly more sophisticated, as described below.

National Warning Systems

In order to improve coordination and communication among all levels of government and the public in the fight against terrorism, the President signed Homeland Security Presidential Directive 3 in March of 2002, creating the Homeland Security Advisory System (HSAS). This advisory system was established to serve as the foundation for a simple communications structure to dissemination information regarding possible terrorist attacks aimed at any levels of government, as well as against our nation's citizens. It was replaced by the National Terrorism Advisory System (NTAS) in April of 2011. Both the HSAS and NTAS are explained below.

The United States has many federal alert systems in America, and each is tailored uniquely to a different sector of U.S. society: transportation, defense, agriculture, and weather, for example. These alert systems all provide vital and specific information in a variety of emergency situations.

The HSAS provided a coordinated national framework for these systems, allowing government officials and citizens to communicate the nature and degree of terrorist threats. This advisory system characterized appropriate levels of vigilance, preparedness, and readiness, in a series of graduated threat-condition levels.

The protective measures that correspond to each threat condition served to help local governments and their citizens decide what actions they should take to respond to, and counter, possible terrorist activity. Based on the threat level, federal government agencies implemented appropriate safeguards and protective measures. State and municipalities were encouraged to adopt compatible local preparedness and response systems.

State and local officials were informed in advance of national threat advisories whenever possible. The Department of Homeland Security (DHS) conveyed relevant information to Federal, state, and local public officials, as well as to the private and nonprofit sectors. Heightened threat levels could be declared for the entire nation, or for a specific geographic area, functional, or industry sector. Changes in assigned threat conditions were made whenever the DHS deemed them necessary.

These threat conditions characterized the risk of a possible terrorist attack based on the best information available. Protective measures are the steps that should be taken by government and the private sector to reduce their respective vulnerabilities. The HSAS contained five threat conditions with associated suggested protective measures. They were:

- Green: Low Condition
- Blue: Guarded Condition
- Yellow: Elevated Condition
- Orange: High Condition
- Red: Severe Condition

Since September 11, 2001, the United States has been at Threat Condition Orange—High Condition—only a few times. HSAS warnings were regional and/or functional in their nature and scope. When the nation went to Threat Condition Orange, and this threat level was not limited to specific geographic areas, public officials in cities would take steps so citizens knew that their municipal officials were making an effort to protect them under this threat condition.

The NTAS replaced the color-coded HSAS. The new warning system is designed to communicate information about terrorist threats by providing timely, detailed information to the public, government agencies, first responders, airports, and other transportation hubs, and to the private and nonprofit sectors. The new advisory system recognizes that Americans all share responsibility for the nation's security, and that they should always be aware of the heightened risk of terrorist attack in the country and what they should do to prepare for, and respond to, disasters and emergencies.

The new national alert system is designed to warn public officials and citizens of a credible terrorist threat against the United States. These alerts will include the statement that an imminent danger or elevated threat exists. Using available information, the alerts will provide a concise summary of the potential threat, information about actions being taken to ensure public safety, and recommended steps that individuals, communities, businesses, and governments can take to help prevent, mitigate, or respond to the threat.

All NTAS alerts, the secretary states, will be based on the nature of the threat. In some cases, alerts will be sent directly to law enforcement agencies or affected areas of the private sector, while in others, alerts will be issued more broadly to the American people through both official and media channels. National alerts under this system also contain a sunset provision—that is, an individual threat alert will be issued for a specific time period and then it will automatically expire. It may be extended if new information becomes available or if the threat evolves. Also, as threat information changes, the Secretary will announce updated alerts. Updated alerts will be distributed in the same way as the original alerts were to ensure that the same public officials and citizens receive the updated information.

Details of the alert have been standardized, and the Secretary will follow a uniform alert format that contains a summary of the threat, indicating whether an imminent or elevated threat is likely. Each alert statement will also specify a duration, after which it either will expire or be officially extended by the DHS.

The next section of the alert notes details of the actual or pending danger, as well as a description of the affected geographic areas and the sectors involved. Finally, the last section of the new national alert document will describe how the public can help authorities, how public officials and citizens should plan for the emergency, and how public officials and citizens can stay informed. These new warnings also include instructions on how public officials and citizens can get additional information, the role of public safety and community leaders, and will provide links to appropriate DHS Web sites.

The new national alert system is based on the recommendations of a bipartisan task force of security experts, state and local elected and law enforcement officials, and other key stakeholders, which assessed the effectiveness of the previous national color-coded alert system. The results of this nationwide assessment, initiated by the Secretary of DHS, formed the basis of our nation's new National Terrorism Advisory System (commonly referred to as NTAS). Lastly, DHS encourages citizens to follow NTAS alerts for information about threats and to take an active role in security by reporting suspicious activity to local law enforcement authorities through the "If You See Something, Say Something" public awareness campaign.

Citizen Assistance and Support Groups

Since September 11, 2001, and the formation of the Department of Homeland Security (DHS), several citizen assistance and support groups have evolved related directly or indirectly to homeland security. Chapters of these groups are active invirtually in every state, and they work closely with their sponsoring and/or supporting federal agency. The federal agencies involved with these groups include the Department of Homeland Security (DHS), the Federal Bureau of Investigation (FBI), the Federal Emergency Management Agency (FEMA), the Department of Justice (DOJ), and the Department of Health and Human Services (HHS). Each of these eight citizen assistance and support groups is highlighted and explained below. It would behoove public officials to know which groups are located in their community so that when an emergency or disaster takes place, they can take advantage of the volunteer services available from the organizations within their own community.

Citizen Corps (CC)

Following the attack of September 11, 2001, state and local government officials have increased opportunities for citizens to become involved in protecting their homeland and supporting local first responders. President Bush launched this group in January 2002—four months after the terrorist attacks. Citizen Corps was created to help coordinate volunteer activities that will make communities safer, and better prepared to respond to emergencies.

It provides opportunities for people to participate to keeping their communities safer from threat of terrorism, as well as from natural disasters of all kinds. Citizens receive training in first aid, emergency skills, and volunteer to assist local first responders. The CC currently has more than 1,200 chapters nationally. This program is coordinated by the U. S. Department of Homeland Security (DHS).

Community Emergency Response Team (CERT)

This program, which FEMA administers, educates citizens about disaster preparedness and trains them in basic disaster response skills, such as fire safety, light search and rescue practices, and disaster medical operations. Using their training, CERT members can assist others in their neighborhood or workplace following an event and can take a more active role in preparing their community for both natural and man-made emergencies. CERT has more than 1,900 chapters throughout the nation.

Fire Corps (FC)

This program promotes the use of citizen advocates to enhance the capacity of resource-constrained fire and rescue departments at all levels of public service, including volunteer, combination, and career. Citizen advocates can assist local fire departments in a range of activities including fire safety outreach, youth programs, and administrative support services. Fire Corps provides resources to assist fire and rescue departments in creating opportunities for citizen advocates, and promotes citizen participation. This group has nearly 1,100 chapters throughout the country. It is funded through DHS and is managed through a partnership between the National Volunteer Fire Council (NVFC), the International Association of Fire Fighters (IAFF), and the International Association of Fire Chiefs (IAFC).

USAonWatch (USAOW)

This group, which includes the nationwide network of Neighborhood Watch Programs (NWP), works to provide information, training, and resources to citizens and law enforcement agencies throughout the country. In the aftermath of September 11, 2001, NWPs have expanded beyond their traditional crime prevention role to help neighborhoods focus on disaster preparedness, emergency response, and terrorism awareness.

These groups also go by many other names, such as Crime Watch, Block Watch, and Business Watch, and have thousands of neighborhood chapters located in cities throughout the United States. USAonWatch-Neighborhood Watch is administered by the National Sheriff's Association (NSA) in partnership with the Bureau of Justice Assistance (BJA), Office of Justice Programs (OJP), and the U. S. Department of Justice (DOJ).

Medical Reserve Corps (MRC)

This program's purpose is to strengthen communities by helping medical, public health, and other volunteers offer their expertise on a long-term basis, as well as during local emergencies and other types of community need. MRC volunteers work in coordination with existing local emergency-response programs, and also supplement existing public health initiatives, such as outreach and prevention, immunization programs, blood drives, case management, care planning, and other efforts. This program, which has nearly a thousand chapters throughout the nation, is administered by the federal Department of Health and Human Services (HHS).

Volunteers in Police Service (VIPS)

The VIPS program provides support and resources for state and local law enforcement agencies interested in developing and/or enhancing a volunteer program, and for citizens who wish to volunteer their time and skills to assist a law enforcement agency. The program's ultimate goal is to enhance the capacity of these law enforcement agencies to use citizen volunteers. There are more than 2,200 VIPS chapters nationally. This program is funded by the U. S. Department of Justice (DOJ), and managed by the International Association of Chiefs of Police (IACP) in partnership with the Bureau of Justice Assistance (BJA), Office of Justice Programs (OJP), in the DOJ.

Corporation for National and Community Service (CNCS)

CNCS promotes volunteer service initiatives and activities that support homeland security and community safety. They are a federal agency that operates nationwide service programs such as AmeriCorps, Senior Corps, and Learn and Serve America, among others. Participants in these programs may support Citizen Corps Council activities by helping to establish training and information delivery systems for neighborhoods, schools, and businesses, and by helping with family preparedness and crime prevention initiatives in a single community or across an entire region. Tens of thousands of citizens presently participate in these national, federally-sponsored, programs. This organization is coordinated nationally by the U. S. Department of Homeland Security (DHS).

InfraGard (IG)

InfraGard is an information-sharing and analysis effort serving the interests and pooling the knowledge bases of a wide range of members. Administered by the Federal Bureau of Investigation (FBI), it is an association of businesses, academic institutions, state and local law enforcement agencies, and other participants all dedicated to sharing information and intelligence to prevent hostile acts against the United States, with its top priorities being the protection of cyber and public infrastructures. The chapters are linked with 56 FBI field office territories and have more than 47,000 members throughout the nation.

Homeland Security and the Future

The new field of homeland security is both dynamic and evolving. It has impacted public officials and citizens in local and state governments throughout the nation in many ways, and continues to do so. The United States has a new national warning system, the National Terrorism Advisory System (NTAS), and community and regional citizen groups that are actively involved in homeland security, emergency management, and assisting first responders in their job responsibilities. It behooves local public officials, especially first responders, to know about these groups, and the services that they provide, especially those located within their own community.

Today there is a greater level of engagement and involvement among law enforcement agencies, and between other first responders, in city, county, state, and federal governments. There are now more meetings and disaster exercises that involve different levels of government, both separately and jointly, than ever before in our nation's history. Also, everyone from public officials to first responders has an expanding awareness of the services available from local and regional nonprofit organizations. The practices and influence of first responders have been greatly enhanced in recent years by both profit-making businesses and nonprofit organizations. It is critical for public officials to know the full range of resources and services available to them when they respond to emergencies and disasters, either natural or man-made.

Lastly, the field of homeland security has influenced the layout and construction of public buildings and facilities at all levels of government. Current and future government buildings, for example, are less likely to provide underground public parking. In many cases, land permitting, public parking space is provided away from public buildings and facilities.

Vehicular access to public buildings is also limited for obvious reasons—i.e., to deter carbomb attacks. In addition, heating and air conditioning systems in new public buildings are no longer accessible by the public from ground floors or exterior locations. Citizen access to such systems is now restricted for security purposes. Lastly, many government buildings are being designed to blend in better with their surrounding community, and not stand out as targets by being the largest and tallest buildings in the immediate area.

The field of homeland security has become nationally introspective in nature, since many recent illegal acts have been committed by home-grown "terrorists" rather than individuals sent or directed from abroad. While border security has increased in importance, law enforcement agencies at all levels of government—federal, state, and local—are working more closely to monitor and track down illegal activities, and plans for carrying them out, hopefully before they take place. In this regard, government officials at every level increasingly rely on reports and leads from alert private citizens. This activity may prove crucial to successfully preventing attacks on homeland targets in the future, since many of these are planned and conducted entirely within the country, rather than by outside terrorists who enter the United States illegally.

Our computer systems, and their record-keeping applications, have also become targets for computer hackers both foreign and domestic. The danger of cyber attacks is one of the biggest threats that the United States faces today. Computer systems, and their automated databases, are decentralized and can face intrusion and possible destruction from miles away. It is often difficult to even determine the source of an attempted intrusion, much less the individuals responsible for creating malware and viruses designed to perform illegal acts. More and more public officials are creating duplicate records and databases so as to have back-up systems available in case of cyber attack emergencies.

This is becoming a common practice throughout U.S. public agencies. Increasingly, private companies, too, are threatened by potential computer intrusions and cyber attacks. No sector, be it public, nonprofit, or private, will go untouched by this trend. Everyone must be prepared. Steps such as continuous monitoring of computer use, and routine creation of duplicate systems to back-up records and databases, are likely to become commonplace over the next few years.

Sources Available for Further Information
Citizen Assistance and Support Group Websites

- Citizen Corps (CC)—http://citizencorps.gov/
- Citizen Emergency Response Team (CERT)—http://citizencorps.gov/cert/
- Fire Corps (FC)—www.firecorps.org/
- USAonWatch (USAOW)—www.usaonwatch.org/
- Medical Reserve Corps (MRC)—www.medicalreserve-corps.gov/
- Volunteers in Police Service (VIPS)—www.police-volunteers.org/
- Corporation for National & Community Service (CNCS)—www.serve.gov/
- InfraGard (IG)—www.infraguard.net
- Federal Government Websites
- Customs and Border Protection (CBP)—http://cbp.gov/
- Department of Homeland Security (DHS)—www.dhs.gov/
- Disaster Assistance Programs (DAP)—www.disaster-assistance.gov/
- Emergency Preparedness for Citizens (EPS)—www.ready.gov/
- Federal Emergency Management Agency (FEMA)—www.fema.gov/
- First Responder Information (FRI)—www.dhs.gov/xfrstresp/

- National Terrorism Advisory System (NTAS)—www
  .dhs.gov/files/programs/ntas.shtm
- Transportation Security Administration (TSA)—www
  .tsa.gov/

Critical Thinking

1. What are the potential benefits and drawbacks of merging
   22 federal agencies into one department?
2. Why was the color-coded National Security Advisor System
   eliminated?
3. What roles do role citizen assistance and support groups have
   in homeland security?
4. How has homeland security evolved since 9/11?

Create Central

www.mhhe.com/createcentral

Internet References

Department of Homeland Security
 www.dhs.gov/national-terrorism-advisory-system

Homeland Security Research
 www.homelandsecurityresearch.com/2008/09/global-homeland-security
-past-present-and-future/

U.S. House of Representatives Hearings
 http://homeland.house.gov/hearing/hearing-dhs-intelligence-enterprise
-past-present-and-future

ROGER L. KEMP, PhD, is a career city manager, having served in California, New Jersey, and Connecticut. He is the editor of *Homeland Security: Best Practices for Local Government* (Int'l City/County Management Association, 2010). Dr. Kemp served on the USDOJ's Anti-Terrorism Advisory Council, and was appointed by the Governor to the Homeland Security Working Group, State of Connecticut. He can be reached via email at rlkbsr@snet.net.

Kemp, Roger L. From *World Future Review*, vol. 4, no. 1, Spring 2012, pp. 28–33. Copyright © 2012 by World Future Society. Reprinted by permission.

Article

Prepared by: Thomas J. Badey, *Randolph-Macon College*

Changing Homeland Security: In 2010, Was Homeland Security Useful?

CHRISTOPHER BELLAVITA

Learning Outcomes

After reading this article, you will be able to:

- Identify the four main issues that have helped define homeland security.

- Describe the basic requirements for the creation of an academic discipline.

- Discuss the role of paradigms in the formation of academic disciplines.

- Understand what has to happen in order to continue to advance Homeland Security as an academic discipline.

What do the concept of homeland security and the intellectual program surrounding that concept actually contribute to the nation's security?

Since 2004 I have asked each new homeland security class at the Naval Postgraduate School what is working in homeland security and what needs to be improved. I ask the questions again eighteen months later when they are about to graduate.

Over the years, the answers to both questions—and at both times—tend to constellate around the same issues:

- Collaboration—among people, agencies, disciplines, jurisdictions and increasingly, nations;
- Information sharing and intelligence;
- Preventing terrorism—arising from international and domestic sources;
- Preparedness—in its many guises, including most recently "resilience";
- Transportation security—aviation, rail, other public transportation;
- Border control—northern, southern and coastal;
- Illegal immigration;
- Technology—its role in homeland security; what problems it solves and creates;
- Risk management—to include risk assessment and risk informed decision-making;

- Resources—where they come from, how they are allocated, how they are used to sustain progress;
- Critical infrastructure protection—the interface between public and private sectors;
- Leadership—at all levels in the homeland security enterprise.

Our master's degree participants—all of whom work in a homeland security-related public safety discipline—believe the nation is continuously improving its ability to prevent attacks, respond to disasters, and recover from a variety of incidents. They also believe we have much more work to do, work that will never be completed.

As I reviewed what happened in the homeland security enterprise during 2010, and compared that with previous "Year in Review" articles, I saw something similar to what our master's participants observed.[1] Most of the issues that helped to define homeland security have remained fairly consistent over the past five years:

- The meaning of homeland security,
- The nature of the threat,
- Surprise (anticipating and responding to), and
- The strategic approaches to achieving the various homeland security missions.

Those concerns—along with the other issues noted above—outline what I consider to be the enduring problems in homeland security. The dynamic contours of the homeland security enterprise are shaped largely by the shifting attention and neglect these issues receive.[2]

I have little doubt we are better prepared as a nation to prevent attacks and respond to disasters than we were on September 10, 2001. But it seems to me most of that progress has more to do with the work of homeland security artisans—practitioners skilled in both the practice and theory of what they do—than homeland security intellectuals.[3]

Public and private sector professionals, exercising the knowledge and skills they earned through discipline-specific training, education, and experience make the nation safer and more secure than it was a decade ago.

Report Documentation Page		*Form Approved* *OMB No. 0704-0188*
Public reporting burden for the collection of information is estimated to average 1 hour per response, including the time for reviewing instructions, searching existing data sources, gathering and maintaining the data needed, and completing and reviewing the collection of information. Send comments regarding this burden estimate or any other aspect of this collection of information, including suggestions for reducing this burden, to Washington Headquarters Services, Directorate for Information Operations and Reports, 1215 Jefferson Davis Highway, Suite 1204, Arlington VA 22202-4302. Respondents should be aware that notwithstanding any other provision of law, no person shall be subject to a penalty for failing to comply with a collection of information if it does not display a currently valid OMB control number.		

1. REPORT DATE **2010**	2. REPORT TYPE	3. DATES COVERED **00-00-2010 to 00-00-2010**
4. TITLE AND SUBTITLE **Changing Homeland Security: In 2010, Was Homeland Security Useful?**		5a. CONTRACT NUMBER
		5b. GRANT NUMBER
		5c. PROGRAM ELEMENT NUMBER
6. AUTHOR(S)		5d. PROJECT NUMBER
		5e. TASK NUMBER
		5f. WORK UNIT NUMBER
7. PERFORMING ORGANIZATION NAME(S) AND ADDRESS(ES) **Naval Postgraduate School, Monterey, CA, 93940**		8. PERFORMING ORGANIZATION REPORT NUMBER
9. SPONSORING/MONITORING AGENCY NAME(S) AND ADDRESS(ES)		10. SPONSOR/MONITOR'S ACRONYM(S)
		11. SPONSOR/MONITOR'S REPORT NUMBER(S)

12. DISTRIBUTION/AVAILABILITY STATEMENT **Approved for public release; distribution unlimited**

13. SUPPLEMENTARY NOTES **HOMELAND SECURITY AFFAIRS, VOLUME 7, ARTICLE 1 (FEBRUARY 2011)**

14. ABSTRACT

The failure of public safety disciplines to prevent the September 11, 2001 attack gave "homeland security" its chance to emerge as a competing paradigm for organizing the nation's security. But the other disciplines that contribute to the homeland security enterprise have not simply waited for this new discipline to emerge. They responded to the twenty-first century's national security threats by getting better at what they do. They may be eliminating the need for homeland security as a distinct public safety/national security paradigm. At the end of 2010, we were better prepared as a nation to prevent attacks and respond to disasters than we were a decade ago. But that progress may have more to do with the work of homeland security practitioners than with homeland security intellectuals. If homeland security is to become a useful academic and professional discipline, it has to demonstrate how looking at enduring problems through a homeland security framework adds significant value not provided by other disciplines.

15. SUBJECT TERMS

16. SECURITY CLASSIFICATION OF:			17. LIMITATION OF ABSTRACT	18. NUMBER OF PAGES	19a. NAME OF RESPONSIBLE PERSON
a. REPORT **unclassified**	b. ABSTRACT **unclassified**	c. THIS PAGE **unclassified**	**Same as Report (SAR)**	**11**	

Standard Form 298 (Rev. 8-98)
Prescribed by ANSI Std Z39-18

It is less apparent to me what value "homeland security" as a distinct—albeit still emerging—body of knowledge or discipline has contributed to that progress.

If homeland security is to become a useful academic and professional discipline, I think it has to demonstrate how looking at enduring problems through a homeland security framework adds significant value not provided by other disciplines. If it is unable to demonstrate value, homeland security may devolve into a legacy concept, like the now largely forgotten idea of civil defense.[4]

Homeland Security as a Discipline

The idea of homeland security as a distinct discipline took root initially because of the federal government's reaction to September 11, 2001. The homeland security concept was premised on the assumption that public safety disciplines operated too much in isolation from each other. That separation created vulnerabilities al Qaeda exploited.[5] Homeland security was supposed to prevent something like that from ever happening again.[6]

Shortly after the government acted, some educational institutions explored whether there was—or could be—enough substance in the homeland security idea to construct an academic discipline around its constituent concerns.[7] By 2010, more than 200 colleges and universities (as well as a few high schools) offered courses and programs in homeland security.[8]

An academic discipline minimally requires:

- A set of problems to work on;
- A body of knowledge to apply to those problems;
- Scientifically legitimate research about the problems;
- Textbooks that aggregate the core knowledge of the discipline;
- Programs to educate students at the undergraduate and graduate levels, including developing PhD programs to advance knowledge in the field.[9]

I believe people interested in homeland security as a potential academic discipline have made modest advances in each of those areas, with the possible exception of educating homeland security PhDs.

But the other disciplines that contribute to the homeland security enterprise have not simply stood around waiting for a new discipline to emerge.[10] They responded to the twenty-first century's national security threats by getting better at what they do. They may be eliminating the need for homeland security as a distinct public safety/national security paradigm.

I still believe there is a place for homeland security as a professional and intellectual discipline. But it is a belief based increasingly more on faith than evidence.[11]

Homeland Security and Paradigms

As has been argued elsewhere, homeland security can be seen as a pre-paradigm discipline.[12] In the world of practice and in the academy, it must compete against the more mature perspectives offered by the other disciplines in the homeland security enterprise.

Thomas Kuhn uses "paradigm" in two senses that I will adapt for this essay. [13]

A paradigm symbolizes: 1) *the entire constellation of beliefs, values, [and] techniques . . . shared by members of a given community [of practice].*

A paradigm describes: 2) *the concrete puzzle solutions which, employed as models or examples, can replace explicit rules as the basis for the solution of the remaining puzzles of normal science.*

Translated into a homeland security context, a paradigm is a fundamental way of thinking about a discipline's theories and practices. Each traditional discipline in the homeland security enterprise (for example, law enforcement, emergency management, fire service, public health, and so on) has particular knowledge, skills, and preferred ways to think about the issues its members attend to. Because "each group uses its own paradigm to argue in that paradigm's defense,"[14] paradigms provide raw material for constructing the disciplinary stovepipes one continues to find within the homeland security enterprise.

The second part of Kuhn's definition refers to a discipline's "best practices." For example, some people believe the incident command system and its National Incident Management System extension should be the foundational model for all incident response. The National Response Framework holds a similar position as disciplinary exemplar. Both models provide general solutions to a broad set of problems; they do not provide inviolate rules.[15]

Each of what can be termed the participating homeland security disciplines brings with it an "articulated body of problems" and a commitment to use particular values, knowledge, skills and practices to (i.e., paradigms) to address those problems.[16]

For the routine problems practitioners encounter, they can use their discipline's "normal science,"[17] tested and proven behaviors that reflect successful solutions to similar problems. This approach works as long as practitioners face "tame problems," situations characterized by relatively well-defined problems, obvious stopping points, and solutions that can be objectively judged as right or wrong.[18] The strategies are less effective for "wicked problems": ambiguously defined situations generated by nested social and political complexity, disagreements about what a solution looks like, and so on.[19]

The most intractable issues in the homeland security enterprise are related more closely to wicked problems than to tame ones, constraining the ability of traditional disciplines to apply normal problem solving methods to enduring problems.[20]

But looked at from the perspective of someone who is not an advocate for homeland security as a discipline, one could argue there are very few public safety activities undertaken after September 11, 2001 that were not done in some form prior to the attack. Information was being shared—maybe not as effectively as it could have been, but it was being shared. Agencies were collaborating. Grants were being awarded and spent. Plans were being written and exercised. Lessons were being learned and incorporated into new procedures. Each discipline was practicing its version of normal science.

The central difference between then and a decade later is all those practices have improved across the board. Yes there is room for additional improvement. But critical security practices in this nation are better than they used to be. That progress may be enough to obviate the need for a distinct homeland security discipline.

Is There a Need for a New Paradigm?

What would justify bringing a new paradigm into an enterprise that may no longer need it? What, asks Kuhn, causes a community to abandon one paradigm for another? What must people do "to convert the entire profession . . . to their way of seeing science and the world?"[21]

Existing paradigms (represented in this discussion by traditional public safety disciplines) continue unchallenged as long as they satisfactorily address the problems they face. "Paradigm testing occurs only after persistent failure to solve a noteworthy puzzle has given rise to a crisis."[22]

September 11, 2001 was the initial crisis that opened the door to homeland security as a potential new discipline. Hurricane Katrina created a second crisis. Pandemic flu (H1N1) created another opportunity for homeland security to step forward and demonstrate how the framework it provides is in any way superior to traditional security approaches. That (arguably unrealized) opportunity may be vanishing.

Paradigm change begins with anomalies: when gaps arise between expectations about what should happen and the reality of what actually does happen. Anomalies typically have to be "sufficiently fundamental" to invoke the unease and dissatisfaction that leads to the next step in paradigm change: a crisis.[23]

"Sometimes,"notes Kuhn, "an anomaly will clearly call into question explicit and fundamental generalizations of [a dominant paradigm]."[24] But an anomaly does not always have to challenge fundamentals before it sparks a change. If the normal science practiced by a discipline inhibits important work, the anomaly is worthy of "concerted scrutiny."

"When . . . an anomaly comes to seem more than just another puzzle of normal science [that can be solved using existing frameworks], the transition to crisis . . . has begun."[25]

Said less elegantly, when business as usual gets in the way of doing what needs to be accomplished, it may be time to challenge basic assumptions. This is precisely what homeland security as an intellectual framework was supposed to do.

Is the Nation Over Its Security Crisis?

Efforts to address what I called the enduring problems of homeland security can be seen from a "glass half-full"and a "glass half-empty" perspective.

Is the nation (as a whole) generally content with the incremental progress made in addressing many of the enduring problems outlined at the start of this essay and visible in the hundreds of homeland security-related incidents and activities that occurred in 2010?[26] Or is there a significant demand for more substantial and more rapid improvement in most, if not all those areas?

Anomalies morph into crises ("the common awareness that something important has gone wrong")[27] when the normal way of dealing with problems is unsatisfactory. The "failure of existing rules [to solve problems] is a prelude to a search for new ones."[28]

With the exception of continuing—and important—problems at the southern border and with aviation security, I am not aware of significant national dissatisfaction during 2010 with existing rules for addressing the enduring problems. The traditional disciplines in the homeland security enterprise, relying on their normal (and improved) paradigms, may have passed through last decade's doubts about the appropriateness of their conceptual dominance.

An outcome like that is compatible with Kuhn's claim about how paradigm crises end.[29]

Sometimes existing paradigms eventually solve or ameliorate the problems that provoked a crisis.

As one example, in 2010—and after some controversy—fusion centers improved their ability to balance information sharing and privacy protection.[30] This kind of gradual improvement based largely on trial, error, and correction happens routinely throughout homeland security.

Sometimes problems resist almost all attempts at solution and the "problem is . . . set aside for a future generation with more developed tools."[31]

One could argue many important homeland security-related issues have so far been impervious to solutions: for instance, trying to measure preparedness in a way that will satisfy congress and accountants; figuring out how to formally incorporate social media into prevention and response activities; reducing illegal immigration; controlling the southern, northern, and coastal borders; and reducing the number of congressional committees that have a stake in homeland security. Perhaps these problems are best left to future generations of (homeland security?) scholars and practitioners to address.

A crisis might also end, writes Kuhn, "with the emergence of a new candidate for paradigm and with the ensuing battle over its acceptance."[32]

Here is how that part of the change process works:[33]

A new interpretation of some part of the world "emerges first in the mind of one or a few individuals." These are men and women who typically are new to an enterprise, and who are attracted by a "crisis provoking" problem.[34]

Applied to homeland security, this might refer to undergraduate and graduate students who study homeland security, and to scholars and practitioners who may be at the sociological margins of one of the traditional disciplines: people who for a variety of reasons are not satisfied with the established way of addressing national security concerns. Because they are either comparatively new to the field or are dissatisfied with existing approaches, they are less committed to a traditional discipline's ways of thinking about and working on issues.

The failure of existing disciplines—and the paradigms they embody—to prevent the September 11, 2001 attack gave "homeland security" its chance to emerge as a competing paradigm for organizing the nation's security. Homeland security acted as a symbolic catalyst to trigger reflection and change in traditional disciplines. Maybe the homeland security concept has served its social purpose. Maybe it has contributed all it reasonable can to the question of how to establish a more secure nation.

Are We Finished with Homeland Security?

Thomas Kuhn wrote, "The single most prevalent claim advanced by the proponents of a new paradigm is that they can solve problems that have led the old [paradigms] to a crisis."[35]

That assertion creates a fair test for advocates of a homeland security paradigm: How does a homeland security perspective (whatever that may mean in practice) help solve any of the enduring problems outlined at the start of this essay? How are ideas derived from that perspective superior to the approaches championed by other disciplines in the homeland security enterprise?

Kuhn also wrote, "In the development of a scientific field . . . a number of schools [of thought] compete for domination. . . . [In] the wake of some notable scientific achievement, the number of schools is greatly reduced . . . and a more efficient mode of . . . practice begins."[36]

This provides another test for homeland security's claim to be a discipline: What have been its notable scientific achievements?

To the best of my knowledge, there have been no notable scientific achievements—either theoretical or practical—as a result of looking at security-related issues from a homeland security academic or intellectual framework.

But one can ask the same question of law enforcement, fire services, emergency management, public health and the other allied disciplines—and get the same answer. There have been no notable scientific achievements over the past decade (that I am aware of) generated by their traditional paradigms that suggest any of homeland security's enduring problems will soon disappear.

I believe the opportunity remains for a "homeland security perspective" to make distinct and valuable intellectual contributions to national security. But I do not think it has much time to convincingly demonstrate its utility.

Where to From Here?

I get my persisting belief in the potential of homeland security—and in the difficulty it faces realizing that potential—from Thomas Kuhn's historical analysis.

> Philosophers of science have repeatedly demonstrated that more than one theoretical construction can always be placed upon a given collection of data. History of science indicates that, particularly in the early developmental stages of a new paradigm, it is not even very difficult to invent such alternates. But that invention of alternates is just what scientists seldom undertake except during the

pre-paradigm stage of their science's development and at very special [crises] occasions during its subsequent evolution. So long as the tools a paradigm supplies continue to prove capable of solving problems it defines, science moves fastest and penetrates most deeply through confident employment of those tools. The reason is clear. As in manufacture so in science—retooling is an extravagance to be reserved for the occasion that demands it. The significance of crises is the indication they provide that an occasion for retooling has arrived.[37]

I believe a homeland security perspective can be the means to retool significant parts of public safety for the twenty-first century.

Here is a path I think those who are committed to homeland security as a distinct discipline might productively travel. Some of these activities already are underway.

1. Clarify the set of problems the discipline does and should work on: what we know about causes, consequences, and approaches to addressing those issues.
2. Clarify the foundational knowledge to be applied to those problems. This work should also incorporate categories Kuhn outlines in his "disciplinary matrix:"[38]
   • Shared values and ethical principles;
   • Symbolic generalizations that (potentially) unite the discipline [e.g., Risk $= f$ (Threat, Vulnerability, Consequence)];
   • Shared commitments to certain beliefs, analogies, and metaphors;
   • Shared examples and cases that students encounter from the start of their homeland security education demonstrating how homeland security work is done, and highlighting the link between problem and solution;
3. Systematically gather and feature exemplars of quality homeland security research;
4. Write textbooks that feature the discipline's core knowledge;
5. Educate homeland security PhDs.

On December 30, 2010, "Wired Science" featured the top scientific breakthroughs of 2010. The article reminded readers that in 2010 scientists made a reasonable interpretation of the color of a dinosaur, created a synthetic self-replicating form of life, decoded another drug resistant superbug, produced a human embryo with genetic material from three parents, created an HIV drug that seems to have remarkable success, and found millions of tons of water on the moon.[39]

Notes

1. Christopher Bellavita, "Changing Homeland Security: The Year in Review—2007" *Homeland Security Affairs* IV, no. 1 (January 2008), www.hsaj.org/?article=4.1.1; Bellavita, "Changing Homeland Security: The Year in Review—2008." *Homeland Security Affairs* V, no. 1 (January 2009), www.hsaj.org/?article=5.1.1; Bellavita, "Changing Homeland Security:

Twelve Questions From 2009," *Homeland Security Affairs* VI, no. 1 (January 2010) www.hsaj.org/?article=6.1.1.

2. These issues are not the only important concerns for the homeland security agenda. The items in the list are meant as suggestive descriptions of broad problem areas, with each topic having multiple sub-dimensions. On the shifting attention and neglect of issues, see Anthony Downs, "Up and Down With Ecology: The 'Issue-Attention Cycle,'" *The Public Interest,* 28 (Summer 1972): 38–50, and a synthesis of Down's argument in Christopher Bellavita, "Changing Homeland Security: The Issue-Attention Cycle," *Homeland Security Affairs* I, no. 1 (Summer 2005), www.hsaj.org/?article=1.1.1.

3. Donald A. Schon, *The Reflective Practitioner: How Professionals Think in Action* (Ashgate, September 1995). Also on this point, see the Letter to the Editor from Nick Castranzos, "Security for Artisans," in Volume 7 (February 2011) of *Homeland Security Affairs.*

4. U.S. Department of Homeland Security, *Civil Defense and Homeland Security: A Short History of National Preparedness Efforts* (2006), 4–16. See also, "Homeland Security as a Legacy Concept," www.hlswatch.com/2010/10/12/homeland-security-as-a-legacy-concept/.

5. National Commission on Terrorist Attacks upon the United States, *The 9/11 Commission Report: Final Report of the National Commission on Terrorist Attacks Upon the United States,* 1st ed. (New York: Norton, 2004); Paul C. Light, "The Homeland Security Hash," *Wilson Quarterly* (Spring 2007).

6. Prevention was the first priority of the first national homeland security strategy. United States Office of Homeland Security, *National Strategy for Homeland Security* (Washington, D.C.: Office of Homeland Security, 2002).

7. John Rollins and Joseph Rowan, "The Homeland Security Academic Environment" (Homeland Security and Defense Education Consortium, September 2007).

8. James Ramsay, Daniel Cutrer, and Robert Raffel, "Development of an Outcomes-Based Undergraduate Curriculum in Homeland Security," *Homeland Security Affairs* VI, no. 2 (May 2010), www.hsaj.org/?article=6.2.4; Cheryl J. Polson, John M. Persyn, and O. Shawn Cupp, "Partnership in Progress: A Model for Development of a Homeland Security Graduate Degree Program," *Homeland Security Affairs* VI, no. 2 (May 2010), www.hsaj.org/?article=6.2.3; Gregory Moore, et al., "Homeland Security-Related Education and the Private Liberal Arts College," *Homeland Security Affairs* VI, no. 2 (May 2010), www.hsaj.org/?article=6.2.1. See also the Homeland Security and Defense Education Consortium website at www.hsdeca.org/about/.

9. For a creative perspective about how social science disciplines emerge as a type of fractal around certain core and stable issues, see Abbott, Andrew Delano Abbot, *Chaos of Disciplines* (Chicago: University of Chicago Press, 2001).

10. I am using discipline to refer to activities governed by shared expectations, training, education and rules. I use discipline and profession interchangeably in this essay (although there are significant differences between the two). I am not aware of a definitive list of what "disciplines" should be included within the homeland security enterprise. One might infer certain disciplines from Appendix A in "Quadrennial Homeland Security Review Report," *Quadrennial Homeland Security Review* (U.S. Department of Homeland Security, February 2010). For several years, a colleague, William Pelfrey, has maintained a listing of core and peripheral disciplines in homeland security. His list includes people whose job responsibilities range from having a lot to do with homeland security-related issues to those who have rare and tangential involvement: law enforcement, emergency medical services, fire service, hazardous waste operations and emergency response, emergency dispatch communications, health services, emergency management, governmental administrators, public health, public works, business continuity, cyber-security and information technology infrastructure protection, educational institutions and organizations, homeland security, private security, loss prevention, major event security and public safety, Red Cross, volunteer and non-governmental organizations providing public assistance, public information, media management, public places and major facilities, financial institutions, prosecutors, risk management, skilled trades, transportation services, public/private utilities, and military. (Personal correspondence, 2009)

11. Thomas S. Kuhn—whose ideas provide much of the foundation for the argument I make—writes, "The man [or woman] who embraces a new paradigm at an early stage must often do so in defiance of the evidence provided by problem-solving. He must . . . have faith that the new paradigm will succeed with the many large problems that confront it, knowing only that the older paradigm has failed with a few. A decision of that kind can only be made on faith." Thomas S. Kuhn, *The Structure of Scientific Revolutions,* 3rd ed. (University Of Chicago Press, December 1996), 158.

12. Christopher Bellavita and Ellen M. Gordon, "Changing Homeland Security: Teaching the Core," *Homeland Security Affairs* II, no. 1 (April 2006), www.hsaj.org/?article=2.1.1.

13. Kuhn, *Structure of Scientific Revolutions,* 175. For the purpose of the argument I make in this essay, I am using "paradigm" less precisely than would a philosopher or historian of science.

14. Kuhn, *Structure of Scientific Revolutions,* 94.

15. For information about the National Information Management System, see www.fema.gov/emergency/nims/. Information about the National Response Framework is located at www.fema.gov/emergency/nrf/.

16. Kuhn, *Structure of Scientific Revolutions,* 136.

17. I am using "science" in this paper in a general sense: systematic knowledge about subjects gained through observation, experience, experimenting (testing) and theorizing. I am using "normal science" to describe the routine work of the disciplines I discuss in this paper. My use of the phrase is much less precise that Kuhn's use. Kuhn, *Structure of Scientific Revolutions,* 5–6.

18. H. Rittel and M. Webber, "Dilemmas in a General Theory of Planning," *Policy Sciences* 4 Amsterdam: (Elsevier Scientific Publishing Company, 1973): 155–169.

19. Ibid.

20. Christopher Bellavita, "Changing Homeland Security: Shape Patterns, Not Programs," *Homeland Security Affairs* II, no. 3 (October 2006), www.hsaj.org/?article=2.3.5.

21. Kuhn, *Structure of Scientific Revolutions,* 144.

22. Ibid., 147.

23. Ibid., 82.

24. Ibid.

25. Ibid.

26. I think the best, and most easily available, source for watching the changing dynamics of homeland security is the Homeland Security Institute's weekly newsletter—found at www.homelandsecurity.org/NewsletterArchives.aspx. In 2010, they celebrated their tenth year of monitoring news for the homeland security enterprise; www.homelandsecurity.org/bulletin/100709.htm.

27. Kuhn, *Structure of Scientific Revolutions,* 181.

28. Ibid., 68.

29. Ibid., 84.

30. Chris Strohm, "Most Domestic Intel Centers Lack Privacy Plans," *Government Executive,* October 18, 2010, www.govexec.com/story_page.cfm?articleid=46336&dcn=e_hsw.

31. Kuhn, *Structure of Scientific Revolutions,* 84.

32. Ibid.

33. Ibid., 144.

34. In my view, the following 2010 events produced "crisis provoking problems" in the way I use that phrase in the essay: the election of twenty-six new U.S. governors (and the impact that may have on state homeland security activities), the Deepwater Horizon leak in the Gulf of Mexico, the Haitian earthquake and subsequent response, release of information by WikiLeaks, the Icelandic volcano eruption (and what something like that might do if it happened within the U.S.), the growth of social media during response activities (for example Ushahidi crowd sourcing), the apparent growth (or is growth overblown?) of violent domestic radicalization, human trafficking, illegal immigration, continued growth of cyber threats and attacks, continued violence along the southern border (yet why is the border city of El Paso, TX one of America's safest cities?), the use of full body scanners at airports, mail bombs on aircraft, the chairman of the Joint Chiefs of Staff called the national debt "our biggest security threat," the official end—according to the World Health Organization—of the H1N1 pandemic, the "end" of the U.S. combat role in Iraq, the continued problems with the U.S. economic recovery, and the absence (again) of a terrorist attack anywhere near the magnitude of the September 11, 2001 attacks. One might also note 2010 saw the end—

without much fanfare—of a formal national homeland security strategy; general direction for the entire enterprise transitioned from remnants of the Bush-era homeland security strategy, to the *Quadrennial Homeland Security Review* and then into the National Security Strategy.

35. Kuhn, *Structure of Scientific Revolutions,* 153.

36. Ibid., 178.

37. Ibid., 76.

38. Ibid., 182–191.

39. "Wired Science: The Top Scientific Breakthroughs of 2010," *Wired,* www.wired.com/wiredscience/2010/12/top-scientific-discoveries/?utm_source=feedburner&utm_medium=feed&utm_campaign=Feed:+wired/index+(Wired:+Index+3+(Top+Stories+2)).

Critical Thinking

1. What are the four main issues that have helped define homeland security?

2. Is there a need for a new paradigm in Homeland Security?

3. Is the United States over its National Security Crisis?

4. What has to happen in order to advance Homeland Security as an academic discipline?

Create Central

www.mhhe.com/createcentral

Internet References

Homeland Security Affairs
  www.hsaj.org/?home
FEMA
  www.fema.gov/
Homeland Security Articles
  www.homelandsecurity.org/staff-articles

CHRISTOPHER BELLAVITA teaches in the Master's Degree Program at the Naval Postgraduate School in Monterey, California. An instructor with twenty years experience in security planning and operations, he serves as the director of academic programs for the Center for Homeland Defense and Security and is the executive editor of Homeland Security Affairs. He received his PhD from the University of California, Berkeley.

Bellavita, Christopher. From *Homeland Security Affairs,* vol. 7, no. 1, February 2011, pp. 1–11. Copyright © 2011 by Naval Postgraduate School Center for Homeland Defense and Security. Reprinted by permission.

Unit II

UNIT

Prepared by: Thomas J. Badey, *Randolph-Macon College*

Threats to Homeland Security

The purpose of this unit is to give the reader a sense of existing threats. The attacks on the World Trade Center and the Pentagon spawned wild speculation and apocalyptic predictions concerning the future of U.S. security. The tragedies and the subsequent anthrax attacks have fueled fears and have led to exaggerations of terrorist capabilities. Although the existing threats cannot and should not be ignored, the U.S. government and the media often project unrealistic images of terrorists, endowing them with capabilities far beyond their actual reach. These articles seek to provide insights into what some believe the future of terrorist threats may look like. Since terrorism is one of the top priorities for homeland security, difficult choices must be made. As policymakers attempt to find ways to reassure a concerned public, choices between spending for security today and preparing for the threats of the future are becoming increasingly difficult.

Terrorism will undoubtedly remain a major policy issue for the United States well into this century. Opinions as to what future perpetrators will look like and what methods they will pursue vary. While some experts warn of the growing threat posed international terrorists, others are more concerned about lone-wolf style attacks perpetrated by so-called home-grown terrorists. While some argue that the traditional methods of terrorism, such as bombing, kidnapping, and hostage taking, will continue to dominate the new millennium, others warn that weapons of mass destruction or weapons of mass disruption, such as biological and chemical weapons, or even nuclear or radiological weapons will be the weapons of choice for terrorists in the future.

The killing of Osama bin Laden in May 2011, although an important political milestone for the United States, may have only a limited impact on al-Qaeda. Since 9/11, al-Qaeda has become increasingly decentralized. As al-Qaeda central has weakened, al-Qaeda branches, affiliates, and small groups of individuals who claim association with al-Qaeda have become more active.

Even without the training and the logistical and financial support traditionally provided by al-Qaeda central, these ideological networks will continue to exist and fan the flame of violent Islamic extremism. Opinions as to what future perpetrators will look like and what methods they will pursue vary significantly. While some argue that the traditional methods of terrorism, such as bombing, kidnapping, and hostage taking will continue to dominate this millennium, others warn that weapons of mass destruction or weapons of mass disruption, such as biological and chemical weapons, or even radiological or nuclear weapons, will be the weapons of choice for future terrorists. Experts believe that there are certain trends that will characterize international terrorism in the coming years. Some scholars predict that the continuing growth of Islamic extremists will give rise to a new generation of violent, anti-American terrorists. Others are more concerned about a potential increase in home-grown terrorism. Most agree that the tactics employed by terrorists will be more diverse. Future terrorism will likely cause more casualties and may involve the use of weapons of mass destruction.

The articles in this unit highlight some of the potential threats. While politicians and the media primarily focus on threats posed by Islamic extremists, both left- and right- wing militant extremists continue to operate in the United States. "Militant Extremists in the United States" offers an overview of four basic categories of militant extremists and the domestic intelligence infrastructure developed to address this threat. The second article examines the phenomenon of the home-grown Islamic terrorism. It attempts to answer the question: Is there an Islamic Wave? In the third article, by a former CIA counter-terrorism official, explores some potential nuclear terrorism scenarios. Finally, David Wood examines the threat posed by the use of improvised explosive devices (IEDs). He argues that the threat posed by IEDs is increasing as they may become the weapon of choice for terrorists in the United States.

Article   Prepared by: Thomas J. Badey, *Randolph-Macon College*

Militant Extremists in the United States

Jonathan Masters

Learning Outcomes

After reading this article, you will be able to:

- Understand the legal ambiguity caused by the lack of a uniform definition of terrorism.

- Identify the four broad categories of domestic extremists used by the Federal Bureau of Investigation.

- Describe the components of the domestic intelligence infrastructure developed since 9/11.

- Discuss what is needed to effectively address domestic militant extremism.

Introduction

The January 2011 shootings—in which a lone gunman killed six people at a Tucson, Arizona, shopping center—served as a reminder of the threat posed by militant extremism in the United States. Similar acts of violence in the last few years—such as the suicide plane crash into an IRS building in Texas and the 2009 shooting at the U.S. Holocaust Memorial Museum—have brought renewed attention to the dangers posed by fringe political extremism. Although the frequency of these types of attacks has decreased in recent years, "lone wolf" violence is on the rise. The FBI is particularly concerned by such threats because they are performed by individuals who are unaffiliated with any larger movement and are, therefore, hard to detect. As with the case of Tucson shooter Jared Lee Loughner, it is difficult for authorities to determine whether such an act of violence falls under the legal definition of "domestic terrorism," a determination that invokes much harsher sentencing guidelines. Some experts criticize a lack of consistency in the way U.S. domestic terrorism laws are applied, which can lead to dissimilar procedures and outcomes for similar cases.

Violent Extremism or "Domestic Terrorism"?

Since September 11, the threat of internationally based Islamic extremist networks has dominated concerns of Homeland Security officials. And while authorities say the threats posed by homegrown Islamic extremism is growing, the FBI has reported that roughly two-thirds of terrorism in the United States was conducted by non-Islamic American extremists from 1980–2001; and from 2002–2005, it went up to 95 percent.

With the enactment of the Patriot Act in 2001, the legal definition of "terrorism" was expanded to include domestic as well as international terrorism. However, alternative definitions still exist at the FBI, Justice Department, Homeland Security Department, and Defense Department. Some descriptive terms (such as "sub-national," "pre-meditated," "noncombatant," etc.) are present in one definition and absent in others. Furthermore, many law enforcement groups, like the FBI, use the labels of domestic terrorism and violent extremism interchangeably. One consequence of this practice is a lack of uniformity in the way domestic terrorist activities are prosecuted. In an effort to improve federal terrorism laws, a Syracuse University-sponsored watchdog organization compared the number of terrorism cases listed by three entities—the courts (310), the prosecutors (508), and the National Security Division (253)—and found that from 2004–2009 only 4 percent of cases were classified as terrorism on all three lists. This suggests that the agency that made the designation, not the facts of the case, determined whether a suspect was prosecuted as a terrorist and, therefore, may have received a harsher sentence. The same report found "little public evidence that the Obama administration has launched a significant effort to deal with the continuing criminal enforcement flaws."

A Spectrum of Militancy

The worst case of domestic extremist violence was the 1995 bombing of the Alfred P. Murrah Federal Building in Oklahoma City that killed 168 people. In the twenty-five years prior, the United States experienced an average of forty-eight such attacks per year. Since 1995, the average attacks per year declined to nineteen. However, the percentage of attacks perpetrated by individuals acting alone, characterized by law enforcement as "lone wolf" offenders, has increased roughly *five-fold.* . . . Defending against these types of attacks is a daunting task for the FBI and police.

The FBI divides domestic extremists into four broad categories, including left-wing, right-wing, single issue groups, and homegrown Islamic. The lone offender phenomenon spans all categories, and the classifications have other overlapping characteristics as well.

Lone Offenders

Violence by lone offenders (*WSJ*) may pose the most immediate threat in the United States. According to an FBI report on terrorism, the lone wolf label refers to individuals "who commit acts of violence outside of the auspices of structured terrorist organizations or without the prior approval or knowledge of these groups' leaders." A Department of Homeland Security study found that attacks by individuals constituted one-third of all extremist acts of violence since 1995, up from just 6.5 percent in the twenty-five years prior. Recent high-profile cases of these attacks include those by Jared Lee Loughner (*NYT*), James von Brunn (*WSJ*), and Abdulhakim Mujahid Muhammad. Because of their isolation from organized extremist groups, lone wolves are particularly hard to track for intelligence agencies. However, their independence often makes them less effective than members who are well connected to large networks.

Left-Wing Groups

The FBI states leftist extremist groups "generally profess a revolutionary socialist doctrine and view themselves as protectors of the people against the "dehumanizing effects" of capitalism and imperialism." From 1960 to the mid-1980s, most acts of extremist violence were committed by leftist factions like the Weather Underground. A wellspring of disaffected, radical youth with ideological roots in the civil rights, women's liberation, and anti-war movements provided these groups with much of their militant fervor. However, broad left-wing violence has been in a marked decline since the fall of the Soviet Union and a successful FBI infiltration campaign in the mid-1980s.

Single-Issue Groups

Single-issue extremists attack targets that embody distinct political issues like environmental degradation, abortion, genetic engineering, or animal abuse. These groups are usually composed of small, autonomous cells that are hard to infiltrate because of rigid secrecy. According to the FBI, so-called eco-terrorists and animal rights groups like the Earth Liberation Front have committed over two thousand crimes and caused losses of over $110 million since 1979. Ecological extremism (*BaltimoreSun*) gained particular notoriety in the 1990s, and in 2004 the FBI declared these groups the No. 1 domestic terrorism threat. Anti-abortion extremists are responsible for seven murders, forty-one bombings, and 173 acts of arson in the U.S. and Canada since 1977, according to the National Abortion Federation, an abortion rights group. While much of this violence peaked in the 1990s (PDF), the 2009 murder of Dr. George Tiller (*NYT*) served as a reminder of the threat still posed by these factions.

RIGHT-WING GROUPS

The most recent swell of extremist violence began to emerge from right-wing militants in the late-1980s and 1990s. According to a 2005 FBI report on terrorism, these groups, which are "primarily in the form of domestic militias and conservative special interest causes, began to overtake left-wing extremism as the most dangerous, if not the most prolific, domestic terrorist threat to the country." Right-wing extremists champion a wide variety of causes, including racial supremacy, hatred and suspicion of the federal government, and fundamentalist Christianity. The Southern Poverty Law Center, which tracks the activities of hate groups, suggests militia groups declined every year since 1996 but have seen a dramatic resurgence since 2008.

Civil Liberties and Counterterrorism

Following the Church Committee hearings of 1975 and the exposure of several illegal U.S. intelligence programs, U.S. lawmakers instituted a number of legal reforms to safeguard civil liberties, including the 1978 Foreign Intelligence Surveillance Act or FISA. This legislation created strict procedures for reviewing government requests for the electronic surveillance of Americans and resident aliens, and sought to end the practice of warrantless wiretapping. It placed the legal burden of proof on the intelligence community to demonstrate that the subject of surveillance is "a foreign power or agent of a foreign power."

Alternative definitions [of what legally constitutes terrorism] still exist at the FBI, Justice Department, Homeland Security Department, and Defense Department.

However, after the September 11 attacks, the FBI shifted its directive (CNN) from law enforcement to terrorism prevention—returning its emphasis to proactive domestic surveillance. The public fear of another large-scale attack ushered in a new privacy-security paradigm, and with it came legislation aimed at broad national security reforms, such as the Patriot Act, the Homeland Security Act, the Intelligence Reform and Terrorism Prevention Act (PDF), and the 2008 FISA Amendment Acts. But despite this overhaul, CFR's Richard Falkenrath suggests, "The federal government has a quite limited domestic intelligence program and capability. The government does not have an unfettered right to collect information on Americans. It's a very complicated legal and executive order framework, which governs when and how the government can collect information of potential threats domestically."

The Domestic Intelligence Infrastructure

September 11 was a seminal event for U.S. intelligence culture. Prior to the attack, critical components of the intelligence infrastructure like the CIA, FBI, and NSA were not sharing essential information. The 9/11 Commission Report cited a number of reasons for this including structural barriers, divided management, lack of common practices, and excessive secrecy. In their effort to reform the system, lawmakers deemed terrorism prevention a national priority that required the integration all elements of the intelligence infrastructure, including local and state entities as well as dedicated federal agencies like the FBI. To fulfill their new role, local police commanders promoted the adoption of "intelligence-led policing" (PDF), a philosophy emphasizing future-oriented, risk-based intelligence.

The conventional wisdom from law enforcement officials is that prevention requires active, exploratory intelligence gathering. But despite the new emphasis, CFR's Falkenrath says the U.S. domestic intelligence system "is still really built around a framework that requires 'predication,' or evidence of a crime that has occurred or is about to occur. This framework works well in a criminal justice setting, but it really struggles when you know there are real threats that don't have clear predication."

In an open-source review (PDF) for the Department of Homeland Security in 2009, the RAND Corporation mapped the domestic intelligence network to identify all the components "involved in the collection, analysis, and sharing of information about individuals and organizations in the United States." This study identifies three principle categories focused on domestic extremists:

- **Department of Homeland Security.** Formed in 2002, DHS is a cabinet-level department that performs a vast number of domestic intelligence activities and initiatives. The Office of Intelligence and Analysis is the core element of its intelligence function. DHS also operates the National Operations Center, which collects and fuses information from more than thirty-five public and private agencies. In addition, Information-Sharing and Analysis Centers or ISACs are an assortment of public-private partnerships designed to protect critical physical and electronic infrastructure from terrorist attacks. For example, DHS launched a cybersecurity operation center in New York in November 2010.
- **Department of Justice.** The Federal Bureau of Investigation is the government's lead agency for domestic intelligence and counterterrorism, but the DoJ also includes the DEA, U.S. Attorneys Offices, U.S. Marshals Service, and the Bureau of Alcohol, Tobacco, Firearms, and Explosives. The FBI intelligence mission is managed at the National Security Branch which, among other things, manages the National Joint Terrorism Task Force and the Terrorist Screening Center.
- **State, Local, and Private-Sector Groups.** The FBI-led Joint Terrorism Task Force and the DHS-supported Fusion Center program are the most prominent federally directed, multiagency initiatives. Both programs use intelligence from multiple entities to leverage information-sharing potential. However, the FBI task force is always the lead agency for domestic terrorism investigations, as demonstrated in the the January 2011 MLK Day attempted-bombing in Washington state. On the other hand, fusion centers may be focused on any number of other concerns outside the realm of terrorism, such as organized crime, immigration, and natural disasters.

The Road Ahead

> "We're at a point where you have to start asking hard questions about changing the law, and/or the executive orders that interpret the law, to be more permissive."
>
> —CFR Adjunct Senior Fellow Richard Falkenrath

Militant extremism in the United States continues to provide grist for the national debate on a number of policy areas. The shootings in Tucson revived the issue of gun control once again, highlighting some of the nation's controversial firearm legislation—like the Arizona law allowing citizens to carry concealed weapons without a permit. In addition, public discussion continues over the legal definition of domestic terrorism and whether it is applied equitably. Questions also remain as to whether the United States has lessons to learn from the counterterrorism experiences of other countries. For instance, should it create an independent domestic intelligence agency (PDF) similar to Britain's MI-5, which does not incorporate a law enforcement function like the FBI?

Efforts to counter homegrown militancy will also continue to drive a conversation on civil liberties. Liberal groups like the American Civil Liberties Union advocate for stricter legal guidelines, "oppos[ing] the broad definition of terrorism and the ensuing authority that flows from that definition." On the other hand, proponents of assertive enforcement capabilities, like CFR's Falkenrath, raise concerns over potentially excessive regulation. "We're at a point where you have to start asking hard questions about changing the law, and/or the executive orders that interpret the law, to be more permissive."

Critical Thinking

1. Why are "lone wolf" attacks more difficult to prevent than organized terrorism?
2. What are the benefits and drawbacks of expanding domestic intelligence capabilities?
3. What can be done to reduce the threat of militant extremism in the United States?

Create Central

www.mhhe.com/createcentral

Internet References

The Challenge of Domestic Intelligence in a Free Society
www.rand.org/pubs/monographs/2009/RAND_MG804.pdf
Congress and the Intelligence Community
http://gai.georgetown.edu/congressintell.cfm
Intelligence-Led Policing
www.ncjrs.gov/pdffiles1/bja/210681.pdf

Article   Prepared by: Thomas J. Badey, *Randolph-Macon College*

Homegrown Terrorism
Is There an Islamic Wave?

Geneve Mantri

Learning Outcomes

After reading this article, you will be able to:

- Discuss the history of domestic terrorism in the United States.

- Identify external factors that may contribute to radicalization

- Discuss how the United States can best respond to the threat posed by domestic terrorism.

U s Representative Peter King's congressional hearings—on Muslim radicalization, the war on terror, and the role of America's Muslims—proceed, provide an opportune time to take stock of a homegrown terrorist phenomenon that has gripped headlines across the country particularly since Christmas Day 2009. Even a cursory look at the past 18 months gives rise to a number of incidents that seem to reflect a view of the United States increasingly under attack, whether it be the Fort Hood shootings, the Christmas Day bomber Abdul Muttalab, or the attempted Times Square bombing by Faisal Shahzad.

The most alarming things about these attempted attacks have been both the apparent ineffectiveness of the Homeland Security apparatus put in place post-9/11 and the rise in what is commonly termed homegrown terrorism: attacks conceived and launched by US citizens on US citizens. The link between some of these attacks and Anwar ai-Awlaki—an American imam living in Yemen—highlights the new threat from the United States' own. Even Michael Leiter, the head of the National Counterterrorism Center, recently described af-Awlaki as the greatest threat to the United States. These attacks, albeit unsuccessful, have punctured a false sense of security that has developed post-9/11, and contested the commonly held narrative that the United States was free from attack for seven years.

A History of Domestic Terror

Firstly, is domestic terrorism in the United States a new phenomenon? While the concept of international terrorism has resonated strongly for many European countries, especially those with post colonial histories, this heady mix of insurgency, terrorism, and bourgeois radicals, such as the Baader Meinhof gang and the Red Army Faction, appears to have no parallel at home. However, previous waves of international terrorism have both been launched from the United States and also terrorized Americans. Clan na Gael (United Irishmen), led by Jeremiah Donovan Rossa, organized and fundraised from the United States in the 1870s. In today's parlance of material support they raised US$23,350 to fund a terrorist campaign. In January 1881, they bombed Salford Barracks, Manchester, killing a seven-year-old boy and injuring three people. From 1881 to 1883, they conducted an indiscriminate bombing campaign of underground and railway stations in the United Kingdom.

Even the US homeland was not immune to violence. In May 1886, an anarchist threw a bomb at Haymarket in Chicago, killing eight police officers and an unknown number of civilians. US President William McKinley was assassinated in September 1901 by another anarchist, Leon Czolgosz. The attacks were linked to a global ideology, and they struck significant political and civilian targets both in the United States and across the world, including former French President Marie-Francois Sadi Carnot in 1894. Throughout the 20th century, US citizens continued to provide material support for terrorists, including arms for the Irish Revolutionary Army (IRA), even when it was abundantly clear they would be supporting a mainland bombing campaign aimed at civilian targets. Americans have also actively participated in supporting international terrorist groups, including Tupac Amaru in Peru.

More recently, even the earlier Al-Qaeda operatives included some local recruits. Jose Padilla, "Abdullah al Muhajir," the millennium bomber Ahmed Ressam, an Algerian living in Montreal, and Ali Mohammed Abdel-soud Muhammed, a former Egyptian military officer who immigrated to America and became a sergeant in the US Army, all worked with Al-Qaeda long before 9/11. While these recruits were luckily few in number, it does belie the notion that the latest outbreak reflects a new tactic which has emerged from nowhere. There are conflicting opinions about the actual role and motivations of John Walker Lindh (the "American Taliban"), but no one contests he was in Afghanistan training with the Taliban while they were supporting Al-Qaeda, three years after the US Embassy bombings in Nairobi and Tanzania in 1998. While there are important differences, it is also worth noting that, apart from radical Islam, there are other major threats to the United States which have resulted in major acts of terror—most notably Oklahoma City, and the 1996 Atlanta Olympic bombing by Eric Rudolph. All this indicates that the United States is facing multidimensional threats which ought to be seen in the context of a much more varied and longstanding threat picture.

The New Wave

Is there truly a wave of homegrown terrorism? At first blush the answer appears to be yes. On the basis of simple cursory scans of headlines it appears that not only are there more attacks, but that a significant proportion of them appear to be led or conceived by Americans targeting other Americans. Before the Fort Hood shooting, there was an attack on a US recruiting station in Little Rock, Arkansas; after Fort Hood, there was the failed Christmas Day attack, the attempted Times Square bombing by Faisal Shahzad, and the attempted attack last Christmas in Portland, Oregon by Somali-born Mohamed Osman Muhamad. Colleen La Rose, "Jihad Jane," was arrested for plotting to murder Swedish cartoonist Lars Vilks, and David Headley, "Daood Sayed Gilani," was arrested for his involvement in the Mumbai attacks, assisting Lashkar-E-Taiba, and for his involvement in plotting an attack on the *Fyllands Posten* newspaper in Copenhagen.

Many of these cases, if not all, were under surveillance by law enforcement and the Federal Bureau of Investigation (FBI); hence it is not clear if there are more plots or if the United States is simply getting better at disrupting them. Some included early FBI work to supply phony devices, which raises civil libertarian concerns about the FBI both luring people who are susceptible, and simultaneously entrapping them. Regardless, if they are operationally successful, is this a cause for concern, celebration, or both?

The answer, unfortunately, is not clear, according to Mike German, a current member of the American Civil Liberties Union (ACLU) and former FBI agent. What appears to be simple repetition of headlines and court eases is, on closer examination, neither as clear cut, nor as linear as it appears. There were fewer plots in 2010 than in 2009, and of those, according to the Triangle Center on Terrorism and Homeland Security, there were over 20 terrorist plots by non-Muslims in the United States in 2010.

Many Forms of the Wave

In the years immediately before and after 9/11, there was a common assumption that the United States and its allies were facing a new and radical threat that was distinct from modern international terrorism by its diffuse nature, vague obscurantist objectives, and total lack of proportionality. However, the wave was apparently foreign-born and bred, and if the United States could figuratively and perhaps literally seal its borders, the wave could be kept out, or at least displaced.

This assumption, focusing on the 9/11 plotters, stemmed largely from foreign-born Al-Qaeda operatives who were able to enter and live in the United States relatively easily due to their lack of prior intelligence records. Other Al-Qaeda operatives involved in the 9/11 plot, such as Ramsi Bin al Shibh, had been denied entry to the United States due to immigration concerns related to their links to Yemen. The core 9/11 conspirators such as Mohammed Atta were attractive to Al-Qaeda precisely because they were western-educated, could mix easily, and had "clean skins"—with no prior evidence of extremism. According to this narrative, the origin and development of the 9/11 plot tended to focus on disillusioned middle-class migrants, such as Mohammed Atta, alienated and living in a largely hedonistic western European sea that at once lured, enticed, and repelled them.

The United States was immune in this schema. The European experience of post-colonial immigration has no relation in the United States, where the melting pot of immigration and integration largely worked in socializing new immigrants to the American dream and offering them opportunities. A key proponent of this view has been Mark Sageman, a French-born American, who spent considerable time with former Jihadis in France, Spain, and Western Europe; he drew sharp contrasts between life chances on the margins of European society and the pathway offered by the American dream.

The more recent US attacks belie this view in their nature as largely domestic and seemingly undirected by Al-Qaeda central. The domestic attacks disprove the idea that the United States, as a nation, is immune from radicalization at home. Even more disturbing has been the concept that this is driven by so called "lone wolf" attacks, of people self-radicalizing through the internet and without the support of a much wider terrorist infrastructure or radical community.

Paths Leading to Terror

Regardless of anecdotes that give rise to concerns about lone wolves who are self-radicalizing on the internet, as Peter Neumann ably points out, terrorism is a group activity. The concern is not only what triggers this involvement, but also what spurs terrorist activities and how they are operationalized. It is still highly improbable that lone individuals sitting in a basement or visiting Home Depot are going to construct terrorist devices for their own use. Much more of a concern are patterns of behavior indicating frequent visits to places where terrorist networks exist and evidence of personal connections that can lead them to institutional and operational help of whatever kind.

David Headley's trip to Pakistan, like the 9/11 bombers before him, served to equip him for his journey into jihad. Military training and activity requires space and at least a semi-state willing to turn a blind eye. Experienced personnel are needed to train and nurture a terrorist along a path, and building and testing bombs takes space. Evidence suggests that there are myriad individual paths to violence that are neither linear nor rapid, and a number of thresholds have to be reached before recruits are able to carry out acts of violence.

Where a willing state is available to provide a de facto sanctuary, the concern increases, as in the case of Pakistan and the

Muslim-American Terrorism Suspects and Perpetrators, 2010

Name	Location	Alleged Plot	Disrupted	Status of Case*
Zarein Ahmedza	NY	Planned subway attack in NYC	Late	Guilty Plea
Adis Medunjani	NY	Planned subway attack in NYC	Late	Trial Pending
Colleen R. LaRose	PA	Planned to attack cartoonists in Europe	Early	Trial Pending
Jamie Paulin-Ramire	CO	Planned to attack cartoonists in Europe	Early	Trial Pending
Sharif Mobley	NJ	Arrested in Yemen	No	Trial Pending
Raja Lahrasib Kha	IL	Spoke of atacking a sports stadium	Early	Trial Pending
Anwar al-Awlaki	Yemen	Incited terrorism in the US and Yemen	No	Convicted in Yemen
Faisal Shahzad	NY	Times Square car-bomb, NYC	No	Guilty Plea
Mohamed Aless	NJ	Planned to join a-Shabaab in Somalia	Early	Trial Pending
Carlos Almont	NJ	Planned to join a-Shabaab in Somalia	Early	Trial Pending
Samir Khan	NC	Joined al-Qa'ida in Yemen	No	Not Yet Charged
Zachary A. Chesse	NY	Planned to join a-Shabaab in Somalia	Early	Trial Pending
Nadia Rockwood	AK	Passed along list of assassination targets	Early	Guilty Plea
Paul G. Rockwood J	AK	Developed list of assasination targets	Early	Guilty Plea
Shaker Masr	IL	Planned to join a-Shabaab in Somalia	Early	Trial Pending
Farah Mohamed Beled	MN	Joined a-Shabaab in Somalia	No	Trial Pending
Abdel Hameed Shehadeh	HI	Planned to join a-Shabaab in Somalia	Early	Trial Pending
Farooque Ahmed	VA	Planned to attack subway in Somalia	Early	Trial Pending
Mohamed Mohamud	OR	Christmas Tree Ceremony attack	Early	Trial Pending
Antonio Martinez	MD	Planned to bomb military recruiting office in Baltimore County	Early	Trial Pending

Triangle Center on Terrorism and Homeland Security; 2011

border regions of Federally Administered Tribal Areas (FATA), or in the case of Yemen. Pakistan's effective use of paramilitary groups in Kashmir gives it a sub-strategic option against India which it will not readily cede, and the lines between domestic and external groups is at best opaque. These groups have received support funding and training from elements of the Pakistani Inter-Services Intelligence, and the same allied structures historically apply to its relationships with groups in Afghanistan as well as Kashmir.

External Factors

A factor that complicates debates further is that discussions about terrorism are often conflated with concerns over Americans, of mainly Somali extraction, joining external groups such as Al-Shabab. The largest concentrations of Somali Americans are clustered around St. Paul, Minnesota. What appears to be a group from that area has emerged in Mogadishu to fight against Ethiopia, a strong US regional ally which invaded Somalia in 2006 to overthrow the Islamic Courts Union. Al-Qaeda and its affiliates have had a long standing presence in East Africa, long before 9/11, and regional links can be drawn to and from Yemen.

However, the end result can best be described as murky. It is not clear who these people are, or what motivates them, but the concern is that once radicalized, trained, and militarized abroad, they might return home. A parallel could be drawn with Muslim foreign fighters who fought in both Afghanistan and Bosnia, and later formed a core group in Al-Qaeda. Another

parallel many draw is to British Pakistani Muslims who apparently trained at camps in Pakistan and have become a source for concern to the UK government.

On the other hand, the United States has had many communities in which young people go abroad for a variety of reasons in search of a calling, adventure, or belonging. In the 1930s, idealistic Americans joined the Lincoln Brigade and fought Franco's fascists, or later joined the Royal Armed Forces' Eagle Squadrons and fought in the Battle of Britain. Americans even fought with Nelson's fleet against the French and Spanish at Trafalgar. The aim of these comparisons is neither to be flippant nor disrespectful, but the reality is that young people are often motivated by many conflicting desires, and while the arrival of Somali American youth on the African battlefield and their return could be a real concern, this should be seen in a larger context. It is also important to note that in most cases, law enforcement agencies learned about these movements from family members who reported their own relatives as missing.

Domestic Response

Domestic groups often complain that the United States' has only responded by spinning a vast web and hoping the terrorists walk into it, citing Christmas Day and the Times Square attempt as lucky breaks. This is in some ways unfair, as the web could also be argued to be so vast that it sucks up chaff which only increases the time it takes to shift, find, and collate accurate and useful data.

The underlying inability of the US government to create adaptive learning environments is also a concern. The prime agencies involved are all products of the 1947 National Security Act or 1960s reforms. Many have effectively become orphans in Washington DC, with no patrons to develop effective systems and promote stability within these agencies. Congress, much like an absentee parent, is neglectful and only appears intermittently to administer beatings or to cut funds. By contrast, it has taken over 200 years of constant building and rebuilding to create the ethos, values, and competence of the US Marine Corps to tackle specific kinetic tasks. It is unreasonable to create a civilian agency haphazardly with none of these advantages and with little care or attention to their growth or development. The enemy operates within a complex adaptive system, and in response we have built massive bureaucracies. What is required is agility, adaptability, flat structures, and open access to foreign talent. What has been produced is arguably the reverse.

A key issue is the inability to create and develop an effective information operations capability countering radical messages effectively. US actions either signal that local support is irrelevant, or that it is taken for granted. In the midst of the Cold War, the United States was awash in Russian linguists, yet ten years after 9/11, knowledge of Arabic, Dari, or Pashtu is extremely limited. Attempts to understand the region are met with cries of appeasement. Local support and knowledge are not irrelevant to the struggle against Al-Qaeda or other terrorist groups; they are a basic building block of success.

The Best Answer

On many occasions, the best intelligence has been garnered from the suspects' own communities, both in the United States and overseas. The prime warnings about David Headley's suspicious terrorist activities came from two of his wives, and Abdul Mutallab was turned in to US authorities by his own father. One can only imagine how much more effective the United States could be if its agencies could harness the innate goodwill displayed towards and received by individual Americans overseas. Despite the best efforts of superb individual officers, great universities, and the world's most creative communications and entertainment industry, the end product of official US government communications efforts is woefully inadequate.

Just as concerning as the external environment are the language and rhetoric used within the United States. The recent hysteria about the cultural center near Ground Zero became a lightning rod for anti-Muslim feeling, and Representative Peter King's House Homeland Security Committee Hearings on American Muslims also serve to present a view of the country's mosques and Muslim communities as hotbeds of extremism.

The reality is exactly the reverse. As President George W. Bush said in the immediate aftermath of 9/11, Muslims were not responsible for the attacks. Furthermore, senior members of his administration, including Fran Townsend and Juan Zarate, two key voices in the Homeland and National Security Council, have publically and privately defended the role and the contributions of American Muslims against violent extremism. However, in a Senate Homeland Security Committee Hearing in the wake of the Fort Hood shooting, Townsend also rightly noted that, while there is extensive cooperation from the Muslim community, they prefer that this be discrete. Muslim Americans are not a threat, but a vital part of the response; attempts to label them will only serve to alienate an entire population of patriotic citizens.

Controlling the Wave

What should our response be? It is important to maintain a sense of proportion. According to Charles Kurzman at the Triangle Institute, there have been about 150,000 murders since 9/11, averaging 15,000 murders per year, a figure which completely dwarfs the threat from other violent incidents. The threat from Islamic terrorism is not going to be defeated by waging a conventional or sub-conventional war. It is a scourge which needs to be contained, depleted, and ultimately eradicated using every tool in the government's arsenal. Civilians are, unfortunately, all too often on the front line both in the United States and around the world, and civil tools must also be used as part of the response—legally, culturally, and socially. Former President George W. Bush is often maligned for telling Americans in the wake of 9/11 that they should go shopping, but in a key sense be was right. Al-Qaeda cannot contribute to the destruction of US values and institutions on its own. In order to pursue its terrorist ambitions, Al-Qaeda needs to place citizens in a state of fear and uncertainty. An important response to terrorism is to keep calm and carry on in the American way of life.

Regardless of the sometimes breathless coverage of domestic incidents, terrorism does not pose an existential threat to the United States, as the Soviet Union did in the Cold War. Al-Qaeda cannot destroy the United States, its institutions, or its way of life. Attempts to build Al-Qaeda up in this way only serve to glamorize the mythology that Osama bin Laden seeks. Terrorists seek mass casualties to wreak havoc, but they also carry a narrative of a romantic struggle which should be systematically attacked and undermined using every tool and resource at the US government's disposal. Al-Qaeda seeks the legitimacy that comes from wearing the mantel of warriors on a battlefield, therefore, the United States should use every attempt to deny them that stature and instead portray them as criminals, misfits, and murderers. This does not mean that US military force should be restrained any more than the police; the judiciary, or any other useful tool, should be restrained, but over-militarizing the response can push other options off the table and will be self-defeating. Regardless of the desire for revenge, terrorists who are executed or the at the hands of jailers are likely to play a bigger role after death as martyrs than they ever would if they were forgotten in prison. Death creates a mythology that is nigh impossible to undercut.

Most crucially, the struggle against Al-Qaeda is a war of ideas and ideology—not just a contest of kinetic military power. The biggest secret weapon in the US arsenal is its large, prosperous, and well-integrated moderate Muslim population. They have provided support, aided with tips, and shared the costs of keeping the United States safe. They can also help shape a counter-narrative against those who threaten the lives of all Americans. The biggest mistake would be to adopt policies which specifically target and label the American Muslim population as a threat, instead of embracing them as citizens and the heart of the solution. The United States has the best system for attracting and assimilating the greatest talent from around the world, including Muslims, and instilling them with American values within one generation. This also sends a powerful international message that the United States is an immigrant society: diversity of views, race, and religion are all strands in the national fabric that keep society healthy and strong, and adherence to the rule of law and American values are the ties that bind the country together. No other country in the world even comes close to this ability, and whatever limits it may have, it remains a core strength that should be harnessed, not stymied, through shortsighted and self-defeating measures.

Critical Thinking

1. Is domestic terrorism a new phenomenon?
2. Is there truly a new wave of homegrown terrorism
3. What factors contribute the radicalization of individuals or groups?
4. How should the U.S. government respond to domestic terrorism?
5. Does domestic terrorism pose an existential threat to the United States?

Create Central

www.mhhe.com/createcentral

Internet References

Threat of Homegrown Islamist Terrorism
www.cfr.org/terrorism/threat-homegrown-islamist-terrorism/p11509

Homegrown Terrorism
http://csis.org/files/publication/120425_Pregulman_AQAMCaseStudy7_web.pdf

Homegrown Terrorism a growing concern for U.S. Intelligence
www.csmonitor.com/USA/2010/0204/Homegrown-terrorism-a-growing-concern-for-US-intelligence

GENEVE MANTRI serves as the Government Relations Director for Terrorism, Counter-terrorism, and Human Rights at Amnesty International. The views of this article do not represent the views of Amnesty International.

Mantri, Geneve. From *Harvard International Review,* Spring 2011, pp. 88–94. Copyright © 2011 by the President of Harvard College. Reprinted by permission via Sheridan Reprints.

Article

Prepared by: Thomas J. Badey, *Randolph-Macon College*

Nightmares of Nuclear Terrorism

ROLF MOWATT-LARSSEN

Learning Outcomes

After reading this article, you will be able to:

- Describe the threat posed by nuclear terrorism.

- Discuss why a group like Al Qaeda may or may not want to use a nuclear weapon.

- Describe three potential scenarios that could lead to nuclear terrorism

When working abroad for the CIA in the early 1990s, I received a senior officer from Washington on a mission to collect an important piece of evidence to help identify the culprits behind the bombing of Pan Am Flight 103. As we sat in a restaurant sipping a glass of wine, "Mike," a veteran counterterrorism agent, enumerated the reasons why the investigation was among the CIA's highest priorities. His eyes narrowed as he recalled that the terrorist attack on the commercial airliner had killed one of our own. "Terrorism is deeply personal business," he sighed. "It will be around as long as there are people with scores to settle." He continued, "Terrorists embarrass politicians, and their attacks are always painful for the families of their victims. But terrorism isn't a strategic problem. It won't affect our way of life, and it isn't a threat to our national security."

That might have been true at the time, but on 9/11, Al Qaeda rewrote the terrorist playbook by executing mass casualty attacks against strategic U.S. targets. In essence, these attacks ended one era and ushered in a new one. It is an age in which a few terrorists hold the means to alter the course of history with a single blow. Having set a standard that dares to change the world, it is likely only a matter of time before 9/11 is eclipsed by an even more devastating event.

So why has it not happened yet?

For starters, having pulled off such a complex and successful operation as 9/11, Osama bin Laden may find it problematic to settle on anything lesser—or riskier—that might damage his movement's almost mythological standing in the annals of terrorist lore. Al Qaeda is a conservative, risk-averse organization. The group's leadership apparently recognizes that it is better to not attack at all, than to do so in a way that falls short of the lofty goals they have set for themselves. And for now at least, the

Al Qaeda leadership may have few credible options for making good on threats to disrupt the global economy and to convince their adversaries that they are fighting a war that cannot be won.

A further—and highly unsettling—explanation of Al Qaeda's extraordinary patience is that group members think time is on their side. They probably believe they have drawn the United States into a deepening commitment to fight a protracted insurgency in Afghanistan. Moreover, Saddam Hussein was deposed, opening up long-term possibilities for an Islamic theocracy in Iraq. Gen. Pervez Musharraf is out of power in Pakistan, and the domestic instability there is growing every day. These developments create opportunities to change the global status quo. In other words, Al Qaeda may be waiting for a perfect storm in the alignment of targets, opportunity, and timing to launch another game-changing attack. If they do so, it will certainly be based on a calculation that the moment is ripe to try to force Washington's hand in ways that favor Al Qaeda's long-term goals.

In this light, the group's long-held intent and persistent efforts to acquire nuclear and biological weapons represent a unique means of potentially fulfilling its wildest hopes and aspirations. As bin Laden declared in 1998, it is his duty to obtain WMD. He apparently understood at this early juncture that using such weapons might become necessary at some stage of his confrontation with the United States and its allies. With this in mind, Al Qaeda feverishly pursued nuclear and biological weapons capabilities before 9/11. These efforts were managed by the group's most senior leadership, with a sense of purpose and urgency that suggests it was important to make progress on possessing WMD prior to its 2001 attack on the United States. Yet in spite of bin Laden's declaration and Al Qaeda's subsequent efforts to acquire nuclear and biological weapons, the threat is not widely being treated as a clear-and-present danger that requires an urgent response.

Nuclear terrorism detractors point out that the threat has been hyped. Unfortunately, it is true that some have used the WMD threat to incite fear and to justify extreme tactics to combat terrorism. Skeptics argue that there were no WMD in Iraq, so why should people believe intelligence that terrorists are seriously trying to acquire them? Plus, if terrorists have such a weapon, why haven't they used it? They also argue that it is impossible for men in caves to acquire and detonate a nuclear bomb. They acknowledge some nuclear material may be missing from global stocks, but they exude confidence that it is surely not available in sufficient enough quantities to constitute a real threat, and that in any case, it is preposterous to believe that primitive, unsophisticated terrorists might be able to construct a bomb capable of producing a nuclear yield.

Let us hope the skeptics are right, because in terms of organizing the international community to confront the threat posed by large-scale WMD terrorism, not much has been accomplished. Intelligence and law enforcement agencies, in the United States and abroad, have been slow to dedicate resources and leadership to the problem. For example, there is a widespread assumption that terrorists will employ small-scale, crude forms of chemical, biological, and radiological weapons because they are easier to acquire and use. But the weight of the evidence suggests the opposite is true—i.e., terrorists choose weapons best suited for the targets they intend to strike. The history of Al Qaeda strikes against the United States bears this out. The group historically has utilized a remarkably diverse arsenal of weapons in its attacks against the United States: The embassy bombings in Kenya and Tanzania were ground attacks; the U.S.S. *Cole* bombing was a sea attack; and the World Trade Center and Pentagon bombings were air attacks. It chose the desired weapons based on operational considerations, most notably a weapon's capacity to destroy the intended target.

Another dangerous bias in assessing the threat is the belief that once terrorists obtain a nuclear bomb, they will use it. Thus, the following argument is proffered: Since Al Qaeda has yet to use a nuclear weapon, it does not possess one. This might comfort the doubters, but terrorists may not agree that it is difficult to stash a nuclear or biological weapon in a safe place for future use, without fear of discovery. After all, it has proved exceedingly difficult to find bin Laden and his lieutenant Ayman al-Zawahiri, and we have a pretty good idea of where they might be hiding. Plus, nothing in Al Qaeda's behavior suggests that its leaders follow predictable patterns concerning the means and timing of attacks.

But accepting that nuclear terrorism can happen does not mean that it is inevitable. The odds are stacked against a terrorist successfully acquiring a nuclear bomb. That said, in a twenty-first-century world of rare and unpredictable events, prudent risk management must prioritize threats based on both the probability of an event and its potential consequences. Accordingly, terrorists must be denied any possibility, however remote it might seem, from ever succeeding in their quest to launch a nuclear or large-scale biological attack on any city. Better still, if we can anticipate how a nuclear terrorist threat might unfold, it stands to reason that we might be able to prevent such an attack from happening.

The following scenarios are the nuclear nightmares that keep me up at night.

Pakistan Loses Control of Its Bomb

Allegations that the threat posed by Pakistani "loose nukes" has been hyped and that the Pakistani military has everything under control may sound soothing, but they obscure the fact that

South Asia is replete with violent extremists. Mix in a rapidly expanding arsenal of nuclear weapons and growing domestic instability, and there is a greater possibility of a nuclear meltdown in Pakistan than anywhere else in the world.

It is a good thing then that the Pakistani military approaches nuclear security with great professionalism, for Pakistan has fewer margins for error than any other nuclear state. For comparison's sake, in the United States, it was widely recognized that significant nuclear security upgrades had to be made after 9/11. Specific attention was given to the possibility that terrorists could gain access to a nuclear weapons–related facility, particularly with the assistance of insiders working at the facility. Accordingly, large increases in funding were allocated to assure a much higher U.S. nuclear security standard, including an increased emphasis on intelligence and counterintelligence programs. Nonetheless, in recent years, there have been appalling lapses in controls over nuclear weapons and the compromise of nuclear weapons–related information—e.g., a U.S. Air Force B-52 mistakenly and unknowingly flew six nuclear-tipped cruise missiles across the country (from North Dakota to Louisiana) in August 2007. With this in mind, U.S. concerns about Pakistani vulnerabilities should not be interpreted as finger-pointing or meddling; it obviously can happen in the United States as well. Some broader trends in Pakistan, however, elevate the risks of compromised nuclear security.

The Burgeoning Pakistani Nuclear Arsenal

A growing domestic nuclear program means more nuclear activity taking place in more places—necessitating more materials, weapons, facilities, transportation, and storage. In short, there are now more places where something can go wrong.

Increased Extremism

Growing levels of extremism means higher numbers of potential insiders in the nuclear establishment willing to work with outsiders to provide access to facilities and exfiltrate nuclear-related materials and weapons. Recent warnings by the Taliban and Al Qaeda that Washington will seize Pakistan's nuclear weapons amount to a clever recruiting pitch to insiders to collaborate with extremists. In an attempt to stoke such groundless fears, A. Q. Khan, the father of the Pakistani nuclear program, and Bashiruddin Mahmood, the radical CEO of Khan's rogue nuclear supplier network, both recently called upon Pakistan to expand its arsenal of nuclear weapons, implying that they guarantee sovereignty and assure Islamabad's standing as a leading Islamic nation.

The Perilous Military-Civilian Relationship

Although Pakistan's nuclear National Command Authority is controlled by the military, the Pakistani constitution delegates certain nuclear weapon responsibilities to the civilian government. This creates the potential for a military-civilian standoff over nuclear assets during a crisis, especially in the event that extremist elements assume power. Moreover, there are no guarantees of how the military and government would react to all contingencies they may encounter in a rapidly unfolding crisis. For instance, how would they respond to a breakdown in internal communication, or with the outside world? Unconfirmed news reports of a seizure of nuclear weapons in transit? A takeover of a facility by a rogue military unit? Taliban penetration of a nuclear weapons storage site? More importantly, how would India interpret and react to such developments? Along these lines: Are current communication mechanisms between Islamabad, New Delhi, and Washington robust enough to be reliable during a crisis?

At least in Pakistan, the risks are well-known and extra precautions are being taken to avert nuclear compromise. That is not the case for the next scenario.

North Korea Sells the Bomb

The discovery of Syria's Al Kibar reactor, believed to be built with North Korean assistance, was a wake-up call that Pyongyang does not possess strong self-imposed constraints on transferring nuclear technologies to other parties—a sobering, if unsurprising, reality. After all, North Korea routinely prints counterfeit U.S. currency, traffics narcotics, and starves its own people. So it is not unexpected that it would provide nuclear-related technologies for profit. If anything, North Korea's erratic and irresponsible behavior makes it a leading potential source—on a witting or unwitting basis—for terrorist acquisition of nuclear-related technologies and materials.

The extraordinary level of secrecy in handling intelligence concerning the North Korean-Syrian project at Al Kibar helped ensure that knowledge of its existence did not leak before Israel could effectively neutralize the reactor militarily in September 2007. Unfortunately, secrecy also restricted the international community's ability to run down all leads on the reactor before the North Koreans discovered that it had been compromised. So an opportunity was lost to begin an early examination of active proliferation pathways flowing from Pyongyang. Nonetheless, there are three broad implications of North Korean-Syrian nuclear cooperation that should be assessed urgently.

The Viability of the Nonproliferation Regime

To date, the regimes of Kim Jong-il and Bashar al-Assad have suffered no consequences for conspiring to develop a nuclear weapons capability, casting doubts on the viability of the Nuclear Non-Proliferation Treaty and the credibility of the global nuclear order. In fact, U.S. dialogue with Syria improved after the Israeli raid. And the countries participating in the Six-Party Talks with North Korea (the United States, Russia, China, South Korea, and Japan) continue to cajole Pyongyang back to the negotiating table to make new concessions in exchange for more promises the North will not keep. Basically, Al Kibar obliterated all of the red lines thought to exist in terms of nuclear deterrence, accountability, and responsibility, setting a precedent that it is okay to clandestinely provide nuclear-related technologies to other states.

An "A. Q. Kim" Network?

Since Kim Jong-il came close to providing Syria with the building blocks for a nuclear weapon, how confident can the international community be that there is not a long-running "A. Q. Kim" network in North Korea that is analogous to the Khan nuclear supplier network in Pakistan? Clearly, the chapter of proliferation history that suggests Khan was a historical anomaly may need to be rewritten. But what will it say? Today, there is fresh information and new leads that must be explored to determine the full extent of North Korea's proliferation activity.

Intelligence Shortfalls

It is important to remember that the Al Kibar facility was uncovered thanks to a windfall of intelligence and expert analysis. Yet that windfall did not occur until the facility was nearly complete, exposing deficiencies in intelligence collection efforts specific to the nuclear arena. As such, it should create doubts in the international community's ability to identify and neutralize clandestine nuclear sites and networks that might exist in other parts of the world. This inability to reliably assess state-related clandestine nuclear activity further reduces the prospects of uncovering clandestine nuclear trafficking and acquisition efforts of non-state actors, which would have a much smaller footprint than their state program counterparts.

Al Qaeda Acquires the Bomb

It is difficult to objectively assess the feasibility of nuclear terrorism without being suspected of hyping and overdramatizing the threat. It is also hard to set aside fear in contemplating nuclear catastrophe. That said, it is necessary to approach the task with an optimistic mind-set. Methodically sifting through all of the threat's variables can systematically lower the risks—an approach that requires collection and analysis of each potential terrorist nuclear plot pathway, attack indicator, and choke point. Such a dynamic modus operandi can serve as the basis for undertaking anticipatory action that will identify actionable leads, compromise terrorist planning, and neutralize an impending attack.

The chances of identifying indicators of a nuclear terrorism plot are highest in the earliest stages of planning. Over time, the likelihood of interdiction decreases. With this in mind, a premium must be paid to penetrate terrorist leadership, facilitation, and support networks during a plot's most formative stages. Here is how it can be done: Finely tuned terrorist communication intercepts must be used to generate actionable leads. Satellite surveillance and state-of-the-art sensors also must be widely employed to enhance quick detection of nuclear material. And every tool of intelligence tradecraft needs to be focused on finding a logistical and support footprint no larger than that of Mohammed Atta's limited 9/11 plot. Fortunately, the challenges faced by terrorists who want to acquire a nuclear weapon are no less formidable than for the global intelligence agencies that are trying to stop them. In fact, by my count, there are only three pathways to a terrorist nuclear attack.

Sabotage

Terrorists could attack a nuclear facility in hopes of causing a large release of radioactivity—similar to how they used airplanes on 9/11 as an inscrutable weapon. There is evidence that Al Qaeda's leadership considered such a possibility before 9/11, when their operatives reportedly conducted some light casing of U.S. nuclear reactor facilities. But thanks to enhanced security and reinforced defenses at U.S. nuclear sites, the available intelligence seems to indicate that Al Qaeda has concluded that it is too difficult to either (a) crash a plane into a nuclear facility or (b) use a team to penetrate a nuclear facility to gain access to nuclear weapons and materials.

Purchase

After the Cold War ended, the former Soviet Union was an attractive place to shop for nuclear components. In fact, there are credible reports that Ayman al-Zawahiri visited Russia in the mid-1990s. However, al-Zawahiri's announcement in 2001 that Al Qaeda had obtained nuclear devices in the former Soviet Union does not ring true. If the terrorist organization had purchased such weapons, why announce it to the world? Of course, there is a possibility that Al Qaeda's nuclear materials are being held in storage or have not reached their final destination yet. But no credible reporting has surfaced that Russian/Soviet nuclear weapons have been lost, much less that they have found their way into terrorist hands. (Reports of Russian "loose nukes" appear to have been greatly exaggerated.)

Construct

Counting assembled nuclear weapons is far easier than accounting for nuclear material in bulk form. Al Qaeda's experience on the nuclear black market has taught its planners that their best chance at some sort of nuclear or radiological attack is to construct an improvised nuclear device comprised of illegally purchased weapons-usable material—i.e., the direct pathway of finding a "loose nuke" or "suitcase nuke" is riddled with scam artists and intelligence services dangling their wares to terrorists in hopes of landing big fish. So while building a bomb is surely not the preferred course of action, it might be the only realistic pathway for sub-state actors who cannot develop the infrastructure necessary to enrich fissile material. To realistically do so would involve recruiting malicious insiders at nuclear facilities who are in a position to smuggle fissile material from their workplace and patiently combing the nuclear black market for similar material. It also requires enlisting specialists to build a device, rig the explosives, and assemble the pieces, all in complete secrecy. Finally, a suicide bomber is needed to transport the bomb to the intended target. Even if they succeeded in avoiding discovery throughout the planning stages, a terrorist would never know for certain whether his device would reach a nuclear yield or whether he had a viable bomb until he tried to detonate it.

Al Qaeda must understand that the odds are long of conducting a successful nuclear attack. Yet, it is determined to try. And regrettably, time favors intent; if terrorists get something wrong the first time, they can continue to try until they succeed. More likely, however, their plans will be exposed somewhere during the planning stage: Stolen or smuggled fissile material might be interdicted at a port or border crossing equipped with state-of-the-art sensors; a suspicious neighbor might report the curious activities of a rogue scientist from a state weapons program; or an alert analyst might flag the intercept of an unusual container, shipment, or consignment of goods that did not fit the usual patterns. Somehow, though, a clue is likely to emerge that will present an opportunity to disrupt an Al Qaeda nuclear plot—probably when, and where, it is least expected.

In this regard, terrorist use of WMD presents a litmus test of the current state of global counterterrorism response. It is an apt challenge. The prospect of an Al Qaeda nuclear bomb stretches the mind to its limits, as such an attack entails almost unimaginable consequences. As such, it is essential to develop a robust, highly creative capability to identify pathways terrorists might take to obtain a bomb in order to interdict plots before they reach fruition—and to do so quickly. In planning for success, one thing is certain: If we cannot imagine a nuclear catastrophe, we will surely fail to prevent it from happening.

Critical Thinking

1. Why has the threat of nuclear terrorism been "hyped?"
2. Is Al Qaeda likely to develop its own nuclear weapon?
3. How has the government responded to these threats?

Create Central

www.mhhe.com/createcentral

Internet References

Preventing Catastrophic Nuclear Terrorism
www.cfr.org/weapons-of-mass-destruction/preventing-catastrophic-nuclear-terrorism/p10067

The Global Initiative to Combat Nuclear Terrorism
www.state.gov/t/isn/c18406.htm

Preventing Nuclear Terrorism
www.huffringtonpost.com/robert-gallucci/nuclear-terrorism_b_1406712.html

---

ROLF MOWATT-LARSSEN is a senior fellow at the Harvard Kennedy School's Belfer Center for Science and International Affairs. Previously, he spent three years at the Energy Department as the director of intelligence and counterintelligence and 23 years as a CIA intelligence officer. His posts included chief of the Weapons of Mass Destruction Department, Counterterrorist Center; chief of the Europe Division in the Directorate of Operations; and deputy associate director of central intelligence for military support.

Mowatt-Larssen, Rolf. From *Bulletin of the Atomic Scientists*, March/April 2010, pp. 37–45. Copyright © 2010 by Bulletin of the Atomic Scientists. Reprinted by permission of Sage Publications via Rightslink.

Article

Prepared by: Thomas J. Badey, *Randolph-Macon College*

Times Square Bomb
The Growing Threat of "Improvised" Explosives

DAVID WOOD

Learning Outcomes

After reading this article, you will be able to:

- Explain what an IED is.

- Assess the potential impact of the use of IEDs on U.S. counter-terrorist strategies.

- Discuss how the failure of the Times Square bomb may affect other terrorist organizations.

Add Times Square to the growing list of places like Peshawar, Kandahar or any crowded Iraqi market where car bombs, suicide bombers and IEDs are now a deadly threat.

Expertise in making bombs—especially using common materials like those found in the smoldering Times Square truck bomb Saturday night—is spreading like wildfire across the globe with technical data and training widely shared among terrorist groups, experts have found.

In Afghanistan, improvised explosive devices (IEDs) or roadside bombs have killed 89 Americans so far this year. The dead include three in the past week: Army 1st Lt. Salvatore S. Corma, 24, from Wenonah, New Jersey; Marine Lance Cpl. Thomas E. Rivers Jr., 22, of Birmingham, Alabama; and Sgt. Keith A. Coe, 30, of Auburndale, Florida.

But these tragic deaths are only part of a tide of global bomb attacks that are causing a significant increase in dead and wounded, according to the U.S. National Counterterrorism Center. Indeed, the increasing use by terrorists of homemade explosives and yes, "improvised" bombs, like the Times Square device, makes it more likely that what we have gotten used to seeing on our TV screens may soon be happening on our streets.

In the first three months of this year, 837 IEDs were detonated worldwide—*excluding* Iraq and Afghanistan, according to the Pentagon's Joint IED Defeat Organization.

Globally, attacks with explosives, IEDs, vehicle bombs, letter bombs, grenades and firebombs—attacks mostly on civilians—grew by 40 percent between 2005 and 2009, according to the NTIC's global data base. The worse news is that the death toll from those attacks grew in the same period by 30 percent and the number of wounded by 51 percent.

Bloody casualties might have been the case in New York if the dark green 1993 Nissan Pathfinder that was parked in Times Square at 45th Street and Broadway on Saturday night had exploded as intended. The SUV was packed with what one counterterrorism official later described as an "unsophisticated" explosive device made with three propane gas canisters, two cans of gasoline, eight bags of fertilizer, dozens of M–88 firecrackers and two clocks with wires and batteries.

Whoever built the device, Attorney General Eric Holder said Monday, "intended to spread terror across New York . . . we certainly would have seen a substantial loss of life."

In the aftermath of the failed bombing came the usual confusion about who or what group attempted the attack, and why. The Pakistan Taliban, Tehrik-e Taliban, was reported to have issued two videotapes asserting responsibility, but the Taliban spokesman later Monday denied the group was involved.

There was also considerable speculation as to possible motives for the Times Square bombing which seemed inconclusive. What was beyond debate, however, was that the attempted attack was part of an expanding wave of similar attacks around the world "in which terrorist and insurgent bombing campaigns have taken progressively shorter periods to achieve relatively high levels of technical and tactical sophistication," according to a new study on the global IED threat.

The report, issued by the New American Foundation, observes that it took the Irish Republican Army about 30 years to "progress" from crude wire-detonated bombs to radio-controlled detonations. But it took six years for insurgents to make the same technical leap in Chechnya, three years for the fighters in Gaza, and about 12 months for militants in Iraq.

What worries investigators now, however, is that the same kind of accelerating sophistication is taking place in terrorist tactics, not just technology. One shift in tactics adapted by al Qaeda is to use minimally trained agents, rather than well-established extremist cells, in smaller one-time attacks instead of trying to pull off a massive, coordinated attack.

In testimony to the House Intelligence Committee in February, Dennis Blair, director of national intelligence, said that "recent successful and attempted attacks represent an evolving threat, in which it is even more difficult to identify and track small numbers of terrorists" who are newly trained and engaged in short-term plots. It is far easier, Blair acknowledged, "to find and follow terrorist cells engaged in plots that have been ongoing for years."

For example, unlike the 9/11 plot, which drew foreign terrorists into the United States to coordinate their successful skyjacking attacks, recent attempts have suggested that the attackers are more likely to be Americans and thus far more difficult to detect and intercept.

Last month two Americans, Zarein Ahmedzay and Najibullah Zazi, pleaded guilty to planning to blow themselves up using homemade explosives on the New York City subway on the eighth anniversary of 9/11. The guilty pleas of these two Afghan Americans, who had gone home to fight U.S. and allied troops in Afghanistan, revealed that they had been recruited and sent back by al Qaeda.

What is striking about this and other recent cases, according to Bruce Riedel, a former CIA counterterrorism official now at the Brookings Institution, is that it reveals that "al Qaeda has asked all of its allies in the global Islamic jihad, like the Taliban and Lashkar e Tayyiba, and its franchises around the Muslim world, including the one in Yemen, to help it find killers and press the war on America."

What is clear, Riedel writes, "is that al Qaeda still has got the Big Apple in its gun sights. Whether they had anything to do with Saturday's car bomb or not, we know they are determined to strike inside America again."

Critical Thinking

1. Are IEDs more dangerous than conventional explosives?
2. What impact does the increased use of IEDs have on U.S. security at home and abroad?
3. How can the government address the growing threat posed by IEDs?

Create Central

www.mhhe.com/createcentral

Internet References

Time Square Bomb Suspect
www.washingtonpost.com/wpdyn/content/article/2010/06/21/AR20100 62102468.
Time Bomb Could Have Been Devastating
http://abcnews.go.com/WN/Blotter/faisal-shahzads-times-square-bomb -devastating-government-filing/story?id=11759399#.UHWCMK7z6rg
Violent Islamist Extremism
www.hsgac.senate.gov/issues/the-homegrown-terrorist-threat

Unit III

UNIT

Prepared by: Thomas J. Badey, *Randolph-Macon College*

Vulnerabilities

The Department of Homeland security defines vulnerability as a "weaknesses in physical structures, personnel protection systems, processes, or other areas." Both threats (see the previous unit) and vulnerabilities are a key variable in the assessment of potential risk. There is a simple formula often used in the calculation of risk. Threat + Vulnerability + Criticality = Risk. To evaluate threat, one has to ask: How likely is it that someone will attack, or that an event such as a natural disaster will affect a facility or resource? To determine vulnerability, one has to ask: What are the potential weaknesses of this facility or resource? Finally, to establish criticality, one has to ask: What is the likely impact if this facility or resource is lost or harmed? Combined, these factors can be used to evaluate the potential risk for a specific facility or resource.

According to the DHS, "Critical infrastructure are the assets, systems, and networks, whether physical or virtual, so vital to the United States that their incapacitation or destruction would have a debilitating effect on security, national economic security, public health or safety, or any combination thereof."

In December 2003, the Bush Administration issued Homeland Security Presidential Directive 7 (HSPD-7), focusing on infrastructure protection policy and responsibilities. In 2006, the Bush Administration published its National Infrastructure Protection Plan (NIPP). This plan outlines the process that the Department of Homeland Security uses to identify those assets critical to the United States, across all sectors, based on the potential risk associated with their loss to attack or natural disaster. It also prioritizes activities aimed at maximizing the reduction of those risks. In 2009, the Obama Administration released an updated version of the plan, which builds on the framework of the previous plans.

Homeland Security Presidential Directive 7 established U.S. policy for enhancing critical infrastructure protection by establishing a framework for the Department's partners to identify, prioritize, and protect the critical infrastructure in their communities from terrorist attacks.

Currently 18 critical infrastructure sectors have been identified. They include such areas as Banking and Finance, Chemical, Commercial Facilities, Communications, Critical Manufacturing, Dams, Defense Industrial Base, Education Facilities, Emergency Services, Energy, Food and Agriculture, Healthcare and Public Health, National Monuments and Icons, Nuclear Reactors, Materials, Waste, Transportation Systems, and Water. Sector-specific agencies have developed plans that detail the application of the NIPP framework to the unique characteristics of each sector.

The articles in this unit focus on some potential vulnerabilities. The first article in this unit, "Hacking the Lights Out" by David M. Nicol, reminds us that every facet of the modern electrical grid is controlled by computers. He argues that the Stuxnet virus that infected Iran's nuclear program shows just how vulnerable machines are to computer viruses. Nicol warns that an attack could destroy a a significant portion of the U.S. electrical grid. Next, Stew Magnuson offers an overview of new technologies being tested by the TSA Security laboratory to detect explosives hidden in the clothing of airline passengers. Successful attempts to smuggle explosives aboard commercial airliners by Richard Reid and more recently Umar Farouk Abdulmutallab indicate the continuing need to address this vulnerability. Bill Zalud draws our attention to an incident that calls into question the security at U.S. nuclear facilities. In July 2012, three civilians, one of them an 82-year old nun, breached the perimeter protection system at the Y-12 National Security Complex at Oak Ridge. This break-in led to a major shakeup in management and supervisors of security at the facility. Next, an article from an Army medical journal offers an overview of three categories of entomological terrorism, a rarely discussed subcategory of bioterrorism. It offers recommendations as to how military professionals can mitigate the potential threats posed by vector-borne diseases. Finally, Ellen Messmer argues that "America's Critical Infrastructure Security Response System Is Broken". Focusing on a report by the Illinois Statewide Terrorism and Intelligence Center, she highlights potential weakness in the critical infrastructure incident reporting system. Messmer argues that in order for the incident reporting system to be effective, communications between federal agencies, fusion centers, and private-sector industry must be improved.

Article   Prepared by: Thomas J. Badey, *Randolph-Macon College*

Hacking the Lights Out

DAVID M. NICOL

Learning Outcomes

After reading this article, you will be able to:

- Describe the impact of the Stuxnet virus on the Iranian nuclear program.

- Identify specific areas that could be targets of cyberattacks by terrorists.

- Discuss possible responses to cyberattacks.

Last year word broke of a computer virus that HAD managed to slip into Iran's highly secure nuclear enrichment facilities. Most viruses multiply without prejudice, but the Stuxnet virus had a specific target in its sights—one that is not connected to the Internet. Stuxnet was planted on a USB stick that was handed to an unsuspecting technician, who plugged it into a computer at a secure facility. Once inside, the virus spread silently for months, searching for a computer that was connected to a prosaic piece of machinery: a programmable logic controller, a special-purpose collection of microelectronics that commonly controls the cogs of industry—valves, gears, motors and switches. When Stuxnet identified its prey, it slipped in, unnoticed, and seized control.

The targeted controllers were attached to the centrifuges at the heart of Iran's nuclear ambitions. Thousands of these centrifuges are needed to process uranium ore into the highly enriched uranium needed to create a nuclear weapon. Under normal operating conditions, the centrifuges spin so fast that their outer edges travel just below the speed of sound. Stuxnet bumped this speed up to nearly 1,000 miles per hour, past the point where the rotor would likely fly apart, according to a December report by the Institute for Science and International Security. At the same time, Stuxnet sent false signals to control systems indicating that everything was normal. Although the total extent of the damage to Iran's nuclear program remains unclear, the report notes that Iran had to replace about 1,000 centrifuges at its Natanz enrichment facility in late 2009 or early 2010.

Stuxnet demonstrates the extent to which common industrial machines are vulnerable to the threat of electronic attack. The virus targeted and destroyed supposedly secure equipment while evading detection for months. It provides a dispiriting blueprint for how a rogue state or terrorist group might use similar technology against critical civilian infrastructure anywhere in the world.

Unfortunately, the electrical power grid is easier to break into than any nuclear enrichment facility. We may think of the grid as one gigantic circuit, but in truth the grid is made from thousands of components hundreds of miles apart acting in unerring coordination. The supply of power flowing into the grid must rise and fall in lockstep with demand. Generators must dole their energy out in precise coordination with the 60-cycle-per-second beat that the rest of the grid dances to. And while the failure of any single component will have limited repercussions to this vast circuit, a coordinated cyberattack on multiple points in the grid could damage equipment so extensively that our nation's ability to generate and deliver power would be severely compromised for weeks—perhaps even months.

Considering the size and complexity of the grid, a coordinated attack would probably require significant time and effort to mount. Stuxnet was perhaps the most advanced computer virus ever seen, leading to speculation that it was the work of either the Israeli or U.S. intelligence agencies—or both. But Stuxnet's code is now available on the Internet, raising the chance that a rogue group could customize it for an attack on a new target. A less technologically sophisticated group such as al Qaeda probably does not have the expertise to inflict significant damage to the grid at the moment, but black hat hackers for hire in China or the former Soviet Union might. It is beyond time we secured the country's power supply.

The Break-In

A year ago I took part in a test exercise that centered on a fictitious cyberattack on the grid. Participants included representatives from utility companies, U.S. government agencies and the military. (Military bases rely on power from the commercial grid, a fact that has not escaped the Pentagon's notice.) In the test scenario, malicious agents hacked into a number of transmission substations, knocking out the specialized and expensive devices that ensure voltage stays constant as electricity flows across long high-power transmission lines. By the end of the exercise half a dozen devices had been destroyed, depriving power to an entire Western state for several weeks.

Computers control the grid's mechanical devices at every level, from massive generators fed by fossil fuels or uranium all the way down to the transmission lines on your street. Most of these computers use common operating systems such as Windows and Linux, which makes them as vulnerable to malware as your desktop PC is. Attack code such as Stuxnet is successful for three main reasons: these operating systems implicitly trust running software to be legitimate; they often have flaws that admit penetration by a rogue program; and industrial settings often do not allow for the use of readily available defenses.

Even knowing all this, the average control system engineer would have once dismissed out of hand the possibility of remotely launched malware getting close to critical controllers, arguing that the system is not directly connected to the Internet. Then Stuxnet showed that control networks with no permanent connection to anything else are still vulnerable. Malware can piggyback on a USB stick that technicians plug into the control system, for example. When it comes to critical electronic circuits, even the smallest back door can let an enterprising burglar in.

Consider the case of a transmission substation, a waypoint on electricity's journey from power plant to your home. Substations take in high-voltage electricity coming from one or more power plants, reduce the voltage and split the power into multiple output lines for local distribution. A circuit breaker guards each of these lines, standing ready to cut power in case of a fault. When one output line's breaker trips, all of the power it would have carried flows to the remaining lines. It is not hard to see that if all the lines are carrying power close to their capacity, then a cyberattack that trips out half of the output lines and keeps the remaining ones in the circuit may overload them.

These circuit breakers have historically been controlled by devices connected to telephone modems so that technicians can dial in. It is not difficult to find those numbers; hackers invented programs 30 years ago to dial up all phone numbers within an exchange and make note of the ones to which modems respond. Modems in substations often have a unique message in their dial-up response that reveals their function. Coupled with weak means of authentication (such as well-known passwords or no passwords at all), an attacker can use these modems to break into a substation's network. From there it may be possible to change device configurations so that a danger condition that would otherwise open a circuit breaker to protect equipment gets ignored.

New systems are not necessarily more secure than modems. Increasingly, new devices deployed in substations may communicate with one another via low-powered radio, which does not stop at the boundaries of the substation. An attacker can reach the network simply by hiding in nearby bushes with his computer. Encrypted Wi-Fi networks are more secure, but a sophisticated attacker can still crack their encryption using readily available software tools. From here he can execute a man-in-the-middle attack that causes all communication between two legitimate devices to pass through his computer or fool other devices into accepting his computer as legitimate. He can craft malicious control messages that hijack the circuit breakers—tripping a carefully chosen few to overload the other lines perhaps or making sure they do not trip in an emergency.

Once an intruder or malware sneaks in through the back door, its first step is usually to spread as widely as possible. Stuxnet again illustrates some of the well-known strategies. It proliferated by using an operating system mechanism called autoexec. Windows computers read and execute the file named

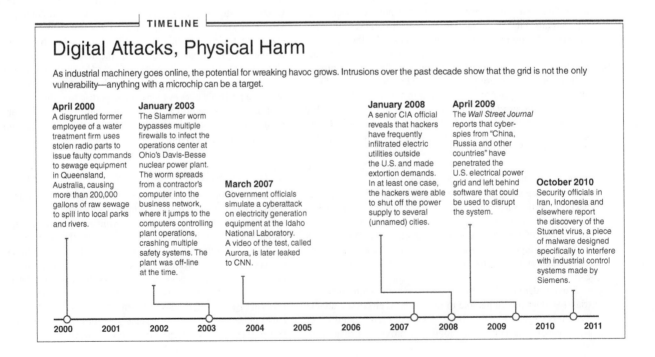

TIMELINE

Digital Attacks, Physical Harm

As industrial machinery goes online, the potential for wreaking havoc grows. Intrusions over the past decade show that the grid is not the only vulnerability—anything with a microchip can be a target.

April 2000
A disgruntled former employee of a water treatment firm uses stolen radio parts to issue faulty commands to sewage equipment in Queensland, Australia, causing more than 200,000 gallons of raw sewage to spill into local parks and rivers.

January 2003
The Slammer worm bypasses multiple firewalls to infect the operations center at Ohio's Davis-Besse nuclear power plant. The worm spreads from a contractor's computer into the business network, where it jumps to the computers controlling plant operations, crashing multiple safety systems. The plant was off-line at the time.

March 2007
Government officials simulate a cyberattack on electricity generation equipment at the Idaho National Laboratory. A video of the test, called Aurora, is later leaked to CNN.

January 2008
A senior CIA official reveals that hackers have frequently infiltrated electric utilities outside the U.S. and made extortion demands. In at least one case, the hackers were able to shut off the power supply to several (unnamed) cities.

April 2009
The *Wall Street Journal* reports that cyber-spies from "China, Russia and other countries" have penetrated the U.S. electrical power grid and left behind software that could be used to disrupt the system.

October 2010
Security officials in Iran, Indonesia and elsewhere report the discovery of the Stuxnet virus, a piece of malware designed specifically to interfere with industrial control systems made by Siemens.

2000 2001 2002 2003 2004 2005 2006 2007 2008 2009 2010 2011

AUTOEXEC.BAT every time a new user logs in. Typically the program locates printer drivers, runs a virus scan or performs other basic functions. Yet Windows assumes that any program with the right name is trusted code. Hackers thus find ways to alter the AUTOEXEC.BAT file so that it runs the attackers' code.

Attackers can also use clever methods that exploit the economics of the power industry. Because of deregulation, competing utilities share responsibility for grid operation. Power is generated, transmitted and distributed under contracts obtained in online auctions. These markets operate at multiple timescales—one market might trade energy for immediate delivery and another for tomorrow's needs. A utility's business unit must have a constant flow of real-time information from its operations unit to make smart trades. (And vice versa: operations need to know how much power they need to produce to fulfill the business unit's orders.) Here the vulnerability lies. An enterprising hacker might break into the business network, ferret out user names and passwords, and use these stolen identities to access the operations network.

Other attacks might spread by exploiting the small programs called scripts that come embedded in files. These scripts are ubiquitous—PDF files routinely contain scripts that aid in file display, for example—but they are also a potential danger. One computer security company recently estimated that more than 60 percent of all targeted attacks use scripts buried in PDF files. Simply reading a corrupted file may admit an attacker onto your computer.

Consider the hypothetical case where a would-be grid attacker first penetrates the Web site of a software vendor and replaces an online manual with a malicious one that appears exactly like the first. The cyberattacker then sends an engineer at the power plant a forged e-mail that tricks the engineer into fetching and opening the booby-trapped manual. Just by going online to download an updated software manual, the unwitting engineer opens his power plant's gates to the Trojan horse. Once inside, the attack begins.

Search and Destroy

An intruder on a control network can issue commands with potentially devastating results. In 2007 the Department of Homeland Security staged a cyberattack code-named Aurora at the Idaho National laboratory. During the exercise, a researcher posing as a malicious hacker burrowed his way into a network connected to a medium-size power generator. Like all generators, it creates alternating current operating at almost exactly 60 cycles per second. In every cycle, the flow of electrons starts out moving in one direction, reverses course, and then returns to its original state. The generator has to be moving electrons in exactly the same direction at exactly the same time as the rest of the grid.

During the Aurora attack, our hacker issued a rapid succession of on/off commands to the circuit breakers of a test generator at the laboratory. This pushed it out of sync with the power grid's own oscillations. The grid pulled one way, the generator another. In effect, the generator's mechanical inertia fought the grid's electrical inertia. The generator lost. Declassified video

shows the hulking steel machine shuddering as though a train hit the building. Seconds later steam and smoke fill the room.

Industrial systems can also fail when they are pushed beyond their limits—when centrifuges spin too fast, they disintegrate. Similarly, an attacker could make an electric generator produce a surge of power that exceeds the limit of what the transmission lines can carry. Excess power would then have to escape as heat. Enough excess over a long enough period causes the line to sag and eventually to melt. If the sagging line comes into contact with anything—a tree, a billboard, a house—it could create a massive short circuit.

Protection relays typically prevent these shorts, but a cyberattack could interfere with the working of the relays, which means damage would be done. Furthermore, a cyberattack could also alter the information going to the control station, keeping operators from knowing that anything is amiss. We have all seen the movies where crooks send a false video feed to a guard.

Control stations are also vulnerable to attack. These are command and control rooms with huge displays, like the war room in *Dr. Strangelove*. Control station operators use the displays to monitor data gathered from the substations, then issue commands to change substation control settings. Often these stations are responsible for monitoring hundreds of substations spread over a good part of a state.

Data communications between the control station and substations use specialized protocols that themselves may have vulnerabilities. If an intruder succeeds in launching a man-in-the-middle attack, that individual can insert a message into an exchange (or corrupt an existing message) that causes one or both of the computers at either end to fail. An attacker can also try just injecting a properly formatted message that is out of context—a digital non sequitur that crashes the machine.

Attackers could also simply attempt to delay messages traveling between control stations and the substations. Ordinarily the lag time between a substation's measurement of electricity flow and the control station's use of the data to adjust flows is small—otherwise it would be like driving a car and seeing only where you were 10 seconds ago. (This kind of lack of situational awareness was a contributor to the Northeast Blackout of 2003.)

Many of these attacks do not require fancy software such as Stuxnet but merely the standard hacker's tool kit. For instance, hackers frequently take command over networks of thousands or even millions of ordinary PCs (a botnet), which they then instruct to do their bidding. The simplest type of botnet attack is to flood an ordinary Web site with bogus messages, blocking or slowing the ordinary flow of information. These "denial of service" attacks could also be used to slow traffic moving between the control station and substations.

Botnets could also take root in the substation computers themselves. At one point in 2009 the Conficker botnet had insinuated itself into 10 million computers; the individuals, as yet unknown, who control it could have ordered it to erase the hard drives of every computer in the network, on command. A botnet such as Conficker could establish itself within substations and then have its controller direct them simultaneously to do anything at any time. According to a 2004 study by researchers at Pennsylvania State University and the National Renewable Energy Laboratory in Golden, Colo., an attack that incapacitated a carefully chosen minority of all transmission substations—about 2 percent, or 200 in total—would bring down 60 percent of the grid. Losing 8 percent would trigger a nationwide blackout.

What To Do

When microsoft learns of a potential security liability in its Windows software, it typically releases a software patch. Individual users and IT departments the world over download the patch, update their software and protect themselves from the threat. Unfortunately, things are not that simple on the grid.

Whereas the power grid uses the same type of off-the-shelf hardware and software as the rest of the world, IT managers at power stations cannot simply patch the faulty software when bugs crop up. Grid control systems cannot come down for three hours every week for maintenance; they have to run continuously. Grid operators also have a deep-rooted institutional conservatism. Control networks have been in place for a long time, and operators are familiar and comfortable with how they work. They tend to avoid anything that threatens availability or might interfere with ordinary operations.

In the face of a clear and present danger, the North American Electric Reliability Corporation (NERC), an umbrella body of grid operators, has devised a set of standards designed to protect critical infrastructure. Utilities are now required to identify their critical assets and demonstrate to NERC-appointed auditors that they can protect them from unauthorized access.

Yet security audits, like financial audits, cannot possibly be exhaustive. When an audit does go into technical details, it does so only selectively. Compliance is in the eye of the auditor.

The most common protection strategy is to employ an electronic security perimeter, a kind of cybersecurity Maginot line. The first line of defense is a firewall, a device through which all electronic messages pass. Each message has a header indicating where it came from, where it is going, and what protocol is used to interpret the message. Based on this information, the firewall allows some messages through and stops others. An auditor's job is partly to make sure the firewalls in a utility are configured properly so that they do not let any unwanted traffic in or out. Typically the auditors would identify a few critical assets, get a hold of the firewall configuration files, and attempt to sort through by hand the ways in which a hacker might be able to break through the firewall.

Firewalls, though, are so complex that it is difficult for an auditor to parse all the myriad possibilities. Automated software tools might help. Our team at the University of Illinois at Urbana-Champaign has developed the Network Access Policy Tool, which is just now being used by utilities and assessment teams. The software needs only a utility's firewall configuration files—it does not even have to connect to the network. Already it has found a number of unknown or long-forgotten pathways that attackers might have exploited.

The DOE has come out with a roadmap that lays out a strategy for enhancing grid security by 2015. (A revision due this year extends this deadline to 2020.) One focus: creating a system that recognizes an intrusion attempt and reacts to it automatically. That would block a Stuxnet-like virus as soon as it jumped from the USB stick. But how can an operating system know which programs are to be trusted?

One solution is to use a one-way hash function, a cryptographic technique. A hash function takes a fantastically huge number—for example, all the millions of 1s and 0s of a computer program, expressed as a number—and converts it to a much smaller number, which acts as a signature. Because programs are so large, it is highly unlikely that two different ones would result in the same signature value. Imagine that every program that wants to run on a system must first go through the hash function. Its signature then gets checked against a master list; if it does not check out, the attack stops there.

The DOE also recommends other security measures, such as physical security checks at operator workstations (think radio chips in identification badges). It also highlights the need to exert tighter control over communication between devices inside the network. The 2007 Aurora demonstration involved a rogue device tricking a generator's network into believing it was sending authoritative commands. These commands eventually led to the destruction of the generator.

These worthwhile steps will require time and money and effort. If we are going to achieve the DOE roadmap to a more secure grid in the next decade, we are going to have to pick up the pace. Let us hope we have even that much time.

Critical Thinking

1. Are terrorist groups likely to use cyberattacks against U.S. resources? Why? Why not?

2. What areas are most vulnerable to cyberattacks?

3. How can the U.S. government prevent cyberattacks from terrorist organization?

Create Central

www.mhhe.com/createcentral

Internet References

Energy Delivery Systems of Cybersecurity
http://energy.gov/oe/downloads/roadmap-achieve-energy-delivery-systems-cybersecurity-2011

Al Qaeda and Cyber Attacks
www.securityweek.com/al-qaedas-calls-cyber-attacks-spark-political-concern

Trustworthy Cyber Infrastructure for the Power Grid
http://tcipg.org/about-tcipg-trustworthy-cyber-infrastructure-power-grid

Scientific American
www.scientificamerican.com/

Article   Prepared by: Thomas J. Badey, *Randolph-Macon College*

Terrorist Loophole: Explosives Under Clothing at Airport Checkpoints

STEW MAGNUSON

Learning Outcomes

After reading this article, you will be able to:

- Describe the changes in airport security measures since 9–11

- Discuss the research that is being done in strengthening airport security

- Identify some of the problems airports have experienced with new technologies

- Assess the potential benefits and drawbacks of the use of Advanced Imaging Technology.

Atlantic City, N.J.—On Dec. 22, 2001, passengers on a flight from Paris to Miami subdued Richard Reid after he attempted to bring down the airplane with a high-top sneaker filled with explosives.

Ever since, travelers at airport checkpoints have been asked to take off their shoes and send them through x-ray machines.

Since the 9/11 hijackings, passengers have submitted to a variety of new Transportation Security Administration (TSA) procedures, and some may have walked through the portals of a few new screening machines. However, the basic technology—metal detectors for the passengers and x-rays for the hand-carried baggage, has remained the same.

The relatively new TSA, meanwhile, has attempted to deploy cutting-edge sensors designed to both increase security and make the procedure smoother for passengers. Its efforts have been marked by notable failures, and few new technologies deployed uniformly throughout the United States. The problem of finding explosives concealed under clothing has not been completely solved.

"One of the hard lessons we've learned is that there is no single technology that is going to detect everything," Clark Kent Ervin, former DHS inspector general and now director of the Aspen Institute's homeland security program, said in an interview.

The United States is capable of developing the technologies needed to both boost security, and make the passenger screening procedure go faster, it just hasn't done so yet, Ervin said.

"Terrorists are on a quick timeline and we have got to be quick," he said. "We are capable of doing these kinds of things."

After 9/11, changes in TSA procedures have come in reaction to terrorist plots to detonate bombs aboard passenger aircraft. The actions of Reid, better known as the "shoe bomber," resulted in the footwear rule. A London-based plan to take down 10 aircraft in 2006 necessitated the banning of large quantities of liquids in hand-carried luggage. The so-called Christmas Day plot, which had Umar Farouk Abdulmutallab allegedly concealing plastic explosives in his underwear, prompted the TSA to dramatically boost the numbers of its new advanced imaging technology machines.

Abdulmutallab's attempt to destroy a Detroit-bound airliner highlighted the biggest vulnerability in passenger screening—the ability to detect explosives carefully hidden underneath clothing.

Scientists and engineers at the TSA Security Laboratory near the Atlantic City airport are conducting basic research on promising technologies, although many of them are several years away from being deployed, if they ever do bear fruit.

"We have people who have spent their whole professional careers here worrying about how to find a bomb," said Susan Hallowell, the lab's director.

Potential screening technologies are put through rigorous testing procedures. The lab has an extensive "library" of real explosives, military grade, or homemade, that it stores in a bunker on site, as well as experts whose job is to construct concealed bombs designed to trip up the machines. (See related story.)

"Everybody wants to get the technology in the field because it's needed," Hallowell said. "But if it's not effective for one reason or another, it breaks down, it's not usable or there is some other defect, it's not of value."

Once the lab gives a new scanning machine the stamp of approval, it is turned over to the TSA for field tests in airports.

"Sometimes you see things that work well in a laboratory, but when you take them to an airport, operationally, they fall down," Hallowell said.

The most glaring example of this was the "puffer" machines.

Beginning in 2004, TSA began to install in some airports portals that shot jets of air over passengers, which would then dislodge trace amounts of explosives from their clothes and bodies. These picogram-sized traces were sucked into a collector that would alert a TSA officer of their presence.

The machines, which ultimately cost taxpayers some $36 million to deploy, began to malfunction as the sensors became clogged with other particles. They also had a high rate of false positives. Jet fuel fumes, for example, set them off, according to Government Accountability Office reports.

Hallowell said the puffer machines were sped into the field prematurely in reaction to the so-called "black widow" bombings in Russia in 2004, when it was believed that Chechen women carrying explosives underneath their clothes made it through Russian checkpoint security and blew up two aircraft. Traces of the military grade hexogen explosives were found on both flights.

TSA was a relatively new agency then, and Hallowell said there was a collective decision to deploy the machines.

"They went to the field too fast and we didn't have a chance to really kick the tires and make sure it was operationally very effective," she said. It was a "lesson learned," and there are now processes in place to ensure the mistake isn't repeated, she added.

The TSA, in the meantime, will rely on three technologies to prevent concealed bombs from making it on to airplanes. The first are the controversial advanced imaging technology (AIT) sensors that peer underneath clothing to look for shapes that may be explosives or other contraband. There are two kinds of AIT machines, one that uses millimeter waves, and another that uses backscatter radiation.

AIT machines were being slowly rolled out at airports throughout the country last year despite being criticized by privacy advocates for creating images that revealed subjects' bodies.

In the wake of the Christmas Day plot, DHS announced the widespread deployment of the machines. Plans now call for the agency to boost AIT numbers from 878 to 1,800 and to make them a third primary screening technology along with the standard metal detectors and carry-on baggage x-ray machines. The goal is to have them in every U.S. airport by 2014.

The Government Accountability Office in a March report warned that the rapid deployment of AIT harkened back to the puffer machines. They too were an example of a technology that was rushed into airports in response to an attack. TSA responded that backscatter x-ray and millimeter wave sensors were further along in the development phase than the puffer machines when they were deployed, and that AIT had been rigorously tested in operational settings.

Ervin said he is not worried about the privacy concerns with AIT technology. DHS said the machines automatically delete the body imagery as soon as a passenger clears the checkpoint. And the TSA officer looking at the data is in another room and cannot see the subject's identity.

"I'm concerned that they are putting so many of their eggs in the basket as far as AIT," Ervin said. "What we have found is that there is no silver bullet technology out there and you have to have a variety," he said.

AIT machines can only sense shapes. The GAO report said it was unclear whether the technology could have detected the explosives in Abdulmutallab's underwear.

Hallowell said the "fairly traditional military explosive" used in the plot was well known, and in the lab's inventory.

"I think the interesting part of that scenario was the attempt to make an artful concealment," she said.

To find carefully hidden explosives, TSA has placed at least one trace explosives detector in every U.S. airport. Like the puffer machines, these devices search for the chemical signatures of explosives. However, they require agents to swab a passengers' hand or luggage, which is a labor-intensive procedure, and slows down the screening process. Because of the time-consuming nature of the technology, TSA is only carrying out this procedure randomly.

During a tour of the Transportation Security Laboratory, scientists demonstrated several potential solutions for ferreting out concealed explosives. There is a sensor in the works using terahertz waves that could potentially peer underneath a passenger's clothing and read the chemical signature of objects hidden there—a combination of the AIT and trace detector's capabilities. Another machine can read the fumes coming off a bottle of liquid to determine if it contains the chemicals needed to mix explosives. These experiments are still being done on lab tabletops and could be years away from being used in airports, Hallowell cautioned.

TSA officials said there are currently no plans to revive puffer machine-like technologies that would allow passengers to walk through a portal and be tested for traces of explosives in a quick, non-intrusive manner. For now, it will be a combination of AIT machines, which are at least four years away from being deployed in all U.S. airports, and random swabbing.

Meanwhile, what about the shoes? Will there ever be a day when passengers don't have to walk through checkpoints while wearing their socks?

TSA is making a renewed effort to remedy this, said Domenic Bianchini, general manager of the TSA's passenger screening program. The agency recently completed an "extensive" market survey to determine what kind of technologies and sensors are currently available. A broad agency announcement has been released seeking proposals.

He wouldn't give a deadline or timeline for when a shoe scanner might reach airports. "But we are very serious about it. We need to understand what's possible, and will this technology meet our requirements at the end of the day."

Hallowell said there have been efforts to solve the shoe problem in the past. The lab has looked at a variety of technologies, everything from trace explosive detectors to scanners that can peer into the shoe. Nothing was deemed "ready for prime time," she said.

Both Hallowell and Bianchini said a solution to the problem will probably require integrating it with a currently deployed machine. The metal detector is at present the only portal that every passenger must pass through, so that is one obvious candidate.

"We have seen some partial solutions that aren't fast enough and the last thing we want to do is put another thing in the airport that will . . . slow down the queue or require another officer to operate," she said.

That's why the integrated approach is necessary, she added.

"I think the game is to make sure that the whole security suite addresses all your threats. The sense now is that shoe scanners will be part of a larger suite, and that's how we're going to end up using it," she said.

Critical Thinking

1. Should the federal government have primary responsibly for security at U.S. airports?

2. What are the limits of technology in the detection of potential threats?

3. What are the benefits and costs of the deployment of new technologies at U.S. airports?

Create Central

www.mhhe.com/createcentral

Internet References

Transportation Security Administration
www.tsa.gov/about-tsa/security-technologies

Airline Pilots Security Alliance
www.secure-skies.org/explosivedetection.php

The ASPEN Institute-Homeland Security Project
www.aspeninstitute.org/policy-work/homeland-security

Article   Prepared by: Thomas J. Badey, *Randolph-Macon College*

Nuclear Facility's Security Breach Draws Attention, Concern

BILL ZALUD

Learning Outcomes

After reading this article, you will be able to:

- Describe the security breach at the Y-12 National Security Complex.

- Examine the implications of this breach for U.S. nuclear security.

- Assess what should be done to prevent future breaches.

It was about 4:30 A.M. in Oak Ridge, Tenn., when sensors on the perimeter intrusion detection and assessment system alarmed. There was an unauthorized entry into a high-security, protected area.

A well-trained and heavily armed guard force responded.

And they found Megan Rice, an 82-year-old nun; Greg Boertje-Obed, 57, a housepainter; and Michael Walli, 63, a gardener, all of whom started reading a statement about their beliefs and opposition to nuclear weapons.

Surprisingly, the trio had simply cut through fencing to hang banners in the dark, splash blood and paint messages on the facility, what turned out to be the $549 million fortress that contains America's primary supply of bomb-grade uranium.

The target: the Y-12 National Security Complex, one of four production facilities in the National Nuclear Security Administration's Nuclear Security Enterprise. Its unique emphasis is the processing and storage of uranium and development of technologies associated with those activities. Y-12 maintains the safety, security and effectiveness of the U.S. nuclear weapons stockpile.

Big Security Shakeup

The break-in, of course, led to the arrest of the three. It also led to a major shakeup in management and supervisors of security at the facility as well as action by the Secretary of the U.S. Department of Energy (DOE). It also spotlights the assignment, and ongoing debate, of contract security at the nation's nuclear

power, government laboratory, poison gas storage and warhead facilities, which demand the highest level of security.

Before they were ordered to halt and kneel, the protesters at Y-12 suggested they break bread with the guards and showed off a Bible, candles and white roses. They also sang.

The incident happened just this past late July and was not greatly covered except for local news reports.

Y-12 spokesman Steven Wyatt has said it was fortunate that no one was hurt or killed in the break-in: "The protesters put themselves at a high risk of losing their life in performing this act. We are thankful that did not occur."

The Obama Administration responded to the break-in and what it called other protection shortfalls at the Y-12 National Security Complex by shifting critical site supervisors and temporarily relieving from duty certain defensive personnel, according to statements by Energy Secretary Steven Chu, adding that the incident "was not consistent with the level of professionalism and expertise we expect from our guard force and all of those federal employees and contractors responsible for security across the [Energy Department] complex."

In a short-term way, the three intruders got what they wanted.

Chu said in early August, "We decided to halt nuclear operations at the site, the guards involved in this incident were suspended, the general manager of the contractor protective force [WSI-Oak Ridge General Manager Lee Brooks] and two members of his leadership team were removed from their positions and all employees at the site are undergoing additional security training. The department has no tolerance for security breaches at any of our sites, and I am committed to ensuring that those responsible will be held accountable."

DOE, however, is sticking with WSI. Steve Hafner will serve as acting general manager. He is vice president and director of safety, security and environment for Mission Support Alliance (MSA) in Hanford, Wash.

MSA is made up of Lockheed Martin, Jacobs and WSI as well as several partners with specialized Hanford expertise. The DOE Hanford site sits on 586 square miles in the desert of southeastern Washington State. The area is home to nine former nuclear reactors and their associated processing facilities. MSA provides integrated infrastructure services for the Hanford cleanup mission, including, but not limited to: roads and transportation services; electrical and water services; facility maintenance; emergency response (fire and patrol) services; network and software engineering; cyber security and records management; as well as environmental compliance and clean energy solutions.

Beyond the Y-12 break-in, the question is proprietary or contract when it some to protecting the most sensitive government facilities. It is also a matter of debate within the Transportation Security Administration, where some airports are choosing private security, often for budgetary reasons.

This article was originally published in the print magazine as "The Nun, the Housekeeper, White Roses and Nuclear Warheads."

Critical Thinking

1. What are the implications of this break-in for U.S. security as a whole?

2. How can the federal government best ensure the security of U.S. nuclear facilities?

3. Does the publication of information about this incident increase or decrease the likelihood of future attacks? Support your answer.

Create Central

www.mhhe.com/createcentral

Internet References

Reuters- Nuclear Bombs
www.reuters.com/article/2012/08/02/us-usa-securtity-nuclear-idUSBRE8711LG20120802

Waging Non-Violence
http://wagingnonviolence.org/2012/08/peace-activists-close-nuclear-facility-cause-historic-security-breach/

Break-in at Nuclear Site
www.nytimes.com/2012/08/08/us/pacifists-who-broke-into-nuclear-weapon-facility-due-in-court.html?_r=0

Y-12 National Security Complex
www.y12.doe.gov/news/release.php?id=303

BILL is the editor emeritus of *Security Magazine*, and he can be reached at (773) 929-6859.

Article   Prepared by: Thomas J. Badey, *Randolph-Macon College*

Entomological Terrorism
A *Tactic in Asymmetrical Warfare*

DEREK MONTHEI ETAL.

Learning Outcomes

After reading this article, you will be able to:

- Define bioterrorism

- Describe entomological terrorism

- Identify potential economic losses that may result from agroterrorism.

- Discuss how vector-borne diseases may be used by terrorist organizations.

Historically, most US wartime casualties have been from disease and nonbattle injuries. If proper precautions are not taken, diseases like malaria, leishmaniasis, giardiasis, and botulism can have a detrimental impact on military personnel, their units, and their missions. Preventive medicine and public health personnel at all levels must remain vigilant during deployments to protect Soldiers from contracting food, water, and vector-borne diseases. The current operational environment, with insurgents using unconventional, indirect attacks against US forces, has caused the military to prepare for a wide array of enemy tactics. Improvised explosive devices (IEDs), vehicle-borne IEDs, snipers, and suicide bombers have all been used against military personnel, local security forces, and various local nationals in the Iraq and Afghanistan theaters. Another unconventional tactic that could be used by our nation's enemies is the use of biological terrorism, also known as bioterrorism.

Bioterrorism is defined as the deliberate release of viruses, bacteria, or other pathogens to cause illness or death in people, animals, or plants.[1] It should be noted that this definition excludes macrobiotic organisms, such as insects, which have been used to attack humans and agriculture. We would expand the Centers for Disease Control and Prevention definition to recognize the history and future of bioterrorism as including all living organisms. Insects have the potential to act as effective instruments for bioterrorism. This article will specifically address the threat posed to both the US civilian population and military personnel from entomological terrorism. Entomological terrorism can be organized into 3 major categories: the use of insects as weapons of direct attacks, as agents of agroterrorism, and as disease vectors.[2] We would note that these categories are not mutually exclusive. For example, a plant disease vector could be an agent of agroterrorism.

Composite risk management (CRM) is the Army's primary decision-making process to identify hazards, reduce risk, and prevent both accidental and tactical loss.[3] The US Army Center for Health Promotion and Preventive Medicine *Technical Guide 288*,[4] used by preventive medicine personnel, applies the CRM concept to vector-borne disease threats encountered by military personnel. Risk management in the Army, regardless of what is being assessed, ultimately seeks to preserve the fighting force for future operations. *Technical Guide 288* provides the framework to assess entomological hazards faced by military personnel, but was not intended to serve as a guide for analyzing entomological terrorist threats to our nation. The tactics used by our adversaries in overseas contingency operations have in many instances focused on targets other than military personnel. Unconventional strategies used by our enemies have included terrorist attacks to our nation on September 11, 2001, our international embassies, and our allies to include the Iraq and Afghan governments. Bioterrorism, including entomological terrorism, can instill fear in a society, devastate economies, and cause disease throughout a populace. Entomological threats should be further evaluated with considerations given to their potential use in attacks by our nation's enemies. Applying the Army's CRM and using *Technical Guide 288* as a guide, examples of each form of entomological terrorism (direct attacks, agroterrorism, and disease vectors) are assessed in this article to illustrate their potential threat to the health of our nation's military, economy, and society.

Direct Attacks

Stinging insects were used for millennia in conflicts as a means of defending fortifications or routing enemies from entrenched positions.[2] It may appear that modern weapons have eliminated the need to conscript insects for such purposes, but such tactics were used by the Vietcong against US troops in Vietnam,[2] and

Entomological Terrorism: A Tactic in Asymmetrical Warfare by Derek Monthei et al.

63

Report Documentation Page

Form Approved
OMB No. 0704-0188

Public reporting burden for the collection of information is estimated to average 1 hour per response, including the time for reviewing instructions, searching existing data sources, gathering and maintaining the data needed, and completing and reviewing the collection of information. Send comments regarding this burden estimate or any other aspect of this collection of information, including suggestions for reducing this burden, to Washington Headquarters Services, Directorate for Information Operations and Reports, 1215 Jefferson Davis Highway, Suite 1204, Arlington VA 22202-4302. Respondents should be aware that notwithstanding any other provision of law, no person shall be subject to a penalty for failing to comply with a collection of information if it does not display a currently valid OMB control number.

1. REPORT DATE **JUN 2010**	2. REPORT TYPE	3. DATES COVERED **00-00-2010 to 00-00-2010**
4. TITLE AND SUBTITLE **Entomological Terrorism: A Tactic in Asymmetrical Warfare**		5a. CONTRACT NUMBER
		5b. GRANT NUMBER
		5c. PROGRAM ELEMENT NUMBER
6. AUTHOR(S)		5d. PROJECT NUMBER
		5e. TASK NUMBER
		5f. WORK UNIT NUMBER
7. PERFORMING ORGANIZATION NAME(S) AND ADDRESS(ES) **US Army Public Health Command (Provisional), Public Health Command Region-West, Entomological Sciences Division, Joint Base Lewis-McChord, WA, 98433**		8. PERFORMING ORGANIZATION REPORT NUMBER
9. SPONSORING/MONITORING AGENCY NAME(S) AND ADDRESS(ES)		10. SPONSOR/MONITOR'S ACRONYM(S)
		11. SPONSOR/MONITOR'S REPORT NUMBER(S)
12. DISTRIBUTION/AVAILABILITY STATEMENT **Approved for public release; distribution unlimited**		
13. SUPPLEMENTARY NOTES		

14. ABSTRACT

The current operational environment presents military forces with enemies that use unconventional warfare to achieve their goals. Although the US government has dedicated significant resources to address threats of bioterrorism, the adaptive nature of our adversaries necessitates additional emphasis on bioterrorism awareness among military health professionals. This article provides an overview of 3 categories of entomological terrorism and examples from each category with a risk assessment.

15. SUBJECT TERMS

16. SECURITY CLASSIFICATION OF:			17. LIMITATION OF ABSTRACT	18. NUMBER OF PAGES	19a. NAME OF RESPONSIBLE PERSON
a. REPORT **unclassified**	b. ABSTRACT **unclassified**	c. THIS PAGE **unclassified**	**Same as Report (SAR)**	**11**	

Standard Form 298 (Rev. 8-98)
Prescribed by ANSI Std Z39-18

---

their use by terrorists in a direct attack is not altogether improbable. More likely, military personnel will have natural exposures to biting, stinging, or toxic insects as part of military deployments in less sheltered conditions and unfamiliar environments. According to *Technical Guide 288*:

> In addition to vector-borne and zoonotic disease, entomological hazards during deployment also include those hazards associated with biting and stinging arthropods, animals, poisonous plants, and pesticide exposure. Biting and stinging arthropods can degrade mission readiness and combat effectiveness even though they are relatively free of vector-borne disease. These arthropods can cause casualties from secondary infections and even death from allergic reactions to their venom. Annoyance from high populations of pests, itching bites, and loss of sleep can also reduce morale.[4(p2)]

One documented threat to military personnel that could be used in a direct attack or encountered in the environment is the

Paederus beetle.[5] *Paederus* is a genus of rove beetles (family Staphylinidae) and are found in the Middle East and the Asian subcontinent. Most species are slender, about 7 mm to 13 mm long, and are distinctly colored with black heads, orange bodies, black abdominal tips, and metallic blue or green elytra[5]. A string of suppurating sores appears when someone brushes away a beetle and inadvertently smears the insect and the toxin, pederin, across the skin. Less than a hundred-thousandth of a gram of this chemical can cause festering lesions.[2] Intense pain and temporary blindness have been reported when pederin is introduced into the eyes. These sores, although not fatal, may result in lost duty time.[6] Ingestion of the beetle leads to severe and even deadly internal damage. Pederin is lethal if injected into the bloodstream.[2]

Military personnel currently conduct operations in environments throughout Iraq that support *Paederus* beetle populations. The entomological hazard assessment[4] for *Paederus* beetles in these areas of Iraq was evaluated based on the severity and probability of exposure. *Paederus* beetles pose a "marginal" hazard to military personnel and the probability of receiving an injury by these beetles would be "occasional," therefore, the risk estimate for this entomological threat is "moderate" in areas with *Paederus* beetle populations. Military personnel can reduce the risk of the typical method of exposure to these beetles by applying an indoor residual spray (permethrin) in tents (D. A. Strickman, PhD, oral communication, January 2010), not working or resting under bright lights during May through July, properly wearing uniforms, and using window screens to help prevent *Paederus* beetles and other insects from traveling toward light sources indoors.[6]

The stings and bites of insects and arthropods are one threat the US Army should be able to manage effectively. Since its adoption, the Geneva Protocol of 1925[7] has prevented most nations from using chemical or biological weapons. The use of insects to vector pathogens is also prohibited under the Protocol. However, terrorists do not bind themselves to such protocols and could possibly employ biological weapons against the United States. The difficulty in the control of biological pathogens indicates that terrorists would probably use them at a location remote from their own territory (ie, against civilians residing in the United States). On the other hand, it is evident that terrorists are willing to both kill their countrymen and to die in attacks against US forces, which suggests that there are no places entirely safe from biological weapons. The 2 main entomological terrorism threats to the United States at home are agroterrorism and vector-borne disease threats.

Agroterrorism

Agroterrorism is defined as:

> the deliberate introduction of an animal or plant disease as well as damage to crops and livestock with the goal of generating fear, causing economic losses, and/or undermining social stability.[8]

Insects can be agents of agroterrorism as they can vector plant or animal pathogens or directly damage economically important crops and livestock. Table 1 identifies plant pests of significant concern in terms of bioterrorist potential. Many insects that are problematic to agriculture are invasive species. Invasive species can be defined as species that have a demonstrable ecological or economic impact and that have become established in a region outside of their native range.[10] Insects that become invasive to the United States can arrive in various ways, including:

- Accidental introductions of a species by global travel or trade
- Species originally released for agricultural or economic gains that later became problematic pests
- Species released in an act of bioterrorism against our nation

Agriculture and livestock remain a vital part of the economic stability of the United States. Although farming employs less than 2% of the country's workforce, 16% of the workforce is involved in the food and fiber sector, ranging from farmers and input suppliers to processors, shippers, grocers, and restauranteurs.[11] The US produces and exports a large share of the world's grain. In 2003, the US share of world production was 42% for corn, 35% for soybeans, and 12% for wheat. Of global exports, the US accounted for 65% for corn, 40% for soybeans, and 32% for wheat.[12]

Economic losses from an agroterrorist incident could have the following effects:

- Value losses in terms of lost production, cost of destroying diseased animals or products, and cost of containment (drugs, diagnostics, pesticides, and veterinary services).[8]
- The imposition of trade restrictions on US exports by foreign nations to prevent the disease or pest from spreading.
- Damage to the US economy as tourism and agriculturally dependent businesses suffer.
- State and federal governments burdened by the significant costs associated with disease or pest eradication, containment efforts, and compensation to farmers for their losses.

The Mediterranean fruit fly (*Ceratitis capitata* Wiedemann), commonly known as the Medfly, is a possible entomological agent that could be used against the United States for the purposes of agroterrorism. The species is found in Hawaii, but is not established on the US mainland. The larvae of this fly eat a wide variety of plants, including avocados, coffee, olives, tomatoes, bananas, citrus, mangos, and peaches.[2] If Medflies were established in California, a total quarantine of California fruits, both nationally and internationally, would result in the loss of 132,000 jobs and $13.4 billion.[13]

Medflies played the central role in a relatively recent entomological threat faced by our nation's citrus growers. In 1989, an ecoterrorist group known as the "Breeders" threatened to release Medflies in California if the state did not stop its pesticide spraying program. The State of California was spraying pesticides, ironically, to remove Medflies that had appeared in the Los Angeles area.[2]

Entomological Terrorism: A Tactic in Asymmetrical Warfare by Derek Monthei et al.

65

Table 1   Exotic plant pests of greatest risk.[a]

Pest Common Name(s): Scientific Name	Expected Range	Ecological Suitability[b]	Survey Difficulty[c]	Taxonomic Difficulty[d]	Primary Damage	Potential Economic Risk	Potential Environmental Impact	Potential for Establishment
Japanese wax scale: *Ceroplastes japonicas*	67% US (eastern and western states)	High	High	Medium	Ornamentals Fruits	High	High	High
Metallic beetle, Oak splendor beetle: *Agrilus biguttatus*	67% US (eastern and western states)	High	High	Medium	Oak Beech Chestnut	High	High	High
Rice cutworm, Cotton leafworm: *Spodoptera litura*	67% US (eastern and western states)	High	Medium	High	Vegetables Field crops	High	(Low)	High
Silvery moth: *Autographa gamma*	50% US (eastern and parts of western states)	High	Medium	High	Vegetables Field Crops Greenhouses	High	(Low)	High
Egyptian cotton leafworm: *Spodoptera littoralis*	67% US (eastern and western states)	High	Medium	High	Cotton Vegetables Ornamentals Forages	High	(High)	Medium-High
Passionvine mealybug: *Planococcus minor*	67% US (western and midwestern states)	Medium	High	Medium	Many crops	High	High	High
Light brown apple moth: *Epiphyas postvittana*	90% US	High	Medium	High	Ornamentals Fruits	High	(Low)	Medium
Khapra beetle: *Trogoderma granarium*	67% US (eastern and western states)	High	Low	High	Stored grain	High	Medium	High
Arrowhead scale: *Unaspis yanonensis*	33% US (eastern, portions of midwest and California)	Medium	High	Medium	Citrus Vegetables Trees	High	Medium	High
Siberian silk moth: *Dendrolimus superans*	80% US (except parts of western states)	High	Low	Medium-Low	Conifers	High	High	High
Ambrosia beetle: *Platypus quercivorus*	33% US (eastern states and Oregon)	Medium	Medium	Medium	Oak Chestnut	High	High	Medium
Summer fruit tortrix moth: *Adoxophyes orana*	25% US (eastern states and Oregon)	Medium	Low	Medium	Fruit	High	High	High
Pink gypsy moth: *Lymantria Mathura*	50% US (eastern and parts of western states)	Medium	Low	Low	Fruit crops Forests	High	High	Medium

[a] Data adapted from the USDA Animal and Plant Health Inspection Service Mini Pest Risk Assessments.[9] There is no comprehensive summary of agricultural threats, although these pests are representative of the agents that could be used for bioterrorism. The ratings of risk presume that each of the listed categories is of equal weight. The qualitative assessments were converted into scores and summed, such that "high" = 3, "medium" = 2; "low" = 1 (in all columns "high" is associated with a quality favorable for bioterrorism). Because potential environmental impact was not explicitly listed for all species, this category was not included in the summed risk score (the authors' estimates for this assessment, based on the USDA descriptions, are shown in parentheses). When totaled scores yielded a tie, potential environmental impact and expected range were used.

[b] Ecological suitability concerns whether the pest's life history accords with climates, soils, and host plants in the United States and the extent to which these ecological conditions are available.

[c] Survey difficulty addresses whether the United States has methods to readily detect the pest (eg, pheromone traps and sampling methodologies) and the extent to which the pest and its damage remain cryptic.

[d] Taxonomic difficulty reflects the ease with which the pest can be differentiated from native insects, the variability of the pest across its life stages, and the availability of supporting materials (eg, taxonomic keys).

[e] Species evaluated in the "mini pest risk assessments" representing lower threats and not included in this table are (in alphabetic order by common name): Chestnut weevil, *Curculio elephas;* European grape vine moth or Grape berry moth, *Lobesia botrana*, False codling moth, *Thaumatotibia leucotreta*, Fruit piercing moth, *Eudocima fullonia;* Giant woodwasp; *Urocerus gigas*; Old World bollworm, *Helicoverpa armigera*; Soft wax scale, *Ceroplastes destructor*

Applying the criteria of *Technical Guide 288,* the severity of damage caused by Medflies to the United States would be "critical" and the probability of this pest occurring and becoming established is "likely," therefore the risk assessment for this pest is "high." There are mechanical, cultural, biological, and chemical control measures that can be used to control and eliminate Medflies, however, preventing the Medfly from establishing itself on the mainland would be less expensive than control measures.

There are ways to mitigate the threat of agroterrorism to our nation. Monitoring, containment, and continued research will help prevent a terrorist event. The following are several suggestions to stop agroterrorism:

- Increase funding for research and eradication programs of invasive species present in the United States.
- Establish or continue monitoring programs for invasive species such as the Medfly, the Emerald Ash Borer (*Agrilus planipennis* Fairmaire*)* (monitoring in adjacent states that have not previously had this pest), and the Khapra beetle (*Trogoderma granarium* Everts), a grain and stored products pest.
- Ensure agencies responsible for monitoring trade and security threats to the United States are trained to identify entomological hazards and deter their entry to the United States. Possible participating agencies include the Food and Drug Administration, Food Safety and Inspection Service, and US Customs and Border Protection. The agency primarily responsible for this function is the US Department of Agriculture (USDA) Animal and Plant Health Inspection Service (APHIS).

Disease Vectors

An intentional release of a vector-borne disease by adversaries of the United States is a realistic threat to our nation. Table 2 provides a list of arthropod-transmitted diseases that could be delivered in a terrorist act that pose significant risks to plant, animal, and human health. The adverse effects caused by the introduction of certain arthropod-vectored pathogens to the United States, whether accidental or intentional, could ultimately result in illness and death from disease or devastation of the economy. This could be compounded if the introduced pathogen became established within our nation's borders and persisted, despite control and eradication efforts. Engineering new strains of viruses would require resources that typical insurgent groups do not possess at present, but many naturally occurring pathogens do exist that would need minimal effort to develop into biological weapons. Furthermore, the delivery of

Table 2 Arthropod-transmitted exotic diseases of potentially significant risk to plant, animal, and human health.[a]

Disease	Vector(s)	Pathogen	Host(s)
Chikungunya	Mosquitoes	Virus	Humans[b]
Yellow fever	Mosquitoes	Virus	Humans[c]
Japanese encephalitis	Mosquitoes	Virus	Humans, pig, birds
Rift Valley fever	Mosquitoes	Virus	Humans, livestock, birds
Lumpy skin	Mosquitoes and other flies	Virus	Cattle[d]
African horse sickness	Biting midges	Virus	Horses
Russian spring-summer encephalitis	Ticks	Virus	Humans[e]
Crimean-Congo hemorrhagic fever	Ticks	Virus	Humans[f]
Cattle tick fever	Ticks	Virus	Cattle
Africans wine fever	Ticks	Virus	Pigs
New World screwworm	Adult screwworms flies	NA	Mammalian livestock[g]
Tomato yellow leaf curl	Whiteflies	Virus	Tomatoes[h]
Citrus chlorotic dwarf	Whiteflies	Virus	Citrus
Citrus variegated chlorosis	Leafhoppers	Virus	Citrus
Lime witches' broom	Leafhoppers	Phytoplasma	Lime
Pierce's disease	Leafhoppers	Bacterium	Grapes
Potato wilt or brown rot	Leafhoppers, beetles, a phids	Bacterium	Potatoes[i]
Citrus greening	Psyllids	Bacterium	Citrus

[a] Data sources: USDA,[9] Frazier and Richardson,[14] Geissler,[15] Pelzel,[16] Wilson et al,[17] and World Health Organization.[18]
[b] Various nonhuman animals can serve as reservoirs.
[c] Other primates can serve as reservoirs.
[d] Insect vectors are highly suspected but have not been specifically identified.
[e] Small mammals can serve as reservoirs.
[f] Small mammals and domestic livestock can serve as reservoirs.
[g] Infestations of screwworms are not a disease in the classic sense but share many important common alities with pathogenic infections.
[h] Localized infections have been found in California, but the disease is not yet established.
[i] Insect vectors are highly suspected based on experiments with closely related diseases but have not been specifically identified.

Entomological Terrorism: A Tactic in Asymmetrical Warfare by Derek Monthei et al.

67

these diseases by terrorists to US soil could be simple and leave little to no evidence of the attack.

Rift Valley fever is an excellent example of a disease that would require little effort to deliver to the United States, and could have devastating effects on the nation's public health and livestock industry. Rift Valley fever (RVF) is caused by a virus in the family Bunyaviridae and occurs in various regions of sub-Saharan Africa and Madagascar.[19] Recent outbreaks in the Arabian peninsula, the first reported cases outside the African continent, have raised concerns that the disease could extend into Asia and Europe[20]. Numerous mosquito species transmit the virus that causes RVF, including those inhabiting North America and the United States.[21] The virus can be passed to an infected mosquito's offspring via transovarial transmission, thus enabling its persistence and maintenance in the environment through long stretches of dry conditions. Eggs infected with the virus can lay dormant until rains arrive when they will then hatch, develop in the larval and pupal stages, and emerge as disease-carrying adults. The public health and economic impacts of a RVF outbreak in the US could far exceed anything experienced by recent West Nile virus events.[2,22] Although these diseases spread in much the same manner, both the infection rate and proportion of those exhibiting severe symptoms are vastly higher in RVF.

The intentional introduction of RVF through infected mosquitoes, humans, and/or livestock represents a serious threat to both our military and civilian populations, whether delivered by a terrorist or through accidental introduction. The RVF virus is transmitted to humans by the bite of an infected mosquito or through contact with animals/meat that are infected. The mild form of RVF observed in most human infection manifests itself in the form of flu-like symptoms. The more severe form of the disease appears in one of 3 syndromes: ocular disease, meningoencephalitis, or haemorrhagic fever. Using RVF's approximate case fatality rate of 1%,[19] the analysis of a hypothetical attack allows us to better understand the implications of such an outbreak. If a small community with a population of just 10,000 people experienced a 10% RVF attack rate, the results would overwhelm the local health care infrastructure. Approximately 1,000 cases of the disease would require medical attention, with approximately 10 people ultimately dying from debilitating symptoms. In this age of constant news streams from cable networks (ie, CNN, MSNBC, Fox News), word of even a small outbreak of RVF would make headlines.

The absence of human cases occurring in a RVF bioterrorist attack would not equate to failure for our adversaries. An intentional release of RVF would also be a form of agroterrorism, for the livestock losses this disease can cause could cripple a large part of our national economy. Cattle, sheep, dogs, and rodents are among the many animals susceptible to RVF. Outbreaks of RVF have been characterized by high attack rates in livestock, with 30% mortality and abortion rates approaching 100%.[23] Corrie Brown, an animal infectious disease specialist who supervised the pathology section of USDA's Plum Island Animal Disease Center in New York, contends that if an outbreak occurred in the United States, domestic beef exports would shut down.[2,24] This impact on the beef industry would result in a $3 billion ($10^9$) loss to the economy.[2,24]

The composite risk assessment for the threat of RVF being delivered in an act of terrorism was estimated to be a "high" due to its "critical" severity and its probability occurrence "likely."[4]

Control measures that can mitigate the risk of RVF include:

- Continue mosquito surveillance programs to both monitor various pathogen infection rates (ie, West Nile and Eastern Equine Encephalitis) in vector populations as well as maintain preparedness in the event of an RVF or other mosquito-borne disease outbreak.

- Monitor conditions suitable for RVF outbreaks (eg, regional flooding, hurricanes) to focus mosquito control and surveillance efforts.

- Develop and rehearse RVF outbreak response plans to be implemented by the Department of Homeland Security (DHS) and Federal Emergency Management Agency.

- Ensure RVF vaccine could be readily available for the public in the event of an outbreak. An inactivated vaccine has been developed for human use. However, this vaccine is not licensed and is not commercially available. It has been used experimentally to protect veterinary and laboratory personnel at high risk of exposure to RVF. Other candidate vaccines are under investigation.[20]

- Institute a mobile, federal vector control force that could respond to such emergencies.

Various state, federal, and international entities have recognized the threat of RVF and have implemented some of the above control measures. Contingency planning, predictive disease modeling, and outbreak response exercises represent some of the recent developments to combat RVF threats in both endemic and potentially exposed geographic regions. The Food and Agriculture Organization (FAO) of the United Nations is just one of the international agencies providing guidelines for development of RVF contingency plans.[25] The FAO provides vital information for animal and human health authorities of individual countries by specifying RVF details regarding risk analysis, prevention strategies, early warning signs, forecasting, and control strategies.

Weather patterns and anomalies have been used recently to model and predict RVF outbreaks. In Africa, outbreaks of RVF are integrally tied to widespread elevated rainfall, and the subsequent flooding and increase in vegetation.[26] Risk mapping using climate and normalized difference vegetation index data led to the first prediction of an RVF outbreak from December 2006 to May 2007.[27] The predicted RVF occurrence provided a warning period of 2 to 6 weeks that facilitated response and mitigation activities. The outbreak that subsequently occurred validated the utilization of risk mapping models to predict future RVF events.

While contingency plans and outbreak predictions provide the logistical framework and science needed, rehearsing the execution of epidemic disease scenarios, with all responding agencies involved, ultimately provides the best gauge of response preparedness. In November 2008, Paul Gibbs, PhD, from the College of Veterinary Medicine at the University of Florida supervised a multiagency test of Florida's response to a hypothetical introduction of RVF (www.flsart.org/rvf/index .htm). Incorporating various state and federal participants, including the DHS, the Federal Bureau of Investigation, and the USDA, the exercise trained major stakeholders to collaborate in response to an introduction of RVF virus into Florida. In light of the original event's success, 2 additional RVF exercises were planned and conducted in Puerto Rico and the Virgin Islands by Dr Gibbs and Dana McDaniel, DVM, in 2010 (Dr McDaniel, oral communication, March 2010).

The control measures discussed could reduce the impact from an RVF outbreak, whether the virus is delivered by terrorists or arrives by accident. Without further scientific advances in RVF forecasting, vaccine development, vector control, and diagnostic capabilities, it may be unrealistic to expect to attain the necessary resources required to build and maintain comprehensive control measures to eliminate the threat to our nation of RVF and similar vector-borne diseases. We conclude that the residual risk associated with the threat of RVF, and other vector-borne diseases, remains "high."

Discussion

Entomological terrorism, regardless of its form, is a current and future threat faced by the United States. The estimated risks of the threats outlined in this article are speculative, however, it would be difficult to argue that the hazards associated with entomological terrorism are negligible. The US government has long recognized the consequences of biological warfare. The federal agencies conducting research and development on vector-borne diseases and crop pests include, but are not limited to the following:

- DHS: National Center for Foreign Animal and Zoonotic Disease Defense, and US Customs and Border Protection
- US Army Medical Research Institute of Infectious Disease (USAMRIID)
- Walter Reed Army Institute of Research
- USDA—Agricultural Research Service (ARS) and Animal and Plant Health Inspection Service

Additionally, some local abatement districts, a few state governments (ie, Florida, California), and numerous universities have also made significant contributions to research on vector-borne infectious diseases.

Merely studying the biology of a disease does not prepare us for response to an actual outbreak. Many aspects of an appropriate response to an entomological emergency still must be addressed, including:

- Is the pest management community prepared for an outbreak with the necessary equipment and knowledge to implement control techniques?
- Can pest management resources be quickly consolidated, mobilized, and deployed to outbreak locations?

- Are emergency organizations prepared with individual response plans for specific entomological threats, especially those posing high risk?

Accidental introductions of invasive arthropod species have a higher likelihood of occurring than intentional deliveries through terrorist plots. Military personnel moving to and from forward deployed environments can do their part in preventing the introduction of invasive species by thoroughly inspecting cargo transported by military transportation vehicles and by conducting retrograde washdowns of vehicles and equipment after a deployment.[28] The importance of preventing invasive species is illustrated by the costs currently incurred by these species in the United States. Damage caused by invasive species currently in the United States is estimated at $120 billion to $138 billion each year.[29] Crop losses and control costs due to invasive insects and pathogens were estimated at $25 billion in 2005.[29] There are approximately 500 invasive insect and mite species in crops and an estimated 20,000 species of microbes, including introduced plant pathogens, that have invaded the United States thus far.[29] Additional invasive species would only compound the problem and costs caused by these pests.

Even with proper systems and technological advances in place to prevent attacks or mitigate the effects of disasters, the United States still faces a deficiency in the number of trained, qualified healthcare professionals. A large portion of the healthcare workforce (including public health professionals, clinicians, and related healthcare fields) in the United States is approaching retirement age.[30] Health professionals are not being trained at a rate needed to fill the loss of retirees.[30] Federal (including the US Army) and state agencies responsible for emergency preparedness and response will soon face personnel challenges requiring additional efforts to educate, train, and retain such public health professionals. A terrorist attack, especially with a biological weapon, would be more devastating if the medical infrastructure is poorly prepared, staffed, and funded.

Conclusion

Vector-borne diseases are a current threat because of the self-perpetuating capabilities and delayed morbidity and mortality following exposure or infection.[31] Most disease causing organisms used as biological weapons, particularly the zoonoses, can be delivered to a target population without risk of immediate detection.[31] This article illustrates that insects and other arthropods can be used by an enemy to attack US military personnel and civilians. Some recommendations on how to mitigate the specific threats given (ie, *Paederus* beetles, Medfly, Rift Valley fever) were presented, however, all military personnel can mitigate vector-borne disease threats by taking relatively simple actions.

- Deploying Soldiers and DoD personnel should practice operational risk management (ORM) for infectious diseases. Excellent resources for understanding and following ORM are *Technical Guide 288*,[4] as well as the website for the National Center for Medical Intelligence (www.phsource.us/PH/MI/index.htm).

Entomological Terrorism: A Tactic in Asymmetrical Warfare by Derek Monthei et al.

69

- Personal Protective Measures should be implemented when training within the United States and when deploying outside the country. Treating uniforms with permethrin, or purchasing uniforms that are pretreated with permethrin, as well as using N,N-diethyl-3-methylbenzamide (deet) on exposed skin can reduce the likelihood of contracting mosquito- or tick-borne diseases during field training. The use of personal protective measures will not only help protect the individual from a new emerging vector-borne disease like RVF, but also prevent Soldiers from contracting Rocky Mountain spotted fever, Lyme disease, West Nile virus, Ehrlichiosis, and other vector-borne diseases present in the United States.

- Military personnel conducting food and water vulnerability assessments[32] or retrograde operations are critical players in security by helping protect food and water from exposure to biological agents and by preventing them, including vectors and invasive species, from entering the country.

Invasive pests and the diseases they may carry represent a threat that is magnified when terrorism is involved. The research conducted by academic institutions, a host of federal agencies (eg, USDA-ARS) and the US military (eg, USAM-RIID), coupled with entities capable of organizing emergency response activities (eg, DHS, Federal Emergency Management Agency, state and local authorities), provide the critical framework needed to address the entomological threats we face. It would be ideal to provide a definitive countermeasure to entomological terrorism, however, this may be unfeasible due to the financial and logistical challenges involved. The most critical countermeasure to entomological terrorism is the same for any form of terrorism—vigilance by the US military, government agencies, citizens, and our allies.[31]

References

1. CDC (Centers for Disease Control and Prevention). Bioterrorism Overview Page. Available at: www.bt.cdc.gov/bioterrorism/overview.asp. Updated February 12, 2007. Accessed December 26, 2009.

2. Lockwood JA. *Six-legged Soldiers: Using Insects as Weapons of War.* New York, NY: Oxford University Press, Inc.; 2009.

3. *Field Manual 5-19: Composite Risk Management.* Washington, DC: Dept of the Army. August 2006.

4. *Technical Guide 288: Entomological Operational Risk Management.* Aberdeen Proving Ground, MD: US Army Public Health Command (Provisional). September 2003. Available at: http://chppm-www.apgea.army.mil/documents/TG/TECHGUID/TG288.pdf. Accessed April 15, 2010.

5. Davidson SA, Norton SA, Carder MC, Debboun M. Outbreak of dermatitis linearis caused by *Paederus ilsae* and *Paederus iliensis* (Coleoptera: Staphylinidae) at a military base in Iraq. *Army Med Dept J.* July–September 2009:6–15.

6. *Just the Facts...Paederus Beetles* 18-071-1108. Aberdeen Proving Ground, MD: US Army Public Health Command (Provisional). November 2008. Available at: http://usachppm.apgea.army.mil/Documents/FACT/PaederusBeetleFactSheet.pdf. Accessed December 28, 2009.

7. Protocol for the Prohibition of the Use of Asphyxiating, Poisonous or Other Gasses, and of Bacteriological Methods of Warfare. Geneva, Switzerland: Conference for the Supervision of the International Trade in Arms and Ammunition; June 17, 1925. Available at: www.icrc.org/IHL.NSF/FULL/280?OpenDocument. Accessed December 26, 2009.

8. Monke J. *Agroterrorism: Threats and Preparedness.* Washington, DC: Congressional Research Service; March 12, 2007:1. CRS Report for Congress Order Code RL 32521. Available at: www.fas.org/sgp/crs/terror/RL32521.pdf. Accessed December 27, 2009.

9. Mini Pest Risk Assessments page. USDA Animal and Plant Health Inspection Service Website. Available at: www.aphis.usda.gov/plant_health/plant_pest_info/pest_detection/mini-pra.shtml. Accessed March 12, 2010.

10. Lockwood JL, Hoopes MF, Marchetti MP. *Invasion Ecology.* Malden, MA: Blackwell Publishing Ltd; 2007.

11. USDA Economic Research Service. Table 1: Key Statistical Indicators of the Food & Fiber Sector, April 2005. Available at: www.ers.usda.gov/publications/agoutlook/aotables/2005/04apr/. Accessed April 19, 2010.

12. US Bureau of the Census. *Statistical Abstract of the United States: 2004–2005.* 124th ed. Washington, DC: US Bureau of the Census Agriculture; 2005. Available at: www.census.gov/prod/2004pubs/04statab/agricult.pdf. Accessed April 19, 2010.

13. Root-Bernstein RS. Infectious terrorism. *Atlantic Monthly.* 1991; May: 44–50.

14. Frazier TW, Richardson DC, eds. Food and agricultural security: guarding against natural threats and terrorist attacks affecting health, national food supplies, and agricultural economics. *Ann New York Acad Sci.* 1999;894:1–232. Theme issue.

15. Geissler E, ed. *Biological and Toxin Weapons Today.* New York, NY: Oxford University Press; 1986.

16. Pelzel AM. Cattle fever tick surveillance in Texas. *NAHSS Outlook* [serial online]. August 2005. Available at: www.aphis.usda.gov/vs/ceah/ncahs/nsu/outlook/issue7/cattle_fever_tick_surveillance.pdf. Accessed April 12, 2010.

17. Wilson TM, Logan-Henfrey L, Weller R, Kellman B. 2000. Agroterrorism, biological crimes, and biological warfare targeting animal agriculture. In: Brown C, Bolin C, eds. *Emerging Diseases of Animals.* Washington, DC: ASM Press; 2000:23–57.

18. World Health Organization. Global early warning system for major animal diseases, including zoonoses. Available at: www.who.int/zoonoses/outbreaks/glews/en/index2.html. Accessed March 24, 2010.

19. Center for Disease Control and Prevention. Rift Valley Fever Fact Sheet. Available at: www.cdc.gov/ncidod/dvrd/spb/mnpages/dispages/rvf/rvf_qa.htm. Updated January 2, 2007. Accessed January 17, 2010.

20. World Health Organization. Rift Valley fever. Available at: www.who.int/mediacentre/factsheets/fs207/en/. Updated September 2007. Accessed January 18, 2010.

21. Gargan TP, Clark CG, Dohm DJ, Turell MJ, Bailey CL. Vector potential of selected North American mosquito species for Rift Valley fever virus. *Am J Trop Med Hyg.* 1988;38:440–446.

22. Selim J. Virus code red. *Discover Mag.* March 2005:14.

23. Patrick KW, ed. *Military Preventive Medicine: Mobilization and Deployment.* Vol 2. Washington, DC: Office of The Surgeon General, Dept of the Army; 2005:825.

24. McGinnis D. Looking for loopholes. *Beef Mag.* July 2004.

Available at: beefmagazine.com/mag/beef_looking_loopholes/. Accessed April 19, 2010.

25. *FAO Animal Health Manual No. 15: Preparation of Rift Valley fever (RVF) contingency plans.* Rome, Italy: Food and Agriculture Organization of the United Nations; 2002. Available at: ftp://ftp.fao.org/docrep/fao/005/y4140e/y4140e00.pdf. Accessed February 18, 2010.

26. Davies FG, Linthicum KJ, James AD. Rainfall and epizootic Rift Valley fever. *Bull World Health Organ.* 1985;63:941–943.

27. Anyamba A, Chretien J, Small J, et al. The first prediction of a Rift Valley fever outbreak. *PNAS: Proc Natl Acad Sci USA.* 106.3 2009:955–959.

28. *Technical Guide 31: Retrograde Washdowns: Cleaning and Inspection Procedures.* Washington, DC: Armed Forces Pest Management Board. March 2008.

29. Pimentel D, Zuniga R, Morrison D. Update on the environmental and economic costs associated with alien species in the United States. *Eco Econ.* 2005;52:273–288.

30. American Association for the Advancement of Science. Center for Science, Technology and Security Policy Page. Available at: http://cstsp.aaas.org/content.html?contentid=2215. Accessed February 17, 2010.

31. Kendall RJ, Presley SM, Austin GP, Smith PN, eds. *Advances in Biological and Chemical Terrorism Countermeasures.* Boca Raton, FL: CRC Press; 2008.

32. *Technical Guide 188: US Army Food and Water Vulnerability Assessment Guide.* Aberdeen Proving Ground, MD: US Army Public Health Command (Provisional). July 2008.

Critical Thinking

1. Is the U.S. prepared to deal with entomological terrorism? Explain your answer.

2. Is bioterrorism more effective than other types of terrorism? Explain your answer.

3. What can/should be done to prepare for this threat?

Create Central

www.mhhe.com/createcentral

Internet References

U.S Army Public Health Command
http://phc.amedd.army.mil/Pages/default.aspx

Paederus Beetle
http://bugguide.net/node/view/21473

FBI Threats: Agroterrorism
www.fbi.gov/stats-services/publications/law-enforcement-bulletin/february-2012/agroterrorism

Center for Disease Control and Prevention (CDC) River Valley Fever (RVF)
www.cdc.gov/ncidod/dvrd/spb/mnpages/dispages/rvf.htm

U.S. Food and Agriculture Organization Preparation for RVF
www.fao.org/docrep/005/Y4140E/Y4140E00.HTM

CPT **Monthei** is a Medical Entomologist, Entomological Sciences Division, US Army Public Health Command (Provisional) Public Health Region–West, Joint Base Lewis-McChord, Washington. CPT **Mueller** is a Medical Entomologist, Entomological Sciences Division, US Army Public Health Command (Provisional) Public Health Region–North, Fort Meade, Maryland. Dr **Lockwood** is Professor of Natural Sciences and Humanities at the University of Wyoming, Laramie, WY. He is the author of *Six-Legged Soldiers: Using Insects as Weapons of War* (2009, Oxford University Press). COL **Debboun** is Program Manager, Medical Education Training Campus Transition, and Chairman of the *AMEDD Journal* Editorial Review Board, US Army Medical Department Center & School, Fort Sam Houston, Texas.

Monthei, Derek, et al. From *Army Medical Department Journal*, April–June 2010, pp. 11–21. Copyright © 2010 by The AMEDD Journal. Reprinted by permission.

Article

Prepared by: Thomas J. Badey, *Randolph-Macon College*

America's Critical Infrastructure Security Response System Is Broken

ELLEN MESSMER

Learning Outcomes

After reading this article, you will be able to:

- Explain the role of fusion centers in the protection of critical infrastructure.
- Describe the potential impact of an attack on a SCADA system.
- Identify potential weakness in the U.S. critical infrastructure incident reporting system.

The flap over the reported water utility hack in Illinois begs the question: Is the reporting system that the U.S. has set up to identify cyberattacks on critical infrastructure broken and in need of re-thinking?

FBI, DHS Say No Evidence of a Hack In An Illinois Water District Pump Failure

Since the year 2000, the Department of Homeland Security (DHS) has encouraged states and cities to establish so-called "Fusion Centers" to operate under local control and collect information from the likes of power companies and water utilities about incidents that might have national-security implications.

There are now 72 of these Fusion Centers in the U.S., which vary in their practices, according to DHS. When one of them, the Illinois Statewide Terrorism and Intelligence Center (STIC), issued a brief report on Nov. 10 titled "Public Water District Cyber Intrusion," it led to a firestorm of controversy, putting what has been a secretive reporting system in the harsh glare of the public spotlight, and highlighting the intrinsic weakness in the way the U.S. critical-infrastructure incident reporting system works today.

The Illinois STIC report said there had been a cyberattack from Russia on a SCADA (supervisory control and data acquisition) system used by an unnamed Illinois water-supply company to control its water pumps, leading to the burnout of a pump as it was repeatedly turned on and off. In addition, the STIC report said an unnamed information technical services company looking at the SCADA system believed the hackers had been going after the SCADA system for several months, trying to get user names and passwords.

The STIC report was sent on to the DHS for its review, which DHS says is the usual process. But the DHS' Industrial Control Systems Cyber Emergency Response Team (ICS-CERT) later said it was only "made aware of" the report on Nov. 16.

The report, shared among those associated with the Illinois STIC, was expected to remain confidential. But the operator of a utility company associated with the Illinois STIC, who was troubled by this report and looking for advice, shared it with a well-known energy-industry consultant, Joe Weiss, head of Applied Control Solutions.

When Weiss mentioned the report in his blog a media firestorm ensued, with the *Washington Post* and other news sources describing it as perhaps the most significant cyberattack on U.S. critical infrastructure.

Once the media blitz erupted, the DHS and FBI took to publicly describing how, in coordination with ICS-CERT, they had sent a team off to the Illinois water facility. The feds were the first to name it as the Curran-Gardner Townships Public Water District in Springfield, Ill., which serves just over 2,000 customers.

ICS-CERT on Nov. 23 issued a bulletin that said once it had received the Illinois STIC report on Nov. 16, the organization "reached out to the STIC to gather additional information. ICS-CERT was provided with a log file; however, initial analysis could not validate any evidence to support the assertion that a cyber intrusion had occurred."

Curran-Gardner itself declines to discuss the matter, but the DHS and FBI now says, "After detailed analysis, DHS and the FBI have found no evidence of a cyber intrusion into the SCADA system of the Curran-Gardner Public Water District in Springfield, Illinois."

The *Washington Post* reported that, too, and later quoted unidentified sources saying the remote SCADA access was from an unnamed contractor for Curran-Gardner that happened to be in Russia at the time.

That contractor, Jim Mimlitz, founder and owner of Navionics Research, has now come forward and publicly said he was in Russia on vacation in June and logged into the SCADA system at the request of Curran-Gardner. He said he didn't mention to them he was on vacation in Russia.

It is unclear how that activity in June came to be perceived as a November hacking attempt in the Illinois CERT report, which Weiss read verbatim to *Network World*. The report is thin on details about the supposed intrusion, the problems with the SCADA system, and what actually happened.

The DHS ultimately concluded: "There is no evidence to support claims made in initial reports—which were based on raw, unconfirmed data and subsequently leaked to the media—that any credentials were stolen, or that any vendor was involved in any malicious activity that led to a pump failure at the water plant. In addition, DHS and the FBI have concluded that there was no malicious traffic from Russia or any foreign entities, as previously reported."

But the DHS does add: "Analysis of the incident is ongoing and additional relevant information will be released as it becomes available."

Several security experts say they find it reprehensible that a SCADA contractor would remotely access a U.S. facility's SCADA system from Russia.

"It's without question a poor security practice, probably the most distressing information out of this investigation," says Andre Eaddy, director of cyber security portfolio solutions at Unisys. "Most organizations would limit access inbound and outbound to certain countries, especially to certain countries like Russia or China." That's because there are so many malware-related attacks associated with them, it isn't worth the risk, and even taking a laptop with contractor information there would not be considered good security, he says.

2011's Biggest Security Snafus

"It is shocking" a contractor would directly access a SCADA system from Russia, Weiss says. But the bigger problem is that "we have no control system forensics and logging," meaning it is hard to get an accurate picture of what happened, where and when after any type of suspected breach.

Weiss says the entire episode, in which the Illinois STIC Fusion Center issued a very direct report that gave no indication it was preliminary or unproven and which had such explosive information, shows how broken the U.S. critical-information reporting system is.

"What Illinois put out is scarier than hell," he says. It's hard to understand how it could be a week or longer for ICS-CERT, DHS and the FBI to step in and say the report was wrong. He also points out that the various Fusion Centers all report different things that seem to circulate only locally before information goes on to DHS in Washington. He wonders why Fusion Centers put out reports without making it clear they're not considered validated.

Weiss thinks the Water-ISAC, a group coordinated by the federal government and the water utilities to share information, should have been informed about the Illinois STIC report. Some in industry think Weiss stepped out of bounds to have even publicly mentioned the Illinois STIC report, but Weiss says he doesn't have any official connection to it and is under no particular obligation to keep the document confidential.

On Nov. 23, ICS-CERT, which works within DHS, issued a security advisory about the "Illinois Pump Failure Report" in which it said: "There is no evidence to support claims made in the initial STIC report—which was based on raw, unconfirmed data and subsequently leaked to the media—that any credentials were stolen, or that the vendor was involved in any malicious activity that led to a pump failure at the water plant."

Without mentioning Weiss by name, ICS-CERT pointed out the impact that public discussion had had on its usual processes, which are typically secret. "Publicly disclosing affected identity names and incident information is highly unusual and not part of ICS-CERT's normal incident reporting and triage procedures. In this particular case, because unconfirmed information had already been leaked to the public, ICS-CERT and the asset owner/operator felt it was in the best interest of the community to collaboratively analyze all available data and disclose some of the findings."

DHS sources say the general assumption about the Fusion Centers is that they are simply places for gathering information and that DHS is the ultimate authority for the validation of that information. Fusion Centers include not just critical infrastructure companies but private-sector partners as well. For instance, Cisco says it belongs to many of the Fusion Centers and would immediately supply information to them if a serious malicious attack was detected.

DHS provides some funding to the Fusion Centers through FEMA grants, but expects the state and local authorities sponsoring a center to carry the basic fiscal and management responsibility. DHS acknowledges the Fusion Centers vary significantly in their activities and practices, though since 2008 there has been a push to try and establish basic guidelines and common toolsets.

However, DHS at this point isn't able to explain exactly what anomalies or security incidents critical infrastructure companies are required to report.

"Right now, it's not a good model," says Gartner analyst John Pescatore of the Fusion Centers. Not only could the intelligence-gathering function be improved, but there should be more "proactive information coming from the other way" that would help private industry definitely know about real threats.

Critical Thinking

1. What is the potential impact of a cyberattack on a SCADA system?

2. What role should the U.S. government play in the protection of critical infrastructure?

3. How can fusion centers help private industry improve security?

Create Central

www.mhhe.com/createcentral

Internet References

Illinois Statewide Terrorism and Intelligence Center
http://publicintelligence.info/IL-STIC.pdf

Supervisory Control and Data Acquisition (SCADA)
www.water.siemens.com/en/products/controls_instrumentation_analyzers/scada/Pages/default.aspx

Industrial Control Systems Cyber Emergency Response Team
www.us-cert.gov/control_systems/ics-cert/

Water Security Network
https://portal.waterisac.org/web/

Unit IV

UNIT

Prepared by: Thomas J. Badey, *Randolph-Macon College*

The Federal Government and Homeland Security

Despite efforts to merge homeland security functions within the Department of Homeland Security (DHS) individual agencies continue to play a critical role in our domestic security. The criticisms of the agencies involved in various aspects of homeland security mirror those of other parts of the federal government. Supporters of a federalist approach to problem solving would argue that only the federal government has sufficient economic, bureaucratic, and legislative resources to effectively address threats to our security. Thus, the federal government must be the primary organizer of homeland security functions. Skeptics warn of unbridled growth, massive bureaucracies, and inefficient spending. They argue that state and local governments should be the focal point of homeland security activities. As students of American history and politics will quickly recognize, this debate is not a new one. It is an integral part of American political culture to question government, particularly the federal government.

The long-term success of homeland security policy is heavily dependent on the ability of federal agencies to contribute to the homeland security mission. Cooperation with local agencies, funding of local projects, and transportation security have been among the areas most often criticized in the press.

The articles in this unit focus on federal government programs that have received some of this media attention. Homeland security fusion centers were established as a bridge between federal, state, and local law enforcement. The program places federal agents from organizations such as the DHS and the FBI alongside state and local law enforcement in local or regional centers funded in part or as a whole by federal grants to gather intelligence on potential threats. Torin Monahan's article identifies potential shortcomings of this approach and argues that these centers should follow clear guidelines and be subject to public scrutiny. As massive government spending spurred the emergence of an endless array of new security, defense, and technology contractors, questions about federal funding of homeland security projects remain unresolved. Kim Murphy's article asks the critical question: Have the $75 billion a year spent on domestic security over the past 10 years have made us safer? It examines how these federal funds have been utilized by both federal and state agencies.

While much of the critiques of homeland security efforts are directed at the executive branch and its agencies, the legislative branch has not been immune to criticism. The third article in this unit thus examines the implications of a 2007 congressional act that mandates 100 percent screening of all air cargo by 2010. It argues that this mandate is impossible to achieve and lacks both "intelligence and common sense."

Finally, the last article in this unit focuses on the much maligned Transportation Security Administration (TSA). A decade after 9/11, the TSA faces increased scrutiny, as poor communications, bad investments, and an inability to adjust in a changing market have undermined public confidence in the federal government's effort to improve passenger screening at U.S. airports.

The Future of Security? Surveillance Operations at Homeland Security Fusion Centers by Torin Monahan

77

Article   Prepared by: Thomas J. Badey, *Randolph-Macon College*

The Future of Security? Surveillance Operations at Homeland Security Fusion Centers

TORIN MONAHAN

Learning Outcomes

After reading this article, you will be able to:

- Describe the role of fusion centers in homeland security.

- Explain the problems associated with activities carried out by fusion centers.

- Discuss the lessons which can be learned from the operation of these fusion centers.

The U.S. "WAR ON TERROR" HAS FUELED REMARKABLE DEVELOPMENTS IN STATE surveillance. In the aftermath of the terrorist attacks of September 11, 2001, the country witnessed a rise in domestic spying programs, including warrantless wiretaps of the communications of citizens, investigations into the borrowing habits of library patrons, infiltration of peace-activist groups by government agents, and the establishment of tip hotlines to encourage people to report suspicious others (Monahan, 2010). Rather than interpret these and similar developments as originating with the "war on terror," scholars in the field of surveillance studies have correctly noted that the events of September 11 provided an impetus for a surge in many preexisting, but perhaps dormant, forms of state surveillance (Wood, Konvitz, and Ball, 2003). Similarly, such domestic surveillance practices neither began nor ended with the George W. Bush administration; instead, state surveillance has grown and mutated in response to changing perceptions of the nature of terrorist threats and the predilections of the Obama administration.

In particular, the Department of Homeland Security (DHS) has renewed its commitment to creating a robust, nationwide network of "fusion centers" to share and analyze data on citizens and others. As of 2010, at least 72 fusion centers existed at the state and regional levels throughout the United States, with many of them listed as "intelligence centers" or "information analysis centers." Officially, such centers prioritize counterterrorism activities, such as conducting "threat assessments" for events and linking "suspicious activities reports" to other data to create profiles of individuals or groups that might present terrorist risks. In this capacity, fusion centers engage in a form of "intelligence-led policing" that targets individuals who match certain profiles and singles them out for further monitoring or preemptive intervention (Ratcliffe, 2003; Wilson and Weber, 2008).

Most fusion centers are located within state and local police departments. Police, FBI, and DHS analysts, whose salaries are usually funded by their respective organizations, typically staff the centers. A common exception is when police representatives are funded in part or completely by DHS grants for the centers. In addition to conducting threat assessments and compiling suspicious-activities reports, fusion center analysts routinely respond to requests for information from state and local police, other fusion centers, or government agencies and organizations such as the FBI, DHS, the Secret Service, or the Department of Defense. When seen as pertinent, fusion centers also share information with private companies, such as those operating public utilities or managing other critical infrastructures (Electronic Privacy Information Center, 2008; Monahan, 2009).

Although the Los Angeles County Terrorism Early Warning Center, established in 1996, is often credited as being the first fusion center (German and Stanley, 2008), most were formed after the release of the September 11 Commission Report in 2004. The early fusion centers built upon and often incorporated the Federal Bureau of Investigation's "Joint Terrorism Task Force" (JTTF) program, thereby hardwiring FBI connections into fusion centers, but allowing for greater information sharing than JTTFs afforded (German and Stanley, 2007). Since their inception, the orientation of many fusion centers has expanded to include "all hazards" and "all threats," such as responding to environmental catastrophes or investigating non-terrorist criminal gangs (Rollins, 2008). One likely reason for this expansion is that the police departments housing fusion centers are trying to translate DHS priorities and apply DHS funds to address local needs (Monahan and Palmer, 2009).

Fusion centers are rapidly becoming a hallmark of the Obama administration's domestic security apparatus. Since 2009, 14 more fusion centers have come on line and the DHS and the Department of Justice have pledged more funding support for fusion centers (Burdeau, 2010; Geiger, 2009). On the surface, the increase in financial and political support for fusion centers should not be that surprising since DHS Secretary Janet Napolitano was a vocal advocate of the well-regarded Arizona-based fusion center, which she helped to create when she was governor of that state (Hylton, 2009). As DHS Secretary, Napolitano (2009) has reaffirmed this support: "I believe that Fusion Centers will be the centerpiece of state, local, federal intelligence-sharing for the future and that the Department of Homeland Security will be working and aiming its programs to underlie Fusion Centers." Attorney General Eric Holder (2010) has also affirmed fusion centers as vital to the ongoing "war on terror": "We are at war. This is the reality in which we live. And our fusion centers are on the frontlines of America's best, and most effective, efforts to fight back."

On a deeper level, fusion centers are probably aligned better with the politics of the Obama administration because its surveillance practices *appear* to be passive, disembodied, and objective. For instance, it has profoundly increased the use of unmanned aerial vehicles (UAVs) internationally and domestically (Wall and Monahan, 2011; Waiters and Weber, 2010). Barring instances of obvious abuse, the fusion and analysis of abstract forms of disparate data do not, in themselves, seem particularly egregious. Indeed, the stated purposes of fusion centers, at least in principle, sound innocuous and rational: "The [fusion] centers' goals are to blend law enforcement and intelligence information, and coordinate security measures to reduce threats in local communities" (U.S. Department of Homeland Security, 2008). Analysts at fusion centers could be thought of as engaging in types of "soft surveillance" (Marx, 2006) that are minimally invasive, at least for most people, and therefore are not nearly as objectionable to the general public as the more invasive articulations of police or state surveillance, such as physical searches, mandatory DNA collection, or telecommunication wiretaps.

Although fusion centers were formed under the Bush administration, largely in response to criticism from the September 11 Commission over intelligence failures leading up to the September 11 attacks, politically speaking this finding of failure was a sore point for President Bush and the relevant security agencies, such as the Federal Bureau of Investigation, the Central Intelligence Agency, and the National Security Agency. Moreover, whereas DHS was established rapidly in 2002, DHS-sponsored fusion centers did not substantially take off until 2005. A case could be made that the supposedly objective, intelligence-led orientation of fusion centers was actually in tension with the general timbre of aggressive, masculinist intervention that characterized many aspects of the "war on terror" under the Bush administration. In contradistinction, the patient police work done by analysts in fusion centers could be viewed as being much smarter and

more reflective, and therefore somewhat feminized compared to other modalities of the "war on terror." DHS officials have explicitly referred to fusion centers as engaging in "thoughtful analysis" (Riegle, 2009) and have implemented workshops and classes to teach fusion center analysts "critical thinking, analytic tools, techniques, and writing" (U.S. Department of Homeland Security, 2008: 16). These articulations are a far cry from the action-oriented counterterrorism myths circulated by entertainment shows like *24,* which were embraced by former White House deputy chief of staff Karl Rove and former DHS Secretary Michael Chertoff, among others (Monahan, 2010). In this light, the operations and concept of fusion centers resonate better with the crafted image of President Obama as a thoughtful, measured, and intelligent leader.

Surveillance of abstract data—or "dataveillance" (Clarke, 2001)—may be perceived as being less intrusive and less threatening than are video cameras, wiretaps, or other technologies that are traditionally associated with surveillance (Ericson and Haggerty, 1997; Marx, 2006). Provided that the data do not involve information considered sensitive, such as pharmacy or bank records, people definitely do not find dataveillance to be as intrusive as physical searches of individuals or individual property (Slobogin, 2008). Nonetheless, these viewpoints neglect the extent to which personal data are constantly being generated, captured, and circulated by the many information systems and technologies with which people come in contact (e.g., cell phones, credit cards, the Internet). When "fused," whether by a marketing firm or a state entity, these data can paint a disturbingly fine-grained representation of individuals, their associations, preferences, and risks. Anyone who has access to such "data doubles" (Haggerty and Ericson, 2006) is in a position to know and act on a great deal of information that might otherwise be considered personal and private. It is perhaps much more personal and private than that which could be gleaned from more traditional surveillance techniques. Even more disconcerting for individuals is the fact that although the data generated by our many information systems are always partial and sometimes grossly inaccurate, they can still negatively affect one's life experiences and chances (e.g., through one's credit score or one's terrorist-risk score).

Therefore, the phenomenon of fusion centers must be situated within the context of surveillance societies. Broadly speaking, surveillance societies operate upon imperatives of data gathering and data monitoring, often through technological systems, for purposes of governance and control (Lyon, 2001; Monahan, 2010; Murakami Wood et al., 2006). These particular logics of surveillance were not invented by U.S. national security agencies in response to the September 11 attacks. Instead, fusion centers and other surveillance-oriented security organizations draw upon existing practices of voracious data collection and fluid information exchange, as exemplified by social networking sites such as Facebook or private-sector data aggregators such as Entersect, a company that actively partners with fusion centers to share its purported "12 billion records on about 98 per cent of Americans" (O'Harrow, Jr., 2008).

Thus, there is also a neoliberal dimension to fusion centers, in that they purchase data from the private sector, sometimes

The Future of Security? Surveillance Operations at Homeland Security Fusion Centers by Torin Monahan

79

hire private data analysts, and share information with industry partners (Monahan, 2009). By forming information-sharing partnerships, analysts at fusion centers seek to "connect the dots" to prevent future terrorist attacks. Meanwhile, government officials are very interested in figuring out ways in which DHS in general and fusion centers in particular can assist the private sector, presumably by enabling and protecting the ability of companies to profit financially (Monahan, 2010). As DHS Under Secretary Caryn Wagner stated in her 2010 testimony before the House Subcommittee on Homeland Security:

> I&A [DHS's Office of Intelligence and Analysis] will continue to advocate for sustained funding for the fusion centers as the linchpin of the evolving homeland security enterprise. While I&A's support to state, local and tribal partners is steadily improving, there is still work to be done in *how best to support the private sector.* We intend to explore ways to extend our efforts in this area beyond the established relationships with the critical infrastructure sectors (Wagner, 2010; emphasis added).

In some respects, fusion centers suffer from a mandate that is too open-ended and from guidelines that are too ambiguous. The task of fusing data to produce "intelligence" that can be used to prevent terrorist acts or respond to "all crimes" or "all hazards" amounts to an invitation for individuals at these centers to engage in almost any surveillance practices that make sense to them. As noted, this flexibility could have the redeeming value of allowing police departments to use DHS and other resources for needs that are perceived as being meaningful for particular jurisdictions (Monahan and Palmer, 2009). However, evidence suggests that people at some fusion centers are also exploiting the significant leeway granted to them to engage in racial profiling, political profiling, illegal data mining, and illegal data collection. The surveillance capabilities of fusion centers enable and invite "mission creep" or "function creep," whereby analysts draw upon the resources at their disposal to exceed the policies and laws that are intended to govern their activities (*Ibid.*). Moreover, the guidelines for fusion centers are quite ambiguous and there is a general absence of oversight regarding their activities (German and Stanley, 2007). In the following sections, I will review in detail a few cases of abuse by fusion centers and discuss the issues raised by such examples.

Fusion Center Abuses

Given the secretive nature of fusion centers, including their resistance to freedom of information requests (German and Stanley, 2008; Stokes, 2008), the primary way in which the public has learned about their activities is through leaked or unintentionally disseminated documents. For instance, a "terrorism threat assessment" produced by Virginia's fusion center surfaced in 2009 and sparked outrage because it identified students at colleges and universities—especially at historically black universities—as posing a potential terrorist threat (Sizemore, 2009). In the report, universities were targeted because of their diversity, which is seen as threatening because

it might inspire "radicalization." The report says: "Richmond's history as the capital city of the Confederacy, combined with the city's current demographic concentration of African-American residents, contributes to the continued presence of race-based extremist groups . . . [and student groups] are recognized as a radicalization node for almost every type of extremist group" (Virginia Fusion Center, 2009: 9). Although the American Civil Liberties Union (ACLU) and others have rightly decried the racial-profiling implications of such biased claims being codified in an official document, the report itself supports the interpretation that minority students will be and probably have been targeted for surveillance. The report argues: "In order to detect and deter terrorist attacks, it is essential that information regarding suspected terrorists and suspicious activity in Virginia be closely monitored and reported in a timely manner" (*Ibid:* 4). Other groups identified as potential threats by the Virginia fusion center were environmentalists, militia members, and students at Regent University, the Christian university founded by evangelical preacher Pat Robertson (Sizemore, 2009).

Another threat-assessment report, compiled by the Missouri Information Analysis Center (MIAC), found "the modern militia movement" to be worthy of focused investigation. The 2009 report predicted a resurgence in right-wing militia activities because of high levels of unemployment and anger at the election of the nation's first black president, Barack Obama, who many right-wing militia members might view as illegitimate and/or in favor of stronger gun-control laws (Missouri Information Analysis Center, 2009). The greatest stir caused by the report was its claim that "militia members most commonly associate with 3rd party political groups. . . . These members are usually supporters of former Presidential Candidate: Ron Paul, Chuck Baldwin, and Bob Barr" (*Ibid.:* 7). When the report circulated, many libertarians and "Tea Party" members took great offense, thinking the document argued that supporters of third-party political groups were more likely to be dangerous militia members or terrorists. In response, libertarian activists formed a national network called "Operation Defuse," which is devoted to uncovering and criticizing the activities of fusion centers and is actively filing open-records requests and attempting to conduct tours of fusion centers. Operation Defuse could be construed as a "counter-surveillance" group (Monahan, 2006) that arose largely because of outrage over the probability of political profiling by state-surveillance agents.

Fusion centers have also been implicated in scandals involving covert infiltrations of nonviolent groups, including peace-activist groups, anti-death penalty groups, animal-fights groups, Green Party groups, and others. The most astonishing of the known cases involved the Maryland Coordination and Analysis Center (MCAC). In response to an ACLU freedom of information lawsuit, it came to light in 2008 that the Maryland State Police had conducted covert investigations of at least 53 peace activists and anti-death penalty activists for a period of 14 months. The investigation proceeded despite admissions by the covert agent that she saw no indication of violent activities or violent intentions on the part of group members (Newkirk, 2010). Nonetheless, in the federal database used by the police and accessed by MCAC, activists were listed as being suspected of the "primary crime" of "Terrorism—anti-government" (German and Stanley, 2008: 8). Although it is unclear exactly what role the fusion center played in these activities, they were most likely involved in and aware of the investigation. After all, as Mike German and Jay Stanley (2008: 8) explain:

> Fusion centers are clearly *intended* to be the central focal point for sharing terrorism-related information. If the MCAC was not aware of the information the state police collected over the 14 months of this supposed terrorism investigation, this fact would call into question whether the MCAC is accomplishing its mission.

Police spying of this sort, besides being illegal absent "reasonable suspicion" of wrongdoing, could have a "chilling effect" on free speech and freedom of association. The fact that individuals were wrongly labeled as terrorists in these systems and may still be identified as such could also have negative ramifications for them far into the future.

Another dimension of troubling partnerships between fusion centers and law enforcement was revealed with the 2007 arrest of Kenneth Krayeske, a Green Party member in Connecticut. On January 3, 2007, Krayeske was taking photographs of Connecticut Governor M. Jodi Rell at her inaugural parade. He was not engaged in protest at the time. While serving as the manager of the Green Party's gubernatorial candidate, he had publicly challenged Governor Rell over the issue of why she would not debate his candidate (Levine, 2007). At the parade, police promptly arrested Krayeske (after he took 23 photographs) and later charged him with "Breach of Peace" and "Interfering with Police" (*Ibid.*). Connecticut's fusion center, the Connecticut Intelligence Center (CTIC), had conducted a threat assessment for the event and had circulated photographs of Krayeske and others to police in advance (Krayeske, 2007). The police report reads: "The Connecticut Intelligence Center and the Connecticut State Police Central Intelligence Unit had briefed us [the police] on possible threats to Governor Rell by political activist [*sic*], to include photographs of the individuals. One of the photographs was of the accused Kenneth Krayeske" (quoted in Levine, 2007). Evidently, part of the reason Krayeske was targeted was that intelligence analysts, most likely at the fusion center, were monitoring blog posts on the Internet and interpreted one of them as threatening: "Who is going to protest the inaugural ball with me? . . . No need to make nice" (CNN.com, 2009). According to a CNN report on the arrest, after finding that blog post, "police began digging for information, mining public and commercial data bases. They learned Krayeske had been a Green Party campaign director, had protested the gubernatorial debate and had once been convicted for civil disobedience. He had no history of violence" (*Ibid.*). The person who read Krayeske his Miranda rights and attempted to interview him in custody was Andrew Weaver, a sergeant for the City of Hartford Police Department who *also* works in the CTIC fusion center (Department of Emergency Management and Homeland Security, 2008).

These few examples demonstrate some of the dangers and problems with fusion centers. Fusion center threat assessments lend themselves to profiling along lines of race, religion, and political affiliation. Their products are not impartial assessments of terrorist threats, but rather betray biases against individuals or groups who deviate from—or challenge—the status quo. According to a *Washington Times* commentary that became a focal point for a congressional hearing on fusion centers, as long as terrorism is defined as coercive or intimidating acts that are intended to shape government policy, "any dissidence or political dissident is suspect to fusion centers" (Fein, 2009). Evidence from the Maryland and Connecticut fusion center cases suggests that their representatives are either involved in data-gathering and investigative work, orare at least complicit in such activities, including illegal spying operations (German and Stanley, 2008). The Connecticut case further shows that individuals working at fusion centers are actively monitoring online sources and interviewing suspects, a departure from the official Fusion Center Guidelines that stress "exchange" and "analysis" of data, not data acquisition through investigations (U.S. Department of Justice, 2006).

One important issue here is that fusion centers occupy ambiguous organizational positions. Many of them are located in police departments or are combined with FBI Joint Terrorism Task Forces, but their activities are supposed to be separate and different from the routine activities of the police or the FBI. A related complication is that fusion center employees often occupy multiple organizational roles (e.g., police officers or National Guard members *and* fusion center analysts), which can lead to an understandable, but nonetheless problematic, blurring of professional identities, rules of conduct, and systems of accountability. Whereas in 2010 DHS and the Department of Justice responded to concerns about profiling by implementing a civil liberties certification requirement for fusion centers, public oversight and accountability of fusion centers are becoming even more difficult and unlikely because of a concerted effort to exempt fusion centers from freedom of information requests. For example, according to a police official, Virginia legislators were coerced into passing a 2008 law that exempted its fusion center from the Freedom of Information Act; in this instance, federal officials threatened to withhold classified intelligence from the state's fusion center and police if they did not pass such a law (German and Stanley, 2008). Another tactic used by fusion center representatives to thwart open-records requests is to claim that there is no "material product" for them to turn over because they only "access," rather than "retain," information (Hylton, 2009).

Although it may be tempting to view these cases of fusion center missteps and infractions as isolated examples, they are probably just the tip of the iceberg. A handful of other cases has surfaced recently in which fusion centers in California, Colorado, Texas, Pennsylvania, and Georgia have recommended peace activists, Muslim-rights groups, and/or environmentalists be profiled (German, 2009; Wolfe, 2009). The Texas example reveals the ways in which the flexibility of fusion centers affords the incorporation of xenophobic and racist beliefs. In 2009, the North Central Texas Fusion System produced a report that argued that the United States is especially vulnerable to terrorist infiltration because the country is too tolerant and accommodating of religious difference, especially of Islam.

Through several indicators, the report lists supposed signs that the country is gradually being invaded and transformed: "Muslim cab drivers in Minneapolis refuse to carry passengers who have alcohol in their possession; the Indianapolis airport in 2007 installed footbaths to accommodate Muslim prayer; public schools schedule prayer breaks to accommodate Muslim students; pork is banned in the workplace; etc." (North Central Texas Fusion System, 2009: 4). Because "the threats to Texas are significant," the fusion center advises keeping an eye out for Muslim civil liberties groups and sympathetic individuals, organizations, or media that might carry their message: hip-hop bands, social networking sites, online chat forums, blogs, and even the U.S. Department of Treasury (*Ibid.*).

Recent infiltration of peace groups seems to reproduce some of the sordid history of political surveillance of U.S. citizens, such as the FBI and CIA's COINTELPRO program, which targeted civil rights leaders and those peacefully protesting against the Vietnam War, among others (Churchill and Vander Wall, 2002). A contemporary case involves a U.S. Army agent who infiltrated a nonviolent, anti-war protest group in Olympia, Washington, in 2007. A military agent spying on civilians likely violated the Posse Comitatus Act. Moreover, this agent actively shared intelligence with the Washington State Fusion Center, which shared it more broadly (Anderson, 2010). According to released documents, intelligence representatives from as far away as New Jersey were kept apprised of the spying:

> In a 2008 e-mail to an Olympia police officer, Thomas Glapion, Chief of Investigations and Intelligence at New Jersey's McGuire Air Force Base, wrote: "You are now part of my Intel network. I'm still looking at possible protests by the PMR SDS MDS and other left wing antiwar groups so any Intel you have would be appreciated. . . . In return if you need anything from the Armed Forces I will try to help you as well" (*Ibid.*: 4).

Given that political surveillance under COINTELPRO is widely considered to be a dark period in U.S. intelligence history, the fact that fusion centers may be contributing to similar practices today makes it all the more important to subject them to public scrutiny and oversight.

Transgressive Data Collection

By now it should be apparent that fusion center personnel are neither objectively assessing terrorist threats nor passively analyzing preexisting data. Fusion centers may appear to be more impartial and rational than previous forms of state surveillance. Yet they have incorporated previous surveillance modalities, including their prejudicial beliefs and invasive techniques, and merged them with dataveillance capabilities that amplify the potential for civil liberties violations and personal harm. Even if fusion center activities were restricted to passive data analysis, which they are not, they could still transgress existing laws that are intended to protect people from unreasonable searches. Specifically, Title 28, Part 23 of the Code of Federal Regulations states that law enforcement agencies "shall collect and maintain criminal intelligence information concerning an individual only if there is reasonable suspicion that the individual is involved in criminal conduct or activity and the information is relevant to that criminal conduct or activity" (in German and Stanley, 2008: 2). When fusion center analysts create profiles of risky individuals and then engage in data mining to identify people who match those profiles, they are effectively bypassing the "reasonable suspicion" requirement for intelligence operations.

Aside from the known cases of abuse, in their official capacity fusion centers are apparently exploiting a technicality in terms of what constitutes "collecting" and "maintaining" criminal intelligence information. The implied reasoning is this: provided that fusion centers merely analyze data stored in databases housed elsewhere, they are not violating the "reasonable suspicion" stipulation even if they are conducting "dragnet" or "fishing expedition" searches that would have been illegal with previous generations of computing technology that did not depend entirely on networks. This rationalization is especially specious when analysts can access police records that are located in the same buildings as the fusion centers. Nonetheless, DHS and Department of Justice guidelines explicitly encourage fusion centers to access as much data as possible, extending "beyond criminal intelligence, to include federal intelligence as well as public and private-sector data" (quoted in German and Stanley, 2007: 7). In an unusually candid statement, Sheriff Kevin Rambosk, who is associated with the Florida fusion center, justifies widespread data sharing as a way to compete with criminals who similarly move across jurisdictional lines:

> We know as law enforcement professionals that there are no jurisdictional boundaries for criminals. . . . And we historically and intuitively know that the more information that we can share with one another, the more cases can be solved, the more crimes can be prevented, and the more information each of our agencies will have to continue to make Collier County one of the safest places in Florida to live (Mills, 2010).

The implication of this assertion is that there should not be any jurisdictional or legal boundaries for law enforcement to collect and share data either, including data from the private sector, which fusion centers in Florida access through a system called "Florida Integrated Network for Data Exchange and Retrieval" or "FINDER" (*Ibid.*).

Conclusion: Surveillance Iterations

Although criminals or terrorists may be crossing jurisdictional boundaries and breaking the law, state agencies and agents do more harm than good when they ignore existing legal constraints or seek out exemptions from public oversight. The few problematic cases reviewed in this article illustrate that without due respect for the "reasonable suspicion" provision on police intelligence-gathering activities, fusion center personnel engage in or endorse racial, political, and religious profiling; they perceive challenges to the status quo as threatening and possibly "terrorist"; they support the investigation and arrest of law-abiding individuals, marking them as "terrorists" in official databases, perhaps in perpetuity; and they exert a chilling effect on free speech in that activists and others are more likely to temper their activities to avoid similar kinds of harmful scrutiny.

It is important to note that the politics of those being targeted by fusion centers spans the spectrum from right-wing militia members to left-wing anti-war activists. Some may be surprised that individuals supporting progressive causes would be seen as threats during a Democratic presidency. Yet these cases underscore that the politics of many environmentalists, anti-war activists, and other progressives are still radical vis-à-vis the mainstream politics of contemporary Washington. Moreover, law enforcement cultures are typically quite conservative (Greene, 2007; Reiner, 2010) and, similar to other organizations, slow to change (Zhao, He, and Lovrich, 1998). Thus, the outcomes of national elections are unlikely to produce discernable near-term changes in the cultures of these organizations.

If today's surveillance state were to fully embody Barack Obama's campaign rhetoric of respect for "the rule of law," fusion centers would differ markedly. The blurring or suspending of the law are supposedly practices that characterized the "war on terror" under the Bush administration. Impatience with bureaucratic constraints upon counterterrorism efforts or frustration with the burden of protecting civil liberties are similarly more readily associated with the masculinist orientation of the previous administration. Fusion centers could strictly follow stipulations on intelligence gathering; they could erect barriers between public and private databases; they could embrace transparency and accountability by complying with, rather than avoiding, freedom of information requests.

Instead of romanticizing the ideals that could have been achieved, or might yet be achieved, I prefer to conclude by highlighting what can be learned from the example of fusion centers. First, fusion centers show the ways in which the logics of "surveillance societies" pervade all aspects of social life, including the operations of government organizations. Imperatives to collect, share, analyze, and act on data increasingly shape the activities of public institutions, private companies, and individuals. The capabilities of new media technologies simply augment this particular drive, which is unchecked or under-regulated in most domains, and the realm of national security is no different. If governments are reluctant to impose serious restrictions on data sharing more generally, except perhaps for particularly sensitive data such as those contained in medical records, one should not be surprised that government agencies would avail themselves of similar data-sharing functions (Regan, 2004). Second, the unstandardized composition and mission of fusion centers may afford them ample flexibility, but it also allows particularistic biases to shape their activities. When made public, such biases may embarrass fusion center officials, but they are undoubtedly more damaging to the targets of unwarranted surveillance and intervention. The latter must contend with legal battles and fees, emotional stress, and perhaps even physical abuse associated with being marked as terrorist suspects (Guzik, 2009). For surveillance states to be more democratic, their police apparatuses should possess and follow clear guidelines that respect the law, and subject their activities to routine public scrutiny. To do otherwise is a recipe for abuse.

References

Anderson, Rick 2010 "Watching the Protesters." *Seattle Weekly News* (June 9). At www.seattleweekly.com/2010-06-09/news/watching-the-protesters/1.

Burdeau, Cain 2010 "Holder: Intelligence-Sharing Centers Vital." *Associated Press* (February 23). At www.washingtonexaminer.com/local/ap/holder-intelligence-sharing-centers-vital-85071812.html.

Churchill, Ward and Jim Vander Wall 2002 *The COINTELPRO Papers: Documents from the FBI's Secret Wars Against Dissent in the United States.* Cambridge, MA: South End Press.

Clarke, Roger 2001 *While You Were Sleeping . . . Surveillance Technologies Arrived.* At www.anu.edu.au/people/Roger.Clarke/DV/AQ2001.html.

CNN.com 2009 "Are You on the List?" (September 30). At www.cnn.com/video/?/video/crime/2009/09/30/willis.fusion.centers.cnn.

Department of Emergency Management and Homeland Security 2008 Department of Emergency Management and Homeland Security Coordinating Council Meeting Minutes. Hartford, CT. At www.ct.gov/demhs/lib/demhs/docsuploaded/cood_council_minutes/cc_mins_9_18_08.pdf.

Electronic Privacy Information Center 2008 "Information Fusion Centers and Privacy." At http://epic.org/privacy/fusion/.

Ericson, Richard V. and Kevin D. Haggerty 1997 *Policing the Risk Society.* Toronto: University of Toronto Press.

Fein, Bruce 2009 "Surveilling for Clues of Evil Intent." WashingtonTimes.com (April 1). At www.washingtontimes.com/news/2009/apr/01/surveilling-for-clues-of-evil-intent/.

Geiger, Harley 2009 "Fusion Centers Get New Privacy Orders Via DHS Grants. December 15." At www.cdt.org/blogs/harley-geiger/fusion-centers-get-new-privacy-orders-dhs-grants.

German, Michael 2009 Testimony in Support of Senate Bill 931 Before the Joint Committee on Public Safety and Homeland Security. Boston. At www.scribd.com/doc/24658143/MikeGerman-Former-FBI-testimony-sb931MA-Fusion-Center-2009.

German, Michael and Jay Stanley 2008 ACLU Fusion Center Update. July. At www.aclu.org/pdfs/privacy/fusion_update_20080729.pdf.

2007 "What's Wrong with Fusion Centers?" (December). At www.aclu.org/files/pdfs/privacy/fusioncenter_20071212.pdf.

Greene, Jack R. 2007 "Human Rights and Police Discretion: Justice Service or Denied?" *Sociology of Crime Law and Deviance* 9: 147–169.

Guzik, Keith 2009 "Discrimination by Design: Predictive Data Mining as Security Practice in the United States' 'War on Terrorism.'" *Surveillance & Society* 7, 1: 1–17.

Haggerty, Kevin D. and Richard V. Ericson 2006 "The New Politics of Surveillance and Visibility." K.D. Haggerty and R.V. Ericson (eds.), *The New Politics of Surveillance and Visibility.* Toronto: University of Toronto Press: 3–25.

Holder, Eric 2010 "Attorney General Eric Holder Speaks at the Fourth Annual National Fusion Center Conference." New Orleans, LA: Department of Homeland Security. At www.justice.gov/ag/speeches/2010/ag-speech-100223.html.

Hylton, Hilary 2009 "Fusion Centers: Giving Cops Too Much Information?" Time.com. At www.time.com/time/nation/article/0,8599,1883101,00.html.

Krayeske, Ken 2007 "And Justice for All . . ." At www.the40yearplan.com/article_052507_And_Justice_For_All.php.

Levine, Dan 2007 "Arresting Development." *Cal Law* (January 12): 5. At www.the40yearplan.com/pdf/annotation.pdf.

Lyon, David 2001 *Surveillance Society: Monitoring Everyday Life.* Buckingham, England; Philadelphia: Open University.

Marx, Gary T. 2006 "Soft Surveillance: The Growth of Mandatory Volunteerism in Collecting Personal Information—'Hey Buddy Can You Spare a DNA?'" T. Monahan (ed.), *Surveillance and Security: Technological Politics and Power in Everyday Life.* New York: Routledge: 37–56.

Mills, Ryan 2010 "Fla. Police Agencies to Start Using Data-Sharing Tools." *Naples Daily News* (February 12). At www.policeone.com/police-products/communications/articles/2003592-Fla-police-agencies-to-start-using-data-sharing-tools/.

Missouri Information Analysis Center 2009 MIAC Strategic Report, 02/20/09. "The Modern Militia Movement." Jefferson City, MO. At www.scribd.com/doc/13232178/MIAC-Strategic-Report-The-Modern-Militia-Movement.

Monahan, Torin 2010 *Surveillance in the Time of Insecurity.* New Brunswick: Rutgers University Press.

2009 "The Murky World of 'Fusion Centers.'" *Criminal Justice Matters* 75, 1: 20–21.

2007 "'War Rooms' of the Street: Surveillance Practices in Transportation Control Centers." *The Communication Review* 10, 4: 367–389.

2006 "Counter-Surveillance as Political Intervention?" *Social Semiotics* 16, 4: 515–534.

Monahan, Torin and Neal A. Palmer 2009 "The Emerging Politics of DHS Fusion Centers." *Security Dialogue* 40, 6: 617–636.

Murakami Wood, David (ed.), Kirstie Ball, David Lyon, Clive Norris, and Charles Raab 2006 *A Report on the Surveillance Society.* Wilmslow: Office of the Information Commissioner.

Napolitano, Janet 2009 "Remarks by Homeland Security Secretary Janet Napolitano to the National Fusion Center Conference in Kansas City, Mo., on March 11, 2009." Kansas City, MO: Department of Homeland Security. At www.dhs.gov/ynews/speeches/sp_1236975404263.shtm.

Newkirk, Anthony B. 2010 "The Rise of the Fusion-Intelligence Complex: A critique of political surveillance after 9/11." *Surveillance & Society* 8, 1: 43–60.

North Central Texas Fusion System 2009 *Prevention Awareness Bulletin.* At www.privacylives.com/wp-content/uploads/2009/03/texasfusion_021909.pdf.

O'Harrow, Jr., Robert 2008 "Centers Tap into Personal Databases." *Washington Post* (April 2). At www.washingtonpost.com/wp-dyn/content/article/2008/04/01/AR2008040103049.html.

Ratcliffe, Jerry H. 2003 "Intelligence-led Policing." *Trends and Issues in Crime and Criminal Justice* 248: 1–6.

Regan, Priscilla M. 2004 "Old Issues, New Context: Privacy, Information Collection and Homeland Security." *Government Information Quarterly* 21, 4: 481–497.

Reiner, Robert 2010 *The Politics of the Police.* New York: Oxford University Press.

Riegle, Robert 2009 Testimony of Director Robert Riegle, State and Local Program Office, Office of Intelligence and Analysis, before the Committee on Homeland Security, Subcommittee on Intelligence, Information Sharing, and Terrorism Risk Assessment, "The Future of Fusion Centers: Potential Promise and Dangers." Washington, D.C. At www.dhs.gov/ynews/testimony/testimony_1238597287040.shtm.

Rollins, John 2008 *Fusion Centers: Issues and Options for Congress.* Washington, D.C.: Congressional Research Service. At www.fas.org/sgp/crs/intel/RL34070.pdf.

Sizemore, Bill 2009 "Report: Region May Be a Hotbed for Terrorist Recruiting." *The Virginian-Pilot* (April 26). At http://hamptonroads.com/2009/04/report-region-may-be-hotbed-terrorist-recruiting.

Slobogin, Christopher 2008 "Government Data Mining and the Fourth Amendment." *The University of Chicago Law Review* 75, 1: 317–341.

Stokes, Jon 2008 "Fusion Center Meltdown: Feds Stifling Open Government in VA?" *Ars Technica* (March 24). At http://arstechnica.com/security/news/2008/03/fusion-centermeltdown-feds-stifling-open-government-in-va.ars.

U.S. Department of Homeland Security 2008 "DHS' Role in State and Local Fusion Centers Is Evolving." Washington, D.C.: U.S. Department of Homeland Security. At www.dhs.gov/xoig/assets/mgmtrpts/OIG_09-12_Dec08.pdf.

U.S. Department of Justice 2006 "Fusion Center Guidelines: Developing and Sharing Information and Intelligence in a New Era." Washington, D.C.: U.S. Department of Justice. At www.iir.com/global/products/fusion_center_guidelines_law_enforcement.pdf.

Virginia Fusion Center 2009 *Virginia Terrorism Threat Assessment.* Richmond, VA: Department of State Police. At www.rawstory.com/images/other/vafusioncenterterrorassessment.pdf.

Wagner, Caryn 2010 Testimony of Under Secretary Caryn Wagner before the House Subcommittee on Homeland Security on the President's Fiscal Year 2011 Budget Request for the Department's Office of Intelligence and Analysis. Washington, D.C.: Department of Homeland Security. At www.dhs.gov/ynews/testimony/testimony_1267716038879.shtm.

Wall, Tyler and Torin Monahan 2011 "Surveillance and Violence from Afar: The Politics of Drones and Liminal Security-Scapes." *Theoretical Criminology* 15, 3: 239–254.

Walters, William and Jutta Weber 2010 "UCAV Surveillance, High-Tech Masculinities and Oriental Others." *A Global Surveillance Society?* Conference at City University London.

Wilson, Dean and Leanne Weber 2008 "Surveillance, Risk and Preemption on the Australian Border." *Surveillance & Society* 5, 2: 124–141.

Wolfe, Gavi 2009 "What We Know about Recent Surveillance of Lawful First Amendment Activity." Massachusetts: American Civil Liberties Union of Massachusetts. At http://aclum.org/sos/aclu_domestic_surveillance_what_we_know.pdf.

Wood, David, Eli Konvitz, and Kirstie Ball 2003 "The Constant State of Emergency? Surveillance after 9/11." K. Ball and F. Webster (eds.), *The Intensification of Surveillance: Crime, Terrorism and Warfare in the Information Age.* London: Pluto Press: 137–150.

Zhao, Jihong, Ni He, and Nicholas P. Lovrich 1998 "Individual Value Preferences among American Police Officers: The Rokeach Theory of Human Values Revisited." *Policing: An International Journal of Police Strategies & Management* 21, 1: 22–37.

Critical Thinking

1. In what way do fusion centers contribute to homeland security?

2. Does the potential for abuse outweigh the potential benefits fusion centers offer?

3. How could the activities of fusion centers be modified to address the concerns of their critics?

Create Central

www.mhhe.com/createcentral

Internet References

FBI Joint Terrorism Task Force (JTTF)
www.fbi.gov/about-us/investigate/terrorism/terrorism_jttfs

National Security Agency
www.nsa.gov/

DHS Office of Intelligence and Analysis
www.dhs.gov/about-office-intelligence-and-analysis

Modern Militia Movement
http://modernmilitiamovement.com/

National Fusion Center Association
www.nfcausa.org

TORIN MONAHAN is Associate Professor of Human and Organizational Development and Medicine at Vanderbilt University (e-mail: torin.monahan@vanderbilt.edu). He is a member of the International Surveillance Studies Network. Among his books are *Surveillance in the Time of Insecurity* (Rutgers University Press, 2010), *Schools under Surveillance: Cultures of Control in Public Education* (Rutgers University Press, 2010), *Surveillance and Security: Technological Politics and Power in Everyday Life* (Routledge, 2006), and *Globalization, Technological Change, and Public Education* (Routledge, 2005).

Acknowledgment—This material is based upon a research project being conducted by the author and Priscilla Regan. The work is supported by the National Science Foundation under grant number SES 0957283.

Article

Prepared by: Thomas J. Badey, *Randolph-Macon College*

Is Homeland Security Spending Paying Off?

A Decade After The Sept. 11 Attacks, Federal And State Governments Are Doling Out About $75 Billion A Year On Domestic Security. Whether The Spending Spree Has Been Worth It Is The Subject Of Increasing Debate.

Kɪᴍ Mᴜʀᴘʜʏ

Learning Outcomes

After reading this article, you will be able to:

- List some of the projects funded by the Department of Homeland Security.

- Analyze the effectiveness of homeland security spending.

- Discuss the impact of homeland security funds on state and local government.

- Discuss how homeland security funds should be allocated.

Reporting from Ogallala, Neb.—On the edge of the Nebraska sand hills is Lake McConaughy, a 22-mile-long reservoir that in summer becomes a magnet for Winnebagos, fishermen and kite sailors. But officials here in Keith County, population 8,370, imagined this scene: an Al Qaeda sleeper cell hitching explosives onto a ski boat and plowing into the dam at the head of the lake. The federal Department of Homeland Security gave the county $42,000 to buy state-of-the-art dive gear, including full-face masks, underwater lights and radios, and a Zodiac boat with side-scan sonar capable of mapping wide areas of the lake floor.

Up on the lonely prairie, Cherry County, population 6,148, got thousands of federal dollars for cattle nose leads, halters and electric prods—in case terrorists decided to mount biological warfare against cows.

In the Los Angeles suburb of Glendale, where police fear militants might be eyeing DreamWorks Animation or the Disney creative campus, a $205,000 Homeland Security grant bought a 9-ton BearCat armored vehicle, complete with turret. More than 300 BearCats—many acquired with federal money—are now deployed by police across the country; the arrests of methamphetamine dealers and bank robbers these days often look much like a tactical assault on insurgents in Baghdad.

A decade after the Sept. 11, 2001, attacks on the World Trade Center and the Pentagon, federal and state governments are spending about $75 billion a year on domestic security, setting up sophisticated radio networks, upgrading emergency medical response equipment, installing surveillance cameras and bombproof walls, and outfitting airport screeners to detect an ever-evolving list of mobile explosives.

But how effective has that 10-year spending spree been?

"The number of people worldwide who are killed by Muslim-type terrorists, Al Qaeda wannabes, is maybe a few hundred outside of war zones. It's basically the same number of people who die drowning in the bathtub each year," said John Mueller, an Ohio State University professor who has written extensively about the balance between threat and expenditures in fighting terrorism.

"So if your chance of being killed by a terrorist in the United States is 1 in 3.5 million, the question is, how much do you want to spend to get that down to 1 in 4.5 million?" he said.

One effect is certain: Homeland Security spending has been a pump-primer for local governments starved by the recession, and has dramatically improved emergency response networks across the country.

An entire industry has sprung up to sell an array of products, including high-tech motion sensors and fully outfitted emergency operations trailers. The market is expected to grow to $31 billion by 2014.

Like the military-industrial complex that became a permanent and powerful part of the American landscape during the Cold War, the vast network of Homeland Security spyware, concrete barricades and high-tech identity screening is here to stay. The Department of Homeland Security, a collection of agencies ranging from border control to airport security sewn quickly together after Sept. 11, is the third-largest Cabinet department and—with almost no lawmaker willing to render the U.S. less prepared for a terrorist attack—one of those least to fall victim to budget cuts.

The expensive and time-consuming screening now routine for passengers at airport boarding gates has detected plenty of knives, loaded guns and other contraband, but it has never identified a terrorist who was about to board a plane. Only 14 Americans have died in about three dozen instances of Islamic extremist terrorist plots targeted at the U.S. outside war zones since 2001—most of them involving one or two home-grown plotters.

Homeland Security officials say there is no way to compute how many lives might have been lost had the nation's massive security apparatus not been put into place—had the would-be bombers not been arrested before they struck, or deterred from getting on a plane because it was too hard.

"We know that they study our security measures, we know they're continuously looking for ways to get around them, and that's a disincentive for someone to carry out an attack," said John Cohen, the department's deputy counter-terrorism coordinator.

"Another way of asking the question is: Has there been a U.S. airplane that has exploded?"

State and local emergency responders have undergone a dramatic transformation with the aid of $32 billion that has been dispensed in Homeland Security grants since 2002, much of it in the early years spent on Hollywood-style tactical gear, often with little connection between risk and outlay.

"After 9/11, it was literally like my mother running out the door with the charge card," said Al Berndt, assistant director of the Emergency Management Agency in Nebraska, which has received $163.7 million in federal anti-terrorism and emergency aid grants. "What we really needed to be doing is saying, 'Let's identify the threat, identify the capability and capacity you already have, and say, OK, what's the shortfall now, and how do we meet it?'"

10 Years After: Are We Safer?
A Key Sept. 11 Legacy: More Domestic Surveillance

Is Homeland Security spending paying off? The spending has been rife with dubious expenditures, including the $557,400 in rescue and communications gear that went to the 1,500 residents of North Pole, Alaska, and a $750,000 anti-terrorism fence—fashioned with 8-foot-high ram-proof wrought iron reinforced with concrete footers—built around a Veterans Affairs hospital in the pastoral hills outside Asheville, N.C.

West Virginia got $3,000 worth of lapel pins and billed the federal government for thousands of dollars in cellphone charges, according to the Center for Investigative Reporting, which compiled a state-by-state accounting of Homeland Security spending. In New York, $3 million was spent on automated public health records to help identify bioterrorism threats, but investigators for the department's inspector general in 2008 found that employees who used the program weren't even aware of its potential bioterrorism applications.

In some cases, hundreds of millions were spent on ill-fated projects, such as when Homeland Security Secretary Janet Napolitano earlier this year pulled the plug on the Secure Border Initiative, a Boeing Co. contract that was to set up an ambitious network of surveillance cameras, radar and sensors as a 2,000-mile-long "virtual" barrier across the U.S.-Mexico border. Originally intended to be in place by 2009, the endeavor was plagued with cost overruns and missed deadlines and wound up costing $1 billion before it was canceled.

Large sums of Homeland Security money, critics complain, have been propelled by pork barrel politics into the backyards of the congressionally connected. Yet the spending has also acted as a cash-rich economic stimulus program for many states at a time when other industries are foundering.

Utah is getting a $1.5-billion National Security Agency cyber-security center that will generate up to 10,000 jobs in the state. The Pentagon in July launched bidding for a $500-million U.S. Strategic Command headquarters at Offutt Air Force Base in Nebraska, which likes to point out that former President George W. Bush flew here for shelter after the Sept. 11 attacks.

Officials in Nebraska have insisted that no one is immune. A virus dropped at a cattle feed lot could wipe out a big part of the nation's food supply, they point out, while an attack on the dam at Lake McConaughy would cut off the main interstate linking New York and San Francisco and the biggest rail switching yard in the country.

"It would take out Kearney, Grand Island, the power grid, stuff like that. It could definitely do a lot of damage in what I call homeland America, and that's where these guys want to hit," said Ralph Moul, chief of the nearby Keystone-Lemoyne fire department.

Officials here say Nebraska and other places in Middle America not necessarily in Al Qaeda's gun sights have been able to improve traditional emergency response agencies that in many cases were under-equipped and whose workers were poorly trained—a benefit of Homeland Security grants that have required the money to be spent on responses to all kinds of emergencies, not just terrorist attacks.

"I think it's important to understand the homeland security equipment wasn't bought to be tucked away for the day there would be some terrorism event," said Harold Peterson, Keith County's emergency management director in Ogallala.

The Lake McConaughy dive team is so well-equipped it has been called out on several drownings around the state. A radio network built with Homeland Security funding paid off during widespread grass fires earlier this year by allowing departments from around the state to easily communicate with each other. And when a massive tornado struck Joplin, Mo., in May, the city was able to get its phones running with the aid of an emergency communications trailer bought with some of the region's $3.1 million in department grants.

Glendale, likewise, has not left the BearCat in the garage. They haven't caught any terrorists, but last fall, police rolled it out for a pre-dawn assault on an apartment in Echo Park where a suspected armed robber and others were thought to be hiding. Instead of having to pound on the door—risking officers' safety—they were able to park on the lawn and call for surrender on loudspeakers.

"The neighbors may remember it, but the bottom line is, the neighborhood didn't get shot up in a police action, dangerous suspects were taken into custody without incident, and we ensured the safety of those suspects and the officers involved," department spokesman Tom Lorenz said.

Berndt, the emergency official in Nebraska, said he had kept detailed records of every dollar spent and was convinced the state was safer for it.

"For me to sit here and say all this money was spent wisely is for me to sit here and lie to you," he said. "Could we have done better? Yes. Have we done all that bad? Probably not all that bad, in the overall scheme of things."

Critical Thinking

1. What is the purpose of homeland security spending?
2. Is homeland security spending paying off?
3. Is the U.S. spending too much on homeland security?
4. Should the U.S. spend more on homeland security?

Create Central

www.mhhe.com/createcentral

Internet References

Department of Homeland Security Budget
www.dhs.gov/dhs-budget
Secure Border Initiative
www.cbp.gov/xp/cgov/newsroom/fact_sheets/border/secure_border/
United States Strategic Command
www.stratcom.mil/
National Security Agency
www.nsa.gov/index.shtml

Article   Prepared by: Thomas J. Badey, *Randolph-Macon College*

100 Percent Cargo Screening Was a Stupid Idea

JUSTIN HIENZ

Learning Outcomes

After reading this article, you will be able to:

- Discuss the purpose of the 9/11 Committee Act of 2007.

- Explain the difference between scanning and screening cargo.

- Analyze the potential impact of this legislation on commerce.

- Describe how TSA may have circumvented the intent of the 9/11 Act.

Sometimes you have to call a spade a spade, no matter who you're talking to. Dear Congress, 100 percent cargo screening was a stupid idea.

In 2007, Congress passed the Implementing the Recommendations of the 9/11 Committee Act (9/11 Act), in which it mandated that by 2010, *all* air cargo—whether domestic or foreign in origin—flying on passenger planes in U.S. airspace be screened for explosives and other threatening items. Congress offered little direction and no funding, heaping the burden of their ill-conceived law squarely on America's air carriers and the Transportation Security Administration (TSA).

At first, few in the industry believed the mandate would be enforced. After all, it was such an enormous demand, which posed significant threats to a functioning supply chain, to say nothing of the hefty costs industry would be required to bear. TSA, however, was under no such illusion. This was federal law, and there was no question what Congress demanded. That is not to say they liked the idea (though TSA folks were consistently and professionally tight-lipped in expressing their personal opinions). In time, it became clear that indeed the mandate would be enforced, and industry had better get on board because the deadline was coming whether they believed it or not.

When the deadline arrived in 2010, TSA and the logistics industry met the mandate . . . domestically. Carriers, air forwarders, shippers and many others collaborated under the banner of the Certified Cargo Screening Program, and the deadline came

and went without much disruption to the supply chain. International cargo was another story. For the last two years, every time cargo arrived in the United States from another country without being screened for explosives, it broke federal law.

Advocates (foremost among them Congressman Edward Markey) continued beating the 100 percent screening drum, apparently without any consideration for real-world circumstances like business models, timetables and the free flow of commerce. To be sure, human life is much more important than an LD-3 container of watches from Switzerland or blueberries from Ecuador, but chasing after a 100 percent metric doesn't necessarily achieve total security (which most in the security field would consider unobtainable). Rather, the effort primarily strained industries (aviation and logistics) already facing steep challenges in a difficult global economy.

Under congressional pressure, TSA announced last year that by Dec. 31, 2011, all air cargo arriving from abroad would be screened. Shortly after, in the face of industry input, TSA decided that probably wasn't a feasible deadline and pushed it off. Now, the deadline is back on—Dec. 3, 2012—except this time, there's a good chance the mandate will be met, not because of major advances in screening funding and technology, but because of semantics.

New Agreements, Same Old Screening

Keeping threatening cargo out of the supply chain is in everyone's best interest, no matter the country. Bombs going off in midair is not only devastating to human life; it disrupts commerce, degrades public confidence and adds fuel to the terrorist fire. That's why countries all over the world have made significant time and resource investments in improving their security standards and processes. Air carriers and others have made major investments in screening training and technology; international associations have released best practices and recommendations for global standards; security agencies (beyond just TSA) have developed innovative and effective programs that pull high-risk cargo out of a mass of otherwise safe, legitimate shipments.

Yet, despite the effort, it still falls short of Congress' 100 percent screening mandate. Either it meets the legal definition outlined in the U.S. mandate or it's against the law. But here's a secret few outside the industry (including many in Congress) understand—*screening ain't scanning*.

When our elected representatives were drafting the mandate, their word choice was somewhat inaccurate. It called for 100 percent "screening," though it seems clear from the legislative text that what the lawmakers meant was 100 percent "scanning." Scanning is physically inspecting cargo, either by hand, with dogs, with technology or through other methods. Screening simply means sorting through all the cargo, looking for dangerous items sent with mal-intent. That might include the use of scanning methods but could also mean other approaches, such as intelligence-driven risk-based screening.

This is where TSA has found a way past the 100 percent mandate. If TSA deems other countries' *screening* efforts to be commensurate with America's cargo screening, it allows TSA to tell Congress all cargo arriving from abroad has been screened at the 100 percent level.

In the last month, TSA has signed agreements with Canada, Switzerland and the European Commission stating that their air cargo screening efforts were mutually acceptable. These are important developments, as it shows TSA is harmonizing its approach with those of other countries, and reducing redundancies while streamlining operations, all of which is important for security and a rapid supply chain. Under these agreements, when air cargo arrives from the European Union or Canada, TSA considers it to have been screened in full (i.e., 100 percent). But that doesn't mean foreign countries are putting every piece of cargo through a rigorous physical scan.

Thousands of tons of cargo arrive in the United States on passenger planes every day. Scanning that much cargo would not only dramatically slow the supply chain, it would be virtually impossible to enforce. TSA's jurisdiction ends at the U.S. border, and many countries abroad see 100 percent screening as the wrong approach to securing cargo. Who could force these countries to follow U.S. law? No one. What resources were offered to TSA to achieve this? None. So is all this cargo scanned before departure? Of course not, but anyone who thought that was possible in the first place was kidding himself.

All this focus on 100 percent screening has not actually resulted in what the law intended. Assuming the deadline is met by December, it will have been nearly five years of government and industry investment and effort striving for an impossible metric rather than focusing all resources on potentially more effective air cargo security approaches.

To be sure, there have been important and effective advances in international cargo security, among them the harmonization of security approaches under the new international agreements. And intelligence-driven, risk-based security (thanks in large part to CBP) is steadily gaining ground as the more rational and effective approach to keeping dangerous cargo grounded and out of the United States. There are programs like the Air Cargo Advanced Screening Pilot, which TSA and CBP recently decided would go forward as the best approach to singling out high-risk cargo. Industry and security agencies are working together today like never before, collaborating on the best approaches, sharing information, and championing security and supply chain efficiency as equally important. Those and other advances do indeed elevate the level of security for air cargo, but they are not 100 percent screening—at least, not the way Congress imagined it back in 2007.

In the end (and December 2012 appears to be the end), the 100 percent screening mandate did little to improve American security or protect the flying public. It was and remains a nuisance, getting in the way of wiser and more effective air cargo security approaches. On an international level, it's not even possible. In that sense, the mandate was crafted lacking intelligence and common sense, which is the very definition of stupidity.

Critical Thinking

1. Is it possible to scan 100 percent air cargo as congress had intended?

2. What are the potential costs and benefits of 100 percent cargo screening?

3. What is the potential impact of this program on international trade?

Create Central

www.mhhe.com/createcentral

Internet References

Implementing the Recommendations of the 9/11 Committee Act
http://thomas.loc.gov/cgi-bin/bdquery/z?d110:H.R.1:

Transportation Security Administration (TSA)
www.tsa.gov

Certified Cargo Screening Program
www.tsa.gov/certified-cargo-screening-program

Certified Cargo Screening Facilities
www.commercialfreightservices.com/CCSF.aspx

Air Cargo Advanced Screening (ACAS) Pilot Program
www.federalregister.gov/articles/2012/10/26/C1-2012-26031/air-cargo-advance-screening-acas-pilot-program

Article   Prepared by: Thomas J. Badey, *Randolph-Macon College*

TSA's Insensitivity Impedes Security, House Panel Says

JEFF PLUNGIS

Learning Outcomes

After reading this article, you will be able to:

- List some of the criticisms directed at the Transportation Security Agency.
- Identify potential reasons for the cost increases in passenger screening.
- Discuss the impact of increased airport security on airline passenger travel.

E leven years after the terrorist attacks that led to its creation, the U.S. Transportation Security Administration must become a "leaner, smarter organization," Representative Mike Rogers said yesterday.

Rogers, an Alabama Republican who leads the House Homeland Security subcommittee on transportation security, said TSA should rely more on private companies to screen passengers for possible terrorism threats.

"The agency has gone down a troubling path of overspending, limiting private-sector engagement, and failing to sufficiently protect passenger privacy," Rogers said at a hearing yesterday on the anniversary of the Sept. 11 attacks.

Rogers released a subcommittee report that said TSA is bogged down in defending unpopular airport screening procedures that may not match current threats.

The agency has been too reactive, imposing screening procedures that respond to past terror plots while not doing enough to anticipate the next threat, according to the report. Once implemented, procedures aren't revisited to ensure they still make sense, the committee said.

"Eleven years after 9/11, the American people expect to see tangible progress in transportation security, with effective operations that respect both their privacy and their wallets,"the committee report said. "The private sector is best suited to this challenge, not the federal government."

Increased Scrutiny

Yesterday's report and hearing follow 22 other hearings, 15 lawmaker briefings and seven site visits by the subcommittee's members and staff since last year. The agency has been subjected to increased scrutiny as some efforts, such as pat-downs and the addition of screening machines that produced detailed images of travelers under their clothes, provoked consumer outrage.

The TSA is committed to working with industry and regularly seeks advice on policy from airlines, airports and travelers, among others, John Halinski, the agency's deputy administrator, told lawmakers at the hearing.

"As the memories of 9/11 slip by for many, we at TSA cannot afford to forget what our job is," Halinski said. "We cannot be distracted by critics and others who forget we face a threat."

The agency replaced guards hired by airlines with federal employees after Sept. 11 to reassure the public that each passenger and each bag would be screened, said Texas Representative Sheila Jackson Lee, the panel's senior Democrat.

"I do not want us to be lax on procedures that have provided a safe passage for billions of travelers since 9/11,"Jackson Lee said.

Explaining Pat-Downs

TSA hasn't adequately explained why it is using invasive pat-downs, the committee's report said. Americans would be more supportive of the agency's practices if they understood why TSA was implementing a policy or what threat it was addressing, it said.

"Pat-downs have hit a nerve with the general public, and TSA has failed to adequately explain why it continues to use this procedure two years after its initial rollout," the committee said.

Many of the TSA's problems are self-inflicted, and result from the strains of managing its bureaucracy and multibillion-dollar technology contracts, the committee said. It said that after spending $29.6 million on 207 explosive-detecting "puffer" machines in 2006, the agency found the machines wouldn't work in dirty, humid airport environments. The machines were ultimately removed and destroyed.

Passenger Traffic

The TSA's workforce has grown as airline passenger traffic has fallen, the committee said.

"A private-sector entity in the face of a shrinking customer base usually must downsize," the committee said. "TSA, by contrast, has continually grown its ranks despite fewer travelers."

The TSA's costs per passenger have been rising rapidly, said Geoff Freeman, chief operating officer of the U.S. Travel Association, a Washington-based trade group for tourism agencies and providers. The agency's budget increased 68 percent from 2004 to 2011, while the number of passengers was little changed, Freeman said.

With passenger levels expected to double over the next 20 years, TSA needs to balance security with moving travelers through the airport more efficiently, Freeman said. Millions of people avoid travel because of time-consuming, frustrating checkpoints, he said.

"The real threat of terrorism, the economic consequences of inefficient screening, and increase in screening costs, add up to create one of the biggest problems facing the travel industry today," Freeman said.

Critical Thinking

1. Are the criticisms of the TSA justified? Support your answer.
2. Has the TSA become reactive rather than proactive? Explain.
3. Is privatization the solution to the TSA's problems? Why or why not?
4. Are the new TSA procedures such as full-body scans and pat-downs really necessary? Explain.

Create Central

www.mhhe.com/createcentral

Internet References

Transportation Security Administration
    www.tsa.gov/

Transportation Security Administration and Pat-Downs
    www.tsa.gov/traveler-information/pat-downs

U.S. Travel Association
    www.ustravel.org/

John W. Halinski Statement to House Committee on Transportation Security
    www.tsa.gov/sites/default/files/publications/pdf/testimony/080112
_halinski_testimony.pdf

Secretary Napolitano Announces New Measures to Strengthen Aviation Security
    www.tsa.gov/press/releases/2010/04/02/secretary-napolitano-announces
-new-measures-strengthen-aviation-security

Unit V

UNIT

Prepared by: Thomas J. Badey, *Randolph-Macon College*

State and Local Governments and Homeland Security

Major disasters, by definition, tend to quickly overwhelm the resources and capabilities of local governments. When challenged beyond their means, cities and localities have come to rely on state governments for assistance. The involvement of state governments in disaster response is nothing new. Most states have had significant experience in disaster response and emergency management. Through years of trial and error, exposure to natural disasters such as earthquakes, floods, wild fires, tornadoes, hurricanes, and snowstorms, and human-made disasters such as plane crashes, train crashes, and chemical spills, states have managed to build up effective emergency management and disaster response capabilities.

States have developed significant infrastructure to assist in such responses. Command and control facilities, specialized equipment, and designated emergency personnel to include, when needed, National Guard units, are important components of most states' disaster response plans. Existing infrastructure may vary from state to state, based on threat perception and the availability of resources, but is an illusion to think that the federal government is more capable at planning for and organizing local disaster response than those who know the area and have been doing it for years.

The federal government can, nevertheless, play an important role. To effectively expand their response repertoire to include potential threats to homeland security, the two most important things that states need from the federal government are information and funding.

Information is the most important thing the federal government can contribute to state and local efforts. Although a number of federal agencies are working on more effective ways to exploit data collected by local and state police departments, little has been done to eliminate the barriers that prevent the distribution of intelligence to these departments. The lack of information and lack of feedback from the federal government continue to be a source of frustration for state and local authorities. State and local police forces cannot become effective "eyes and ears" for federal homeland security efforts if they aren't told specifically who and what to look for. In addition to timely intelligence and accurate threat assessments, states need improved access to specialized knowledge and training that will allow them to prepare themselves for new types of threats.

One of the biggest sources of contention between state and local governments and the current administration is homeland security funding. Although most states and municipalities support the desire for improved security, few have sufficient economic resources to sustain this effort. In a time of deficits and budget cuts, preparing for future threats while responding to heightened terrorist "alert-levels" has become a near impossible task. Federal money to acquire new specialized equipment, conduct training, and field additional security forces is needed. As federal spending on state and local efforts has slowed, states and municipalities have become increasingly critical of federal government efforts.

Despite the construction of a 700-mile fence on the southern border of the United States, the issue of border security and illegal migration has yet to be resolved. Immigration reform has once again been delayed amidst continuing partisan discord. Some warn of the potential threat of infiltration by Middle Eastern terrorist via our southern border, yet there appears to be little evidence to support such assertions. Although Middle Eastern terrorists are more likely to arrive in the United States by means of a first-class ticket than by a two-day trek through the Mexican desert, the lack of effective border control continues to undermine the federal government's credibility on homeland security.

The articles in this unit focus on the challenges that state and local governments faced in their homeland security efforts. Border states like Arizona have long been affected by the flow of illegal immigrants across its southern border. Criminal activity such as the trafficking of drugs, guns, and human beings, pose particular challenges for towns and cities close to the border. The economic recession has also had a significant impact on these communities. Thus, the issue of border security has become the lightning rod for a myriad of political economic and social issues in the state of Arizona. Some Arizona politicians have used the federal government and the immigration issues as scapegoats for unpopular policies and budget cuts necessary in what has become the second poorest state in the United States.

Although pundits focus most often on the role of the federal government in homeland security, local law-enforcement agencies and first responders are most often on the frontlines of homeland security. The New York City Police Department transit bureau's anti-terrorism is an example of the vital role that local law-enforcement agencies can play in protecting critical transportation infrastructure in major U.S. cities.

Finally, Anne Applebaum provides a more critical perspective. She argues that homeland security funding has become a bonanza for congressional districts. Much of homeland security funding has been wasted or gone to small towns and cities that "face no statistical significant security threat at all." She argues that the DHS should be broken up into its component parts and special funding should be limited to cities and buildings that are at risk.

Article
Prepared by: Thomas J. Badey, *Randolph-Macon College*

Securing Arizona
What Americans Can Learn from Their Rogue State

Tom Barry

Learning Outcomes

After reading this article, you will be able to:

- Examine the demographic and social challenges that Arizona faces.

- Discuss the impact of homeland security issues on Arizona politics.

- Explain how Federal stimulus money has been used in Arizona.

- Discuss the role state and local law enforcement agencies in border security.

Over the past year, a few signature events—the killing last March of border rancher Rob Krenz; the passage the following month of the immigration-control law SB 1070; and the January 2011 massacre in Tucson that killed six people and gravely wounded U.S. Representative Gabrielle Giffords—have focused national attention on the political and social tensions in Arizona. The state's cast of political figures—from Senator John McCain to Maricopa County Sheriff Joe Arpaio—has captured the media spotlight and won Arizona a rogue reputation.

But Arizona may not be such an outlier.

Certainly Arizona's history and geography make it one of a kind. Still, comparable demographic and cultural strife is cropping up almost everywhere in America. Arizona's budget woes, while much worse than most states', are mirrored throughout the country in conflicts over government downsizing and taxes. Hatred, economic stress, and fears of border insecurity are playing out in unusually grand scale in Arizona, yet mostly reflect the sense of vulnerability and uncertainty about personal and national prospects that are felt throughout the country.

Arizona's politics are dominated by a potent mix of three ideological currents: support for a muscular national-security program, libertarian capitalism, and social traditionalism. These ideas have long shaped the wider American conservative movement, so it is hardly surprising that some, such

as the Tea Party, look to the state as a model for the nation. They applaud Arizona as the vanguard of the new conservative revolution; it has taken the challenges of immigration enforcement and border security into its own hands, opposed "Big Government" with its newly invigorated populism, and embraced libertarian principles through privatization and government-spending cuts. Boosters point to a mounting list of Arizona firsts: its anti-immigrant legislation, new law banning ethnic studies programs in public universities, proposals against birthright citizenship, gun-rights bills, and demand for a federal waiver from compliance with Medicaid provisions. SB 1070 copycat bills have been introduced in six states, and legislators in fifteen more have expressed interest in their own imitations.

Others see a spectacularly dangerous project in Arizona's ideological approach to policy. Instead of raising alarm about the state's financial instability, Republican politicians—with the organized support of some prominent sheriffs, right-wing foundations and policy institutes, and the Arizona Tea Party— have exploited widespread resentment about fading wealth and diminishing social services by scapegoating immigrants and blaming Washington.

Arizona faces dire problems, but, rather than address them, its leaders make political hay out of convenient distractions. This dynamic demands close scrutiny, especially if the country is facing its future on the border.

Bust

In the 2010 electoral season, border-security talk boiled over in the Arizona heat. Governor Jan Brewer made unsubstantiated claims about drug-related beheadings; Jesse Kelly, a Tea Party candidate trying to unseat Giffords, accused her of being weak on immigration enforcement and border security; and John McCain repeatedly stressed the need to "secure our borders."

It was only on the margins that anxiety mounted over the fiscal stability of state government and the future of the badly battered Arizona economy.

You can't miss the signs of crisis. Many state parks and offices are shuttered, plastered with "Closed for Stabilization" notices.

Thousands of recently built McMansions stand empty, newly constructed highway ramps lead to empty subdivisions and strip malls, and immigrants, whose cheap labor built now-abandoned housing developments, are fleeing the state as immigration enforcement intensifies.

Arizona was hit particularly hard by the housing bust thanks to its poorly diversified economy. "Five Cs"—copper, cotton, cattle, citrus, and climate—are represented on the "Great Seal of Arizona" with the motto Ditat Deus (God Enriches), but it's been a long time since mining, ranching, and agriculture ruled Arizona. The five Cs have been reduced to one: climate. As retirees flocked to the warm Southwestern sun, a "real estate-industrial complex" took root as the primary economic engine of the state.

Galloping population growth has been a constant in Arizona. Over the past four decades, the state's population has quadrupled. For the past two decades, Arizona has been the second-fastest growing state (following Nevada). Spurred by consumer demand (largely in construction and related areas), Arizona's GDP growth has far outpaced the national average.

Since the mid-1980s, easy, unsecured financing has fueled Arizona's real estate boom. As Arizonans, and later most of America, began to think of their homes as investments, waves of newcomers bought fancy new homes with the conviction that they could trade up. The boom—which outlasted the Savings and Loan scandal of the 1980s that brought heavy criticism to McCain and fellow Arizona Senator Dennis DeConcini—produced hundreds of developments stretching into the vast expanses of desert sands and paving over citrus groves that once surrounded Phoenix and other cities.

In the 1990s Arizona enjoyed enviable budget surpluses as sales and property taxes—stimulated by the housing boom—flooded government coffers. At the same time, Arizona's political leaders curried favor with voters with near-annual tax-cutting bills. As the housing bubble kept expanding and the good times kept rolling, the state legislature faithfully approved new spending packages without allocating revenues that would pay for them.

When the bubble burst in 2007, an epidemic of foreclosures and traumatic declines in housing valuations bred fiscal crisis. In 2007 Arizona was the nation's fourteenth-poorest state, but today it is second only to Mississippi. In 2009 it faced the largest income-spending gap in the nation.

No other state faces such a grave threat to its stability. A Brookings Institution study of state finances in four Western states put Arizona—with its projected 33 percent budget deficit—in far worse circumstances than even California.

According to the Brookings study, in the 2011 fiscal year, Arizona faces a 12 percent cyclical budget deficit, amounting to $1.2 billion; a 21 percent structural deficit, or a cool $2.1 billion; and a loss of $2.4 billion in federal stimulus funds that propped up the state's 2010 accounts.

Instead of raising taxes, the Republican leadership has taken the fiscal crisis as an opportunity to downsize government, cut social services, and privatize. The Supreme Court building and the governor's office tower now belong to private investors, prisons are being sold off, and full-day kindergarten has been eliminated. (For more on Arizona's tightening belt, see Table 1.)

Generation Gap

Other states have suffered from the housing bust, but demographics also conspired against the stability of Arizona.

Even before the Great Recession, the state's two wellsprings of population growth—Latino immigration and Midwest migration—were proving a volatile mix. Surges of snowbirds from the north and immigrants from the south have fed Phoenix and Tucson, with brown immigrant labor building the tile-roofed homes of mostly white transplants who previously had little contact with Latinos.

The two demographic flows complemented each other economically, but the combination has proved politically toxic, especially as immigrant population growth began to outpace migration from other states. Over the last two decades, the Latino population increased 180 percent while the state shifted from from 72 percent to 58 percent white. Currently, Latinos account for 31 percent of Arizona's population (yet only 17 percent of the electorate), with an estimated 7 percent of the population being unauthorized. Immigrant population growth over the past two decades has put Arizona on a fast track toward becoming a minority-majority state—likely by 2020 or sooner. It suggests rising Latino political clout and, along with it, a solid Democratic majority. Alongside Latinos, the college-educated white population has been growing faster than the senior white population and the population without college degrees, a dynamic that also disadvantages Republicans.

These changing demographics have produced a white backlash that, when combined with historically low rates of Latino electoral participation, have contributed to a Republican resurgence in Arizona.

The political backlash in part reflects a "cultural generation gap." Arizona's "swift Hispanic growth has been concentrated in young adults and children," says Brookings' William Frey, creating a population with "largely white baby boomers and older populations." In Arizona 43 percent of children are white, compared to 83 percent of the seniors. The 40 percent gap is the highest in the country, far outstripping the national average of 25 percent. Other states that have experienced rapid immigrant population growth—including Nevada, California, Texas, and Florida—confront comparably wide gaps.

In addition to ethnicity and race, class shapes the state's political divide. And here again, age is a factor. With state, county, and municipal governments all strapped for cash, disparate social sectors are mobilizing to protect their own interests.

Seniors and the state's aging white population have been disproportionately affected by declining housing prices. As a result, while they don't necessarily believe that the budgets for education and indigent medical care should be slashed, they are more concerned about cuts to elderly medical care and pensions, the cost of which has jumped more than 440 percent since 2000. With everything on the chopping block, latent resentments about the disproportionate use of educational and social services by the young, poor, and Latino social sectors have emerged.

Governor Brewer describes her tax reforms as "righteous," appealing to a socially conservative, white-right base that

Table 1   Downsizing Arizona

Already Cut (FY 2008–2010)	**Proposed Budget (FY 2012)**
• Sliced K–12 funding by 12%	• Additional 20% cut in university funding
• Shrunk university budgets by 28%	• Cut state assistance to community colleges by 47%
• Reduced lifetime eligibility for Temporary Assistance for Needy Families from 60 to 36 months	• Eliminate all general-fund assistance to parks
• Eliminated full-day kindergarten	• Eliminate free medical care for 280,000 indigent people
• Cut funding for certain organ transplants under state's Medicaid program	• Slash more than half-billion dollars in state Medicaid spending, rising to more than $1 billion when fully implemented (dependent on waiver by Obama administration, which provides the state $7.8 billion in annual Medicaid assistance)
• Mandated six furlough days/year for 28,000 state employees	

Source: Arizona Republic, January 17, 2011: Brookings Institution, Structurally Imbalanced, January 2011.

abhors the provision of education and emergency-medical services to illegal immigrants. Never mind that, as Arizona State economist José Mendez told *The Arizona Republic,* "Empirical studies have shown, [illegal immigrants] pay more in taxes than the value of services they receive."

Until 2007 economic growth helped to dampen the impact of these cultural and generational pressures. As long as the state could meet its public obligations, there was no reason to get anxious about immigrants ostensibly bleeding the state dry. But since then, sinking revenues from sales and property taxes have set off a frenzy of budget cutting and privatization—a frightening turn for Arizonans accustomed to boom times.

Going Alone

Faced with this fiscal crisis, Arizona Republicans have managed to consolidate power by blaming Washington for the state's problems, exploiting fears of big government, and drawing on the state's history of anti-immigrant animus and vigilantism. Republicans occupy 61 of the 90 seats in the legislature; the governor, attorney general, secretary of state, treasurer, and superintendent of public instruction (an elected position) are all Republicans.

At the start of her new term in January 2011, Governor Brewer set forth her "Renewed Federalism" policy agenda. "Faithful adherence to limited government and populist virtues is a hallmark of Arizona's first hundred years," Brewer declared. She vowed to pursue a model that "limits the growth of the public sector and restrains unnecessary regulatory encroachment upon areas that are outside the rightful scope of government." By "areas" she meant "the affirmative goal of stimulating free enterprise." Brewer asserted that her system "protects [Arizona] and its citizens against an overreaching federal government," and puts the federal government's "constitutional and statutory duties to secure the border and restore integrity to our immigration system" at the top of the policy agenda.

Brewer's program hews closely to the ideology and policy prescriptions favored by the Goldwater Institute in Phoenix, Americans for Prosperity, and other conservative think tanks. The restrictionist Federation for American Immigration Reform (FAIR), for example, worked with leading Republican legislators

and selected sheriffs to fashion the language of SB 1070. Both FAIR and the corporate-friendly American Legislative Exchange Council supported the formulation of SB 1070 as a model of "states'-rights" immigration enforcement that other states could follow.

A key figure in charting the state's economic and social course is Republican State Senator Russell Pearce, chair of the Senate Appropriations Committee and the newly elected Senate president. Named "Taxpayer of the Year" in 2003 by the anti-tax institute Americans for Tax Reform, Pearce is a fiscal conservative, social conservative, law-enforcement hardliner, and, like many key Republican leaders in Arizona, a Mormon. Pearce also closely identifies with the anti-Obama, and anti-big government positions of Americans for Prosperity, which offers state-level logistical support and training to Tea Party activists. He boasts of being a "proud member" of the Tea Party.

Pearce achieved national prominence this year as the main sponsor of SB 1070 and for his outspoken views on immigrants, border security, federalism, and liberalism. A 23-year veteran of the Maricopa County Sheriff's Department, Pearce served as chief deputy under Sheriff Joe Arpaio before leaving the Department in 1994. Pearce brags that he launched the Department's notorious thousand-bed "tent city" for jailed immigrants and other selected county inmates. Since 2004 Pearce has sponsored a series of anti-immigrant measures, including bills to deny social services to unauthorized immigrants, sanction employers who hire them, make English the state's official language, prohibit ethnic-studies programs at state institutions, and deny citizenship rights in Arizona to children of illegal immigrants. Pearce is also a key figure in promoting prison privatization.

While Republican political figures such as Pearce have perfected Arizona's new conservative politics at the state level, a trio of county sheriffs—Arpaio in Maricopa County, Larry Dever in Cochise County, and Paul Babeu in Pinal County—have given critical law-enforcement credibility to border-security hawks who rely on popular anxiety to get elected. On the national level, Dever and Babeu have also given voice to a new border-security populism, inflected more by politically effective appeals to rule of law than blatant anti-immigrant sentiment.

Dever's Cochise County is a vast swath of borderland in Arizona's southeastern corner and the heart of Representative Giffords's congressional district. Towns on either side of the 82-mile border with Mexico share the same Spanish name. In the streets of the old county seat of Tombstone, the famous gunfight at O.K. Corral between feuding gangs of deputized ruffians and rustlers is daily reenacted to crowds of fascinated tourists.

Cochise has only recently become a leading front in the border-security offensive. Since the Border Patrol tightened controls along the traditional corridors of illegal border crossing around El Paso and San Diego in the 1990s, flows of illegal immigrants and drugs have shifted to more inaccessible stretches of the border, such as Cochise.

Typically wearing blue jeans and a cowboy hat, Dever rejects the unholy tradition of quick-on-the-trigger Tombstone sheriffs and draws instead on moral imperative; his department's mission statement quotes Winston Churchill: "It is not enough that we do our best; sometimes we must do what is required." Interviewed at his office outside the borderland town of Bisbee, Dever insisted that local law enforcement must be involved in border control—"at least until [the] federal government decides to do its job."

Even before SB 1070 and the series of anti-immigrant legislative measures that preceded it, Cochise and Arizona were taking immigration and border issues into their own hands. One of Dever's predecessors, Sheriff Harry Wheeler, deputized a posse of Bisbee citizens, largely members of the town's anti-immigrant Loyalty League, to organize the Bisbee Deportation of 1917. The posse rounded up 1,200 suspected immigrants (both European and Mexican) for supporting the ongoing strike organized by the International Workers of the World at the Phelps Copper mine. Wheeler loaded the suspected strikers into boxcars and, in mid-July heat, sent them 200 miles away. They were dumped without provisions or water in the middle of the New Mexico badlands.

Cochise has since proved hospitable to anti-immigrant vigilantes. Glenn Spencer, who led white-supremacist groups in California, moved in 2002 to Sierra Vista, in Cochise, where he formed the self-described citizen militia American Border Patrol "on the front lines."

Spencer befriended ranchers Roger and Don Barnett, who have a 22,000 acre ranch outside Douglas that they patrol with night vision goggles and assault rifles. In 1999 the Barnett brothers formed a 30-member rancher militia called Cochise County Concerned Citizens. In 2009 a federal court found Roger Barnett guilty of a 2004 armed assault on a group of seven Mexican immigrants. For failing to prevent Barnett, a former county deputy, from holding unarmed Mexicans men at "gunpoint, yelling obscenities at them and kicking one of the women," Dever himself was charged but not convicted in a suit organized by the Mexican American Legal Defense and Educational Fund.

Long before anti-immigrant vigilantism took an organized form in Cochise County, white ranching families on the arid cattle spreads of the borderland began lashing out against Mexican immigrants crossing their land. Only a few miles from

where Krentz was murdered in 2010, the father and two brothers of a prominent ranching family of Cochise once turned their rising anger at trespassing immigrants into cruel sport.

I traveled to Cochise in 1976 after reading the preliminary news about the Hanigan brothers, Thomas and Patrick. With the support of their father George, they captured and tortured three immigrants who were passing harmlessly through their ranch on their way to seasonal farm work in northern Cochise. The young Mexican men were beaten, robbed, hanged from a tree, burnt with a flame held to their dangling feet, and threatened with knives grazing their genitals. The Hanigans eventually cut their victims loose and told them to run back to Mexico, letting fly volleys of birdshot as they ran off. With juries sympathetic to the property owners and the alarm about drug smuggling, it took three trials for one of the Hanigans to be convicted and sentenced.

Dever and the politicians in Phoenix rely upon and cultivate this sense of go-it-alone toughness to stoke the fires of anti-immigrant sentiment and convince voters that Arizona has no choice but to come up with a home grown response.

Phoenix Republicans also get their share of help from Sheriff Paul Babeu of Pinal County. "Sheriff Paul's" website urges citizens to "Stand with Arizona!" and help him "fight illegal immigration and secure the border." In frequent appearances on Fox News and any other outlet that will have him, the always-smiling, articulate, shiny-headed sheriff mixes his anti-immigrant, secure-the-border convictions with Tea Party slogans about how the country is "sprinting down the path to socialism."

With its southern edge 80 miles from the border, Pinal is not even a border county. But that doesn't bother Babeu, who is sure that violence is spilling over from Mexico into his jurisdiction and that illegal immigrants are behind a local crime wave. "With the rise in the amount of armed violent encounters in the rural areas of Pinal County, it has created a sense of fear in the general public and has restricted their ability to enjoy the desert and rural areas of the county," Babeu claimed in a recent funding proposal.

Pete Rios, chairman of the Pinal County Board of Supervisors, complains that that the sheriff's department hasn't supported its threat assessment with evidence. "All I want is for the sheriff to back his claims with data, but he hasn't done that yet," Rios told me.

Rios also expressed skepticism about the sheriff's version of the alleged April 30, 2010 shooting of Deputy Louie Puroll by drug smugglers armed with AK-47 rifles. "They never found the AK-47S, the bales of smuggled marijuana, or even any bullet casings," Rios observed, despite helicopter surveillance and a massive dragnet that included the Border Patrol. The wounded deputy was quickly released from the hospital.

Questions about the sheriff's account of the incident and its timing—a week after Brewer signed SB 1070 to a nationwide firestorm of criticism—have since dogged the department. Forensic experts determined that Puroll's wound came from a weapon fired only inches away, fueling accusations that the shooting was a hoax to build support for SB 1070 and the sheriff him self. Babeu fired Puroll in January for tall tales he told a *Phoenix New Times* reporter about supposed contacts with drug cartels, but the sheriff stressed that he still "backed [Puroll] 100 percent" on the shootout story.

Claims by the likes of Dever and Babeu—that the federal government's failure to secure the border has subjected Arizona to spillover violence and immigrant crime—are at the core of the Arizona GOP's approach to winning elections, and Governor Brewer echoed them during the 2010 campaign. In April 2010 she told of unchecked "murder, terror, and mayhem" at the border, and in June she launched the Border Security Enhancement Program, which channels money from the governor's office to border sheriffs. Announcing the program, Brewer declared, "The federal government has failed miserably in its obligation and moral responsibility to its citizens regarding border security."

Border-security hawks and immigrant bashers in Arizona thrive on myths and exaggerations. Over the past decade crime rates in Arizona have dropped while the immigrant population has expanded dramatically—up 62 percent from 2000 to 2009, while Arizona's total population increased 24.6 percent. FBI crime statistics (covering all violent crime, property crime, murder, rape, robbery, assault, burglary, larceny theft, and vehicle theft) show a near-steady 22 percent decline in total crime over that period. Vehicle thefts dropped by half. Even along the border, as immigrant and non-immigrant populations were rising, crime rates fell. Douglas and Nogales, both border towns, are among the state's safest communities.

Arizona's conservative sheriffs routinely point out that the state has become a preferred corridor for illegal immigration. In their alarm about border insecurity, they fail to note the dramatic decline in illegal crossings over the past six years. In 2010 Border Patrol apprehensions of illegal border crossers in Arizona were down by 12 percent from the previous year and were less than hall the number of 2004.

Big Government, Big Help

The threat of escalating border violence isn't the only border myth propagated by Arizona's anti-Washington activists. Border security hawks in Arizona blame the federal government for not doing its job, obligating border sheriffs and the state government to cover security breaches. Brewer contributed to this narrative by establishing her Border Security Enhancement Program, but what she didn't advertise is that the $10 million she distributed to border sheriffs (along with a subsequent $10 million to the Pinal County Sheriff 's Office and other law enforcement agencies) came from the State Fiscal Stabilization Fund, established in 2009 with federal stimulus dollars from the Department of Education.

Although most of the funding was used, as intended, to stabilize the state's education budget, Brewer channeled the first $50 million in the stabilization fund to cover the payroll of the state corrections agency. While Sheriffs Dever and Babeu rail about federal neglect of the border, their departments are awash in federal dollars for border security thanks to the stimulus money and multiple large border-security grants from the Departments of Homeland Security (DHS) and Justice.

Opposition to big government and the Obama administration plays well at the State Capitol. Conveniently missing from this narrative is the back-story of federal subsidies and contracts.

At last count, Arizona received $1.19 in federal spending for every dollar sent to Washington, which makes it a beneficiary state. In contrast, California gets $0.78 back for every federal tax-dollar paid, Nevada just $0.65, and Colorado $0.81, while Utah receives $1.07 and New Mexico $2.03. The taking culture of Arizona includes the state's retired masses, whose Medicare and Social Security payments not only help keep them solvent, but also direct federal government revenue to the state's still thriving medical-care sector.

Big Government came to Arizona's rescue in 2009 with the American Re covery and Reinvestment Act (ARRA), which allocated $4.3 billion—nearly half of Arizona's annual budget—to stabilize the state's finances and stave off economic collapse. The termination of ARRA funding is sending shock waves through state agencies, local governments, and Arizona's education and health providers.

Arizona also benefits economically from Homeland Security contracts to house immigrant prisoners. The state already counts among its residents 2,500–3,000 immigrant detainees, and in 2009 Pinal County received $11.7 million from Immigration and Customs Enforcement to house immigrants in the 1,500-bed county jail. Increased immigration-enforcement and border security operations by the federal government in recent years have proved a boon to both private and public prisons in Arizona, and the per-diem payments offered by DHS for immigration detention will surely increase if SB 1070 is enforced.

Federal dollars also help explain Arizona's historic rise. How else to explain a housing oasis in the northern Sonoran desert? Remarking on this mystery, writer and environmental activist Edward Abbey wrote, "There is no lack of water here, unless you try to establish a city where no city should be."

Big Government made this desert miracle possible with two massive water diversion projects—the Salt River Project and the Central Arizona Project (CAP). Envisioned by Barry Goldwater, CAP is the largest and most expensive aqueduct system ever constructed in the United States. Its exclusive purpose is to feed Colorado River water to parched Central and Southern Arizona. Massive pumping of groundwater, accumulated over the eons in aquifers, further enabled the desert bloom. But depleting groundwater reserves and climate change-induced drought in the Colorado Basin now loom as the most serious threats to the Arizona development model.

Direct federal subsidies also underwrite Arizona agribusiness. The United States is the third-largest producer and number one exporter of cotton mainly because of government subsidies—more than $29 billion between 1995 and 2009, $374 million of which went to Pinal County.

Model State, Failed State

If short-term electoral gain is the standard, Brewer's politics are good politics. But the combination of traditional anti-big government conservatism with backlash ideology may be a recipe for disaster.

For the time being, the proponents of less government and more social Darwinism, such as State Senator Pearce, the *Wall Street Journal* opinion pages, and Americans for Prosperity aren't backing down. They insist that low taxes, immigrant crackdowns, and ridding government of the burden of social services will lead to 21st-century stability and security. Groups such as the American Legislative Exchange Council—which ranked Arizona third in the nation in its Economic Competitiveness Index in 2010—and the Tea Party Patriots continue to laud the Arizona model.

But as stimulus funds dry up and budget gaps widen, Arizonans are facing the stark consequences of their state government's anti-tax ideology and fear mongering. Even Governor Brewer, confronting the impossible challenge of bridging the state's budget-deficit abyss, is taking sober assessment of Arizona's fundamental instability. "We face a state fiscal crisis of unparalleled dimension, one that is going to sweep over every single person in this state as well as every business and every family," Brewer warned in January.

Of course, Arizona is not alone in its budget-crisis woes, which Brewer acknowledges are the worst in the state's history. Many other states and local governments also confront staggering budget deficits. Some of them, such as California and North Carolina, are considering tax increases to balance their budgets. Arizona, however, has refused even to contemplate that possibility.

Most close observers of the fiscal crises besieging state governments agree that tax increases on personal and corporate income must form part of the stabilization solution. That is the position of Arizona State University economist Tom Rex, who argues that raising taxes and fees to address the fiscal crisis in his state would have a far less negative impact than would Brewer's litany of proposed spending cuts, which, he says, will result in widespread job losses. Although tax increases inevitably carry some negative economic consequences, addressing the deficit by increasing taxes would go a long way toward staving off the kind of cyclical volatility that is roiling Arizona.

Last year the state enacted a 1 percent temporary increase in the sales tax—a sign that the Republicans' anti-tax ideology is not inflexible, but a far cry from the progressive tax reform that would help close the structural deficit. Other than that, only budget gimmicks, mandated furloughs for state employees, new debt issues, and reckless privatization schemes—along with the temporary reprieve provided by stimulus dollars—have prevented bankruptcy and government shutdown. The state treasurer is warning that issuing IOUs to state employees and debtors may be the next desperate measure.

Raising taxes is unavoidable, but so too are budget cuts. Like many other states, Arizona spends mainly in four areas: K-12 education, health care, higher education, and criminal justice and corrections. The first three have been cut dramatically, but not the fourth, which arguably creates many of the state's costliest problems. The deepening fiscal crisis could be regarded as an opportunity not only to cut criminal justice and corrections budgets but also to overhaul a penal system that incarcerates nonviolent (and overwhelmingly nonwhite) violators of drug laws.

The ideological and corporate-driven assault on government and the public goods it offers has brought Arizona's government—along with other states'—to its knees. At the same time, that assault has devastated the sense of common identity and community trust that has been the foundation of good governance in the United States.

Arizona as we now know it cannot survive, even if there is another housing boom around the corner and government budgets are stabilized. The Arizona model of sprawling, low-density desert cities was built on the myths of limitless water and perpetually cheap gas and construction labor. The entire country faces the onset of climate change and energy scarcity, but no state will confront as squarely as Arizona the consequences of its patterns of unsustainable development. Instead of moving to meet the challenges of the future, Arizona is decimating educational infrastructure; it is already demonstrating its loyalty to old ideologies over long-term planning.

There are no easy fixes, but a bit of leadership from Washington on the immigration issue might go some way toward generating a problem-solving sensibility. Arizonans, like many Americans, are right to be anxious about the federal government's largely ineffective and immensely expensive policies of border control and immigration enforcement. The surge of illegal immigration over the past two decades has in many ways enriched our economy and communities. But—occurring outside the law and in the absence of a shared national plan of sustainable economic growth—illegal immigration contributed to the erosion of our society's sense of community.

In this context Arizona's institution of SB 1070 may be understandable. But clearly its go-it-alone approach to a common problem only further divides Arizonans and the nation. The Obama administration is right to challenge the law; however, its own avid enforcement of immigration laws—resulting in record-breaking levels of prosecution, incarceration, and deportation of immigrants—is, in any honest assessment, more shameful than Arizona's as-yet unenforced immigration-crackdown.

Immigration control is a federal responsibility, and it is the duty of the Obama administration and federal lawmakers (including the Arizona congressional delegation, led by John McCain) to outline for Americans a vision of sustainable immigration and to pass a just and enforceable immigration-reform package. Similarly, the federal government is responsible for drug policy, and its support for drug prohibition at home and drug wars abroad is a central cause of cross-border smuggling, mass incarceration, and horrific gang related violence across Arizona's border with Mexico—as well as being a major source of the rising political influence of border-security hawks.

In the wake of the Tucson massacre, border-security and anti-immigration rhetoric has been toned down a notch or two. And the enormity of the budget crisis may yet create new political space in Phoenix for realistic, less ideological debate over budget priorities.

Whether Arizona can steady itself remains to be seen. But there is little reason for optimism. America's new model state may already be a failed state.

Critical Thinking

1. Is the Arizona budget crisis the result of illegal immigration? Explain your answer.
2. What factors have contributed to the rise of anti-immigrant vigilantism? Explain your answer.
3. Why have Arizona's legislative initiatives like SB 1070 been criticized? Explain your answer.
4. What role should states and localities play in border security? Explain your answer.

Create Central

www.mhhe.com/createcentral

Internet References

Transportation Security Administration
www.tsa.gov

Transportation Security Administration and Pat-Downs
www.tsa.gov/traveler-information/pat-downs

U.S. Travel Association
www.ustravel.org

John W. Halinski Statement to House Committee on Transportation Security
www.tsa.gov/sites/default/files/publications/pdf/testimony/080112_halinski_testimony.pdf

Secretary Napolitano Announces New Measures to Strengthen Aviation Security
www.tsa.gov/press/releases/2010/04/02/secretary-napolitano-announces-new-measures-strengthen-aviation-security

Article   Prepared by: Thomas J. Badey, *Randolph-Macon College*

Here's an Inside Look at the NYPD's Transit Terror-Fighting Unit

MARC BEJA

Learning Outcomes

After reading this article, you will be able to:

• Describe the role of the NYPD transit bureau anti-terrorism unit.

• Identify potential threats to mass transit systems.

• Discuss the challenges local law-enforcement agencies face protecting public transportation.

A team of 104 NYPD officers is the city's first line of defense when it comes to terror threats on the subway. The NYPD transit bureau's anti-terrorism unit is focused on uncovering threats and thwarting attacks on the subway, which has been under tight security in the 11 years since 9/11.

Whether on foot or scooters, officers in the unit search the MTA's busiest stations, largely during the morning and evening rush hours, for suspicious people and packages.

"Our main focus is the prevention of terrorism within the transit system," said Lt. Jose Medina, a 16-year police veteran who has been with the unit for more than two years. "It's an enormous responsibility, obviously, because we have millions of people who travel through the subway system."

The unit, which started patrolling in 2010 with funding from federal stimulus money, also pitches in on Metro-North.

Though officials wouldn't say how many cases the unit has handled, Police Commissioner Ray Kelly has said there have been at least 14 terror plots thwarted citywide since 9/11, including some targeting the subway.

"Thank god . . . we haven't had any major happenings within the subway system," Medina, 44, said.

Before You Swipe

Riders are accustomed to seeing teams of cops at station entrances, randomly selecting people with bags to see if they're carrying anything that's illegal to bring into the system. Don't try to slip away if you've got a bag, said Capt. Roberto Cruz.

There are always at least two undercover cops watching for anyone trying to avoid police.

Cruz said the team tries to vary when and where it does bag checks, or "surges" of officers at stations, though his unit mostly focuses on the MTA's busiest and most iconic stops, including Herald Square, Times Square and Grand Central Terminal.

"We try to be unpredictable," said Cruz, a 36-year-old former Marine who has been an Air Force reservist since 2009. "It's mostly a show of force to reassure the public that we're out here doing something."

Beyond the Turnstiles

Inside the turnstiles, some officers drive electric scooters that raise them a few feet above most riders' heads.

"People can see you from far," said Officer Marlon Minaya, adding that being able to move up to 12 mph helps him reach incidents quicker.

All the officers also carry radiation detectors.

On the Trains

On a recent Tuesday morning, a sergeant and eight officers lined up outside the doors of each No. 2/3 subway car entering the 42nd Street-Times Square station, and quickly inspected the cars before giving the train's conductor an "all clear." The drill would be repeated dozens of times over the 81/2 hour shift. In a similar operation, officers ride a train and step out at each station.

Sgt. Marc Richardson, who joined the unit at its inception in 2009 after five years as a cop in Jamaica, said the different environment brought challenges.

"You could have a subway slashing in a closed subway full of people. That's very difficult to handle," said Richardson, adding that at times he patrols solo, unlike some officers above ground, who drive around with a partner. "Our backup may be two, three, four stations away."

Another task is to distinguish between visitors snapping photos of subway tunnels and would-be terrorists.

"You could be a tourist, but maybe you're not," said Richardson, 45. "If you're not, I don't know that, but you know I'm looking at you."

Behind the Scenes

Though police get called to inspect about 10 unattended packages each day, "most of it is garbage," Richardson said. "Some of it is people's property. They walk off, they forget they left it there on the bench and another person sees it and calls it in."

And every day, officers inspect dozens of underground emergency exits that lead from subway tunnels up to the street. The cops climb down as many as 20 stories to make sure nobody has snuck onto the tracks.

"You have to be in good shape if you're going to be in this unit," said Medina, after emerging from an exit near the United Nations, where the No. 7 train enters Manhattan. "You probably lost a few pounds walking up those steps."

MTA chief Joe Lhota praised the team's work.

Said Lhota: "Protecting the subway system from all threats is one of the toughest jobs in New York, but the NYPD Transit Bureau's counterterrorism tactics, training and skill give me confidence that more than 5 million riders each day are safe and secure."

Critical Thinking

1. Is the U.S. public transportation system vulnerable to terrorist attacks? Explain your answer.

2. Who should provide security for mass transit in major U.S. cities? Why?

3. What are the most effective ways to protect against terrorist attacks?

Create Central

www.mhhe.com/createcentral

Internet References

NYPD Transit Unit
> www.nyc.gov/html/nypd/html/transit_bureau/transit.shtml

NYPD Counterterrorism Units
> www.nyc.gov/html/nypd/html/administration/counterterrorism_units.shtml

MTA New York
> www.mta.info/nyct/

New York State Department of Homeland Security
> www.dhses.ny.gov/

Article   Prepared by: Thomas J. Badey, *Randolph-Macon College*

Homeland Security Hasn't Made US Safer

ANNE APPLEBAUM

Learning Outcomes

After reading this article, you will be able to:

- Describe how homeland security funds have benefited local communities.

- Discuss the effectiveness of homeland security.

Hardly anyone has seriously scrutinized either the priorities or the spending patterns of the U.S. Department of Homeland Security (DHS) and its junior partner, the Transportation Security Administration (TSA), since their hurried creation in the aftermath of the 9/11 attacks. Sure, they get criticized plenty. But year in, year out, they continue to grow faster and cost more—presumably because Americans think they are being protected from terrorism by all that spending. Yet there is no evidence whatsoever that the agencies are making Americans any safer.

DHS serves only one clear purpose: to provide unimaginable bonanzas for favored congressional districts around the United States, most of which face no statistically significant security threat at all. One thinks of the $436,504 that the Blackfeet Nation of Montana received in fiscal 2010 "to help strengthen the nation against risks associated with potential terrorist attacks"; the $1,000,000 that the village of Poynette, Wisconsin (pop. 2,266) received in fiscal 2009 for an "emergency operations center"; or the $67,000 worth of surveillance equipment purchased by Marin County, California, and discovered, still in its original packaging, four years later. And indeed, every U.S. state, no matter how landlocked or underpopulated, receives, by law, a fixed percentage of homeland security spending every year.

As for the TSA, I am not aware of a single bomber or bomb plot stopped by its time-wasting procedures. In fact, TSA screeners consistently fail to spot the majority of fake "bombs" and bomb parts the agency periodically plants to test their skills. In Los Angeles, whose airport was targeted by the "millennium plot" on New Year's 2000, screeners failed some 75 percent of these tests.

Terrorists have been stopped since 2001 and plots prevented, but always by other means. After the Nigerian "underwear bomber" of Christmas Day 2009 was foiled, DHS Secretary Janet Napolitano claimed "the system worked"—but the bomber was caught by a passenger, not the feds. Richard Reid, the 2001 shoe bomber, was undone by an alert stewardess who smelled something funny. The 2006 Heathrow Airport plot was uncovered by an intelligence tip. Al Qaeda's recent attempt to explode cargo planes was caught by a human intelligence source, not an X-ray machine. Yet the TSA responds to these events by placing restrictions on shoes, liquids, and now perhaps printer cartridges.

Given this reality—and given that 9/11 was, above all, a massive intelligence failure—wouldn't we be safer if the vast budgets of TSA and its partners around the world were diverted away from confiscating nail scissors and toward creating better information systems and better intelligence? Imagine if security officers in Amsterdam had been made aware of the warnings the underwear bomber's father gave to the U.S. Embassy in Abuja. Or, for that matter, if consular officers had prevented him from receiving a visa in the first place.

Better still, DHS could be broken up into its component parts, with special funding and planning carried out at the federal level only for cities and buildings that are actually at risk of terrorist attack. Here is the truth: New York City requires a lot more homeland security spending, per capita, than Poynette. Here is the even starker truth: Poynette needs no homeland security spending at all. The events of 9/11 did not prove that the United States needs to spend more on local police forces and fire brigades; they proved that Americans need to learn how to make better use of the information they have and apply it with speed and efficiency.

1974

The United Nations grants observer status to the Palestine Liberation Organization (PLO), considered a terrorist organization by Israel and the United States.

1976

Chinese revolutionary leader Mao Zedong dies.

1978

Egyptian President Anwar Sadat and Israeli Prime Minister Menachem Begin sign the Camp David Accords, paving the way for peace between two bitter enemies.

Chinese leader Deng Xiaoping begins the Four Modernizations policy.

1979

The Islamic Revolution in Iran overthrows the U.S.-allied shah and ushers in a theocratic Shiite state, sending shock waves through the Middle East.

Critical Thinking

1. Is the Department of Homeland Security spending money efficiently? Defend your answer.

2. Has homeland security spending made us safer? Explain.

3. Should small towns and communities be eligible for homeland security funds? Why or why not?

Create Central

www.mhhe.com/createcentral

Internet References

Department of Homeland Security History
www.dhs.gov/history

Transportation Security Administration
www.tsa.gov/

Department of Homeland Security FY2012 Budget
www.whitehouse.gov/omb/factsheet_department_homeland

Anne Applebaum is a columnist for the *Washington Post* and *Slate*.

Applebaum, Anne. Reprinted in entirety by McGraw-Hill with permission from *Foreign Policy,* no. 184, January/February 2011, p. 57. www.foreignpolicy.com. © 2011 Washingtonpost.Newsweek Interactive, LLC.

Unit VI

UNIT

Prepared by: Thomas J. Badey, *Randolph-Macon College*

Emergency Management and Response

First responders play a critical role in any disaster response. The heroic efforts of firefighters, police officers, and emergency medical personnel in New York City and Washington, DC, on September 11 and the sacrifices that they made are eternalized in the many lives that they helped save. As the United States prepares for future disasters and attacks, the role of first responders clearly merits closer examination. The term *first responder*, however, does not apply only to local emergency personnel. It includes people at various levels that may be directly involved in homeland security efforts.

While the battles over increased federal funding and training for police and fire departments continue, most have come to realize the importance of individuals in homeland security. As the actions of the passengers on United Airlines flight 93, which crashed outside of Pittsburgh, Pennsylvania, on September 11, indicate that, once people understand the nature of the threat, they are willing to become involved, and when necessary, even give their lives to save others. Realizing the plans of the terrorists, the passengers of flight 93 decided that they would rather take their chances fighting the hijackers than be used in a terrorist plot to harm others. The selfless action of these passengers may have done more to prevent another terrorist attack than billions of dollars spent on airport security. Similar stories of heroism have emerged in the wake of Hurricane Sandy, as neighbors risked their lives to save neighbors from the onrushing flood waters rather than wait for overwhelmed rescue crews to respond.

But even beyond response to major disasters, local law enforcement, fire prevention, and medical personnel play an important role in homeland security. They provide a first point of contact for citizens and are in a unique position to detect, report, and help prevent terrorist activity. Respect for people and good policing builds trust and support for police officers in local communities. Information from these communities may help in the early detection of potential threats. Fire departments play a critical role in the early identification of possible vulnerabilities and the planning of emergency responses and evacuations. Their contacts with local businesses and industry put them in a position to conduct emergency response training and help in emergency planning. Local medical personnel are the first point of contact for threats to public health. Specialized training and access to appropriate equipment and resources can help in the early detection and containment of public health threats.

Managing the interactions among the first responders from various levels of government continues to be a challenge. Lack of planning and coordination can lead to conflicts, confusion, and duplication of efforts. As federal emergency management exercises provide opportunities to practice these interactions, the lack of interoperability, communication problems, and jurisdictional disputes continue to impede effective cooperation.

The articles in this unit examine how first responders have adapted to continuing changes in the homeland security environment. One of the key components in developing effective emergency response capabilities is training. The DHS Center for Domestic Preparedness in Anniston, Alabama, offers a variety of training programs for first responders. Lashley's article provides a brief description of some of the training programs available at the center. The second article in this unit describes how to develop an all-hazard emergency action plan (EAP). It outlines the key elements and benefits of such a plan and includes a tabletop exercise designed to help emergency planners develop and check the basic elements necessary for effective disaster response. The next article focuses on the use of computer simulations to conduct large-scale training in highly populated areas like New York City. Since 2007, the New York City Office of Emergency Management has trained over 35,000 emergency responders each year using virtual world simulations software. Hartwell describes the NYCOEM's response to Hurricane Irene and offers recommendations as to how this training can be improved.

The last article in this section shifts the focus to the role and responsibilities that private business owners have in emergency response. Drawing on the lessons of 9/11, this article emphasizes the importance of emergency planning for business owners. It argues that employers should familiarize themselves with the best practices for their industry in order to be able to respond appropriately to any type of emergency situations.

Article   Prepared by: Thomas J. Badey, *Randolph-Macon College*

Real Training for Real Responders: The DHS Center for Domestic Preparedness

JOEL LASHLEY

Learning Outcomes

After reading this article, you will be able to:

- Describe the role of the Center for Domestic Preparedness.

- Identify the different types of training available for first responders.

- Explain the importance of disaster preparedness training.

Want to take another FEMA Incident Command course? Sooner jump out of the moving car on the way to the class? I hear you.

But what if I told you there was a homeland security course you'd actually enjoy? What if it's a hands-on course that could save your life and the lives of those who depend on you?

And what if it won't cost you or your department a dime, because it's a federal program designed for the people who are actually responding? That's right—it's for the ones actually on the ground doing the work, before and after the smoke clears. DHS will even fly you there, house you, feed you and drive you to school in the morning!

The Department of Homeland Security's *Center for Domestic Preparedness* in Anniston, Ala., has already trained thousands of our nation's first responders for the disastrous possibility of a chemical, biological, radiological, nuclear or explosive (CBRNE) attack. Having attended the week-long Weapons of Mass Destruction/ Technical Emergency Response Training (WMD/TERT) and completed the Chemical Ordnance Biological and Radiological (COBRA) training that's part of it, I could never doubt that DHS is serious about training first responders.

Among the CDP's many assets at the sprawling former Fort McClellan U.S. Army base is the Noble Training Facility, which is centered at Fort McClellan's 100-bed hospital. NTF is responsible for training, research and development geared toward ensuring the survival and effectiveness of healthcare personnel and facilities in the event of a terrorist attack or natural disaster.

The CDP offers courses not just for personnel concerned with preventing and detecting threats, but also for those responsible for disaster mitigation and the maintenance and recovery of post-incident assets. By including EMS, fire, police, public works and hospital personnel, and all the people who actually control and run the country's long-term survival assets, CDP helps give the survivors of a catastrophic attack a chance at long-term survival.

Airline transportation from your local airport to Atlanta is prearranged. CDP buses then pick you up for the 90-minute drive to Anniston, which sits between the beautiful Appalachian hills and Talladega National Forest. If you only had the time, it would be a beautiful place to hike and camp.

Housing is in a comfortable clean barracks, with a private bedroom, and a bathroom shared with one neighbor. The officers club is open to all CDP trainees, but it closes early for a reason I'll get to later. Transportation is provided to and from local attractions, stores and restaurants at no charge.

My own connection with CDP is that the hospital I work for, the Children's Hospital of Wisconsin, is a Level 1 regional trauma center and so would presumably play a major role in the aftermath of any disaster in the area. CHW has made the commitment to send all of the security staff and an equal number of the nursing staff to CDP. CHW security personnel go in groups of three, one from each shift, and so far about 10 of the security staff have gone, which is about one-third of our total staff.

At Anniston

If you attend the WMD/TERT and COBRA course at the CDP, you'll train in realistic environments simulating the aftermath of a CBRNE attack. You'll wear a variety of PPE, including SCBA, PAPR and MOPP gear. Cops can take a course to learn how to use their patrol rifles and apply their crowd-control procedures while serving in full chemical suits. EMS personnel practice triage and field medicine in realistic environments and PPE. Responders also learn to use chemical and biological detection and decontamination equipment.

At times it's hard and hot work, dragging heavy training mannequins around and decontaminating them, but once you're finished, you'll have a glimpse of what's expected of you if the real thing ever happens in your community. But hot-zone search and rescue is not all you'll learn at the CDP. Most unsettling for me was a glimpse of the challenges police and healthcare security officers will face if they're ever called on to protect post-incident assets.

According to DHS, the CDP's Chemical, Ordnance, Biological, and Radiological Training Facility (COBRATF) is "the world's only toxic chemical training facility dedicated solely to emergency responders." COBRA, as you might guess, is the part of the course that gets the most attention, so much so that it's even sprouted little cottage industries, as base civilian personnel have taken to selling unofficial COBRA hats and T-shirts to trainees on the side.

According to some of my CDP instructors, the center is the only place in the free world that uses live-agent training. [*Ed.: To my knowledge, there's also a facility in Canada that conducts such training.*] That's right boys and girls, if you have the right stuff, you too can walk through controlled environments filled with deadly nerve agent, while wearing a gas mask and chemical gear, of course.

Yes, I did it and survived, after which I received my coveted COBRA uniform pin, which I'm told goes for a pretty penny on eBay! And yes, I did see some trainees opt out of the COBRA portion. I also saw someone wearing a "100 COBRA Entries and Survived" patch. I think I'll pass on earning one of those, but I am glad I did it once.

After Anniston

All of the CHW healthcare security staff frequently attend local hazmat courses, but we agree that none can compare to the CDP. We now know for sure that our equipment will work, and that we can do the job if the worst happens.

After returning from CDP, CHW senior security officer Mike Bolmes said, "The instructors were entertaining and educational. They were real experts."

His favorite part was the improvised explosives class, which included a simulated methamphetamine lab, complete with booby traps. As for live-agent training, he said, "The COBRA training was extremely beneficial. It boosted my confidence."

Back when he was a sergeant on the Milwaukee County Sheriff's Office, CHW security services supervisor Mike Endter oversaw police operations on the Milwaukee Regional Medical Center campus. In addition, he has participated in large-scale drills involving police, fire and other emergency response assets at MRMC and elsewhere in Milwaukee County. He has participated in drills involving simulated airplane crashes, railroad disasters and large industrial chemical leaks.

Endter had previously attended FEMA training in Washington, D.C., and has had experience managing operations during a major construction disaster. But even with that background, he had this to say about the CDP and the COBRA course: "It was the first time I actually ever wore, much less trained in, full NBC [nuclear/biological/chemical PPE] before. I've trained in SCBA for fire response but this was totally different. . . . It was the best, most realistic training I've ever had."

According to CHW senior security officer Sal Scardino, the best parts were "the food (the mess hall fare has a Southern flair and everyone loved it) and talking with first responders from other areas of the country."

What Scardino didn't like was getting up at 0400 for daily blood draws. During much of the training, our blood had to be monitored for chemical exposures. Applicants for training have to complete a prior medical screening before arriving at the center and then submit to basic medical monitoring during the training cycle. *That's* why the officers club closes early.

Emergency and trauma nurses, too, will be on the front line of disaster mitigation if a CBRNE event happens in their community. Tracy Zierer, RN, an emergency pediatric nurse at Children's, says "Our previous hazmat training was good, but 'The Center' makes such an impression and provides such realistic training. Rescuing dummies in realistic environments and actually decontaminating and triaging them was definitely more realistic . . . thorough. It shows you what it will really be like."

All of us who went through the CDP were trained by instructors with real-life backgrounds in explosive ordnance disposal, chemical warfare, and search and rescue. Tracy highlights the analyses and lectures from experts on the Chechen school incident, the 9/11 attacks, IED attacks in Iraq and other terrorist events.

CHW security services director Mike Thiel and I and other CHW security and nursing staff trained alongside the Georgia Army National Guard's 138th Chemical Company, many of whom had already seen deployments to Iraq and were preparing for another. One of their officers put it to me like this, "If the Army sends us here—and we're chemical soldiers—then you know it's good training. Many of us have been through it more than once. There's a reason we keep coming back."

Thiel intends to continue cycling his officers and supervisors through the training at the CDP. He also requires all CHW healthcare security officers to certify in HICS (the hospital version of the Incident Command System) at the HICS-100 and -200 and NIMS-700 levels, so that any member of the CHW security staff can serve in the incident commander role, until relieved. Who knows who might be on duty when a catastrophe happens, or who might survive to handle it?

Thiel explains the need for this high level of disaster response readiness. "We made the commitment to develop an unparalleled level of expertise in pediatric hospitals. Children's Hospital of Wisconsin and our sister adult hospital, Froedtert Hospital, are the Level 1 trauma centers for southeastern Wisconsin. The Milwaukee regional area and beyond, to Chicago in particular, represent a credible target for modern terrorists and a CBRNE attack."

"I don't understand why everyone isn't sending people to this training opportunity," Thiel says. "It's the best available anywhere, and its free!"

At Children's Hospital of Wisconsin we continue to send our healthcare security, nursing, disaster management and other staff through the CDP. CHW personnel have attended the Hospital Emergency Response Training course, and a few others and I took our ICS-100 and -200 training there. ICS-300 and -400 and other NIMS and ICS courses are also available. The CDP even has non-resident instructors who can be sent to your location for training on some subjects.

At the CDP, Children's Hospital and Health System personnel train alongside firefighters, hazmat teams, law enforcement officers, SWAT teams, bomb squads, and military and EMS personnel from all over the country. We train together because if the worst happens, we'll all be working together, under the worst possible circumstances.

Just ask anyone who has ever survived a disaster. If you go to the CDP, you'll have the opportunity to ask them yourself, because some of them will be your instructors. It doesn't get any more real than that.

Critical Thinking

1. How has disaster preparedness changed since 9/11?

2. Does preparing for terrorist threats aid in preparation for natural disasters? Explain.

3. Should more programs like this exist? Why or why not?

Create Central

www.mhhe.com/createcentral

Internet References

Center for Domestic Preparedness
https://cdp.dhs.gov/

CDP Training
https://cdp.dhs.gov/news/impact/index.html

CDP Indirect Training
https://cdp.dhs.gov/mobile/index.html

CDP Mass Causality Exercise
https://cdp.dhs.gov/pdfs/news/features/SchoolBus.pdf

Article Prepared by: Thomas J. Badey, *Randolph-Macon College*

Learning from Hurricane Irene

Catherine Hartwell

Learning Outcomes

After reading this article, you will be able to:

- Explain the effects of Hurricane Irene on the New York City's early response programs.

- Describe how general safety and response knowledge can be improved.

- Discuss the lesson that can be learned from Hurricane Sandy.

As part of its ongoing monthly seminar series, The Christian Regenhard Center for Emergency Response Studies (RaCERS) at John Jay College in New York City brought together Dina Maniotis, assistant commissioner, New York City Office of Emergency Management (NYCOEM) and Andrew Boyarsky, City University of New York (CUNY) School of Professional Studies.

The speakers discussed the city's planning process for sheltering residents in the event of a disaster and the training requirements for city employees who are called on to staff these shelters in an emergency.

Because parts of New York City are susceptible to hurricane-caused flooding, following Hurricane Katrina the NYCOEM, in partnership with CUNY, developed an innovative training program to prepare city personnel to fulfill roles as shelter managers and staff. These efforts require working directly with Emergency Support Function #6—Mass Care, Emergency Assistance, Housing, and Human Services.

These city staff are not emergency responders, however, but "regular" city employees such as teachers, who are mobilized to perform these functions, aided by medical professionals. (Upon an emergency declaration by the Mayor, city staff may be asked to perform functions outside their usual job titles and are compensated for their work.)

Training in a Virtual World

Training is a vital element to ensure that shelters are well managed. Training programs have been developed for evacuation and shelter managers that can be completed by the necessary personnel in either a classroom or online form. The variety of training platforms, such as classroom, online or simulation, maximizes the various types of audience participants who can become involved, from professionals to civilian volunteers.

Shelter management training is a daunting challenge for the city. The shelters, mostly in schools, can't be disrupted to configure them as shelters for training purposes. Additionally, the number of staff needing training required a flexible system capable of being delivered both routinely and "just in time" prior to an event.

The solution was to use online computer simulation. Virtual world simulation software known as "Second Life" was used to simulate the physical layout of actual shelters. http://secondlife.com/

In an immersive virtual environment, participants could walk through the shelter buildings, see rooms intended for various shelter purposes, and interact with other participants to set up and operate the shelter and solve problems. The training can be adapted for various roles played by participants, up to five of whom can participate simultaneously.

This highly effective simulation training engages the learner in what researchers call the Proteus effect. This occurs when someone is placed in a digital role or persona and assumes behavior appropriate to that role or persona, responding as if they were actually in the virtual environment. Simulations can involve team dynamics where the learner sees another avatar and interacts with them as a team to accomplish an objective.

This is an effective practicum that has trained 35,000 employees every year since the program's inception in 2007.

NYCOEM and CUNY also worked together to create three planning guides to go along with employee sheltering training. These include detailed evacuation information for hurricane shelters, evacuation shelters and special medical needs shelters.

The Training Gets Tested

One week before Hurricane Irene was projected to strike the area, NYCOEM activated their situation room and began the operational checklist. Five days prior to landfall, the agency opened its EOC.

Hospitals, nursing homes and health care facilities had their own evacuation plans and knew where they were going to transfer their patients. In all, 350,000 people and 43 healthcare facilities were ordered to evacuate, and 10,000 residents were sheltered in 65 evacuation shelters, 82 emergency shelters and seven special-needs shelters, with 1,000 residents volunteering to help 5,000 city shelter staff.

With hospital and nursing home patients successfully relocated before landfall, the evacuation was the largest undertaken by the city. The planning efforts and training contributed to a highly successful evacuation, with no loss of life among those sheltered or relocated.

Hurricane Irene was one of the costliest hurricanes on record in the Northeastern United States. The ninth named storm, first hurricane and first major hurricane of the annual hurricane season, Irene originated east of the Lesser Antilles and was designated as Tropical Storm Irene on Aug. 20, 2011.

After making landfall in St. Croix as a strong tropical storm later that day, early on Aug. 21, Irene made a second landfall in Puerto Rico, where it strengthened into a Category 1 hurricane. Shortly before making four landfalls in the Bahamas, Irene peaked as a 120 mph (195 km/h) Category 3 hurricane.

Thereafter, the storm slowly lost intensity as curved northward, being downgraded to a Category 1 hurricane before making landfall on the Outer Banks of North Carolina on Aug. 27. Early on the following day, the storm re-emerged into the Atlantic from southeastern Virginia. Although Irene remained a hurricane over land, it weakened to a tropical storm while making yet another landfall in southeastern New Jersey on Aug. 28. A few hours later, Irene made its ninth and final landfall, in Brooklyn, New York City.

On Coney Island, Irene produced a storm surge of more than 4 feet and a storm tide of 9.5 feet at Battery Park. The Hudson River flooded starting around 9 A.M., overrunning its banks into the city's meatpacking district.

Lessons Learned

The mayor's office convened an after action report to assess sheltering during Hurricane Irene. The majority of areas for improvement were related to administration and decommissioning of shelters. Refinements to policy and training programs are already being designed to address the findings.

Specific recommendations included:

- Improving timekeeping for city employees deployed to shelters;
- Improving labeling of supplies, particularly at shelters that were not filled to capacity;

- Ensuring adequate support for medical waste disposal; and
- Ensuring that private care facilities provide staff to support their residents or patients that were moved to shelters.

The speakers described an innovative process for meeting the needs for human services during an event requiring sheltering of populations. Training using virtual worlds was regarded as a cost-effective solution for training the large numbers of people required in New York's plan.

The field guides developed for shelter operations were also effective, so much so that agencies from other states are requesting them to use as templates to design their own field guides.

The city's after action reporting process enabled the numerous agencies involved in the preparation and response to identify areas for strengthening the city's capability. The use of virtual worlds for training was demonstrated to be an asset, and offers lessons for emergency management training nationally.

Critical Thinking

1. How can citizens be trained to respond to emergencies such as a hurricane?

2. What are the benefits of using virtual simulations to prepare for emergencies?

3. What role should local government play in preparing for disasters?

Create Central

www.mhhe.com/createcentral

Internet References

New York City Office of Emergency Planning
www.nyc.gov/html/oem/html/home/home.shtml
City University of New York
www.cuny.edu/index.html
New York State Department of Homeland Security
www.dhses.ny.gov
New York OEM Simulation Based Training
www.emergencymgmt.com/training/Simulation-Training-Cost-Effectiveness-Flexibility.html
National Hurricane Center
www.nhc.noaa.gov

Article   Prepared by: Thomas J. Badey, *Randolph-Macon College*

The Lingering Shadow of "That Day"—Business Preparedness Lessons from 9/11

RICH COOPER

Learning Outcomes

After reading this article, you will be able to:

- Understand the important role that individuals have in emergency preparedness.

- Identify the basic things that every worker should know in case of an emergency.

- Discuss the resources available to businesses in planning emergency preparedness.

For anyone alive eleven years ago, September 11 will always be a date on the calendar when you immediately remember where you were and what you were doing when all hell broke loose. You feel the chill and pang of sadness for those lost, as well as the anger at the evil unleashed.

History records many unforgettable days, but as the rawness of that day's memories ebbs, the lessons learned continue to ripple in many ways. I don't think there is any doubt that as a nation we are a far better prepared to face 21st century threats than we were 11 years ago, but in the discussion on safety and security, one of the often-overlooked aspects is the impact that day had on business.

Businesses open their doors and turn on their lights each day to serve many kinds of customers. Each of those enterprises—regardless of what they do or where they are located—face a risk that some type of emergency, either known (e.g., a power loss, fire, weather emergency, etc.) or completely unknown is possible. Whatever form it may take, that risk and how prepared business owners and operators are to address and overcome it can mean the difference between being "open for business" and being "closed" for good.

After 9/11 (as well as after Hurricane Katrina), private sector preparedness received a lot of attention. Katrina and the 9/11 terrorist attacks both disrupted hundreds, if not thousands, of businesses. As a result, hundreds of thousands of jobs were lost, and this impacted not just the pocketbooks of the newly unemployed and their families but the economies in which they lived, as well as nationwide. There are no magic spells that to prevent "bad days" from occurring, but what makes a difference on those days is summed up in the old Boy Scout motto: "Be Prepared."

As we reflect on another 9/11 anniversary, we can honor those lost by remembering the lessons this country learned 11 years ago. Every business owner, operator, and employee needs to take the time to find out what to do if an emergency were to occur. We should be asking questions like:

- Where are the emergency exits?
- How do I contact employees during an emergency?
- Which essentials should be stored at your office or at home to sustain each person for a minimum of 72 hours?
- What information can and should be on a backup system at a secondary location?

Depending on your industry or line of work, there may be specific standards and best practices (which can be very detailed) for what your enterprise should do on a "bad day." On those days, ignorance is no excuse; it will not save lives nor will it keep an enterprise operating during challenging times.

Business leaders of all types can operate on any good day, but it is how you handle the bad days that will ultimately reveal your enterprise's resilience. There are a number of excellent resources available; here are two items fit well within any business' budget—after all, they're FREE!

- **Ready Business** [5]—Led by the Department of Homeland Security (DHS) and the Federal Emergency Management Agency (FEMA), Ready Business [5] offers a series of easy to use tools, instructions and exercises to help businesses understand the fundamentals of private sector preparedness. For nearly a decade, Ready Business has been regularly refined to put the best insights and know-how to use so users can create custom plans to prepare their employees and operations for a multitude of risks.

- **Ready Rating Program** [6]—First started by the St. Louis branch of the American Red Cross, the Ready Rating Program provides similar preparedness tools as those in Ready Business, but it takes preparedness several steps further. By offering rating tools and better connecting users to their communities (and those working to be prepared in those areas), Ready Rating fosters like-minded partners and increased coordination in towns where this cooperation is especially essential in an emergency. Given the success of the St. Louis program, and recognizing the impact it could have for communities nationwide, the American Red Cross took the program national in 2010. It continues to grow in reach and impact every day.

Where you get your preparedness information is certainly important, but it's not as important as the step you take to make sure you are truly prepared for the unexpected. If that step is not taken, it leaves you steps behind in recovering and ensuring the "Open for Business" sign is proudly displayed afterwards.

Among the many lingering shadows of "that day" is the resolve that how we prepare can make all the difference. Being realistic about risks and threats, large and small, known and unknown, is important. Being prepared gives you the calm and strength you need when it is needed most, and that's a lesson worth living every day

Critical Thinking

1. Should private industry be responsible for the safety of their workers during natural disasters? Why or why not?

2. Should regular disaster training for employees be the responsibility of private industry? Why or why not?

3. What can businesses do to better prepare for emergencies?

Create Central

www.mhhe.com/createcentral

Internet References

Department of Homeland Security
   www.dhs.gov

Federal Emergency Management Agency
   www.fema.gov

Ready Business
   www.ready.gov/business

Ready Rating Program
   http://readyrating.org

Unit VII

UNIT

Prepared by: Thomas J. Badey, *Randolph-Macon College*

New Technologies in Homeland Security

New technologies have had a tremendous impact on U.S. security. Surveillance cameras, metal detectors, and explosive detection equipment have become commonplace at U.S. airports. Yet, despite the existence of these precautionary measures, the September 11 hijackers managed to board and take over four U.S. aircraft. While some choose to blame the intelligence community for the security failures of 9/11, there has been little or no discussion of the failure of technology. Billions of dollars spent on new security measures and millions spent on new explosive detection equipment, installed at major U.S. airports on the recommendations of the Gore Commission after the crash of TWA Flight 800, did not prevent the attacks of 9/11. As we become increasingly dependent on technology in day-to-day security, we must recognize the limits of technology in homeland security. Technological solutions are expensive. They offer limited solutions to specific problems. Once in place, they are vulnerable to counter-measures. One of the major drawbacks of technology solutions to security issues is cost. Since the first attack on the World Trade Center in 1993, counter-terrorism funding has increased significantly. In the United States, government spending on counterterrorism has risen from less than $1 billion in 1995 to, by some estimates, as much as $75 billion in 2011. As the federal budget deficits increase and counter-terrorism spending reaches its limits, increased attention must be paid to the nature of investments in technology and the associated tradeoffs.

Technological solutions often focus on very narrow problems. Metal detectors may detect firearms but are not likely to detect plastic explosives. Databases that maintain information on potential terrorists are only useful if they capture all possible suspects and if they can be easily accessed by those who need them. Passenger profiling software does not identify terrorists who don't fit a specific profile. Systems designed to protect aircraft against heat-seeking missiles do not protect against other types of shoulder-fired weapons or prevent attacks against targets on the ground. The selection of one technology over another thus automatically determines the limitations of the security system.

Once a new technology is in use, it becomes susceptible to counter-measures. Terrorists have proven themselves extremely adept at circumventing existing security. Billions spent on technology for airport security were circumvented by 99-cent box-cutters. The case of Umar Farouk Abdulmutallab, sometimes referred to as the "underwear bomber," who attempted to detonate plastic explosives hidden in his underwear while on board a Northwest Airlines flight from Amsterdam to Detroit in December of 2009, provides ample evidence that technology has its limits. Despite security precautions in Amsterdam, Abdulmutallab was able to board the plane. In the end it was the actions taken by alert passengers and crew rather than billons spent on technology that ultimate averted another disaster. Systems that monitor the international transfer of funds have been rendered ineffective by traditional barter and exchange systems such as *hawala* and *hundi*. Technology designed to intercept and monitor cell-phone calls has led to the development and use of alternate means of communication. Profiling of terrorists has led to the increased recruitment of individuals who don't meet the profile.

Although technology alone cannot solve the complex problems posed by homeland security, the use of technology can significantly improve and enhance existing security. With this caveat, the articles in this unit examine the potential role of new technologies in homeland security.

The first article in this unit focuses on the question of how to improve passenger screening at airports. Aaron Karp advocates a "risk-based" passenger screening system to improve both the effectiveness and efficiency of airport checkpoints. Next, Sebastian Thaler discusses the Transportation Worker Identification Credential (TWIC) program which uses new, tamper-resistant biometric card for access. He offers a number of recommendations on how to improve this cost-effective, cutting-edge verification technology. Next, Joseph Nevins examines the use of unmanned aerial vehicles (UAV) for surveillance operations along U.S. borders. He discusses the potential benefits and drawbacks of the broader use of drones by U.S. law enforcement and security agencies. X-ray screening of cargo containers is slow, inefficient, and disrupts the flow of commerce. Next, with *Science and Technological Review* discusses work on a new technology that may offer an effective mechanism for quickly detecting even the smallest items in large containers. Finally, Austin Wright discusses the Future Attribute Screening Technology (FAST), a new system being developed by the Department of Homeland Security. Still years from completion, this new technology attempts to use body scanners to look at bodily signals to identify individuals with hostile intent.

Article   Prepared by: Thomas J. Badey, *Randolph-Macon College*

Changing Checkpoints

Aaron Karp

Learning Outcomes

After reading this article, you will be able to:

- Discuss the changes in airport security since 9/11.

- Identify reasons for and against the elimination of current liquid restrictions.

- Explain how risk-based checkpoints could improve airport security.

It seemed simple, and reasonable enough. As had been planned for some time, from April 29 passengers connecting to flights at EU airports from a third country would be allowed to carry through security checkpoints liquids, aerosols and gels purchased either at an airport duty-free shop or onboard a non-EU airline. It was supposed to be a modest, interim step toward the 2013 elimination of the rules, put in place in the US and EU following the uncovering of the transatlantic bomb plot in 2006, that have forced passengers to measure carefully the amount of toothpaste they place in carryon bags.

But as has been learned repeatedly in the nearly 10 years since 9/11, nothing is simple about the ever-more-elaborate systems that have been put in place at airports around the world for screening passengers. As the April 29 deadline approached, the UK government said it would wait until the autumn to implement the change, citing a "continuing high threat" at its airports including London Heathrow. France, Italy and the Netherlands also said they weren't ready to make the change, and the US was skittish about the EU move.

Under intense pressure (including from many airlines that ultimately favor eliminating the liquids rules), the European Commission pulled back on partial relaxation of restrictions at the eleventh hour. "It is clear that a situation at European airports which leads to confusion for air passengers as to whether they can travel or not with 'duty-free liquids,' in particular for connecting flights to the United States, should be avoided," EC VP-Transport Siim Kallas said.

Reason Foundation Director-Transportation Policy Robert Poole, who has done a number of studies on post-9/11 airport security, told *ATW*, "The full implications weren't thought through among the EU countries and it was only when the deadline approached that people said, 'Wait a minute' . . . It

was a good, object lesson in not doing your homework well enough to coordinate such changes. Very disappointing to me because I'd really like to see the liquids ban end."

The scenario demonstrated how difficult it will be to make even small changes to passenger screening checkpoints that don't involve adding more layers of physical inspection to an already burdensome process, typified by the body scanner machines being deployed at massive cost at airports around the US and elsewhere. In a recent report published by RAND Corp., author K. Jack Riley noted that the US Transportation Security Administration will spend an estimated $1.4 billion per year to operate these machines by 2014. That figure is in addition to some $5 billion TSA spends annually "on a workforce numbering an estimated 60,000," he wrote.

Yet from industry to government (including at the highest levels of TSA), there appears for the first time since 9/11 to be a consensus that significant changes in airline passenger screening are necessary, both to enhance security and to facilitate the flow of an increasing number of air travelers.

"Intelligence Driven"

Given that TSA, which essentially has set the global passenger security agenda since its 2001 establishment, through the years often has stubbornly resisted altering its approach, it was quite notable when Administrator John Pistole signaled in March that the current system needs revamping. Formerly the second-ranking official at the US FBI, he took over TSA last June and appears to have concluded that the aviation security apparatus in place is less than optimal.

Speaking before an American Bar Assn. homeland security conference in Washington, Pistole revealed that his agency is developing airport "checkpoint of the future concepts" that will place a greater emphasis on "cutting-edge technology" and intelligence to differentiate passengers based on threat levels. He noted that "TSA screens more than 628 million airline passengers each year at US airports" and "the vast majority of the 628 million present little-to-no risk of committing an act of terrorism."

He added, "If we want to continue to ensure the secure freedom of movement for people and commerce . . . there are solutions that go beyond the one-size-fits-all system. My vision is to accelerate TSA's evolution into a truly risk-based, intelligence-driven organization in every way."

Airlines and airports have embraced Pistole's remarks. "We strongly support a risk-based approach to include a 'trusted traveler' or 'known traveler' type program," US Air Transport Assn. Senior VP-Safety, Security and Operations Tom Hendricks tells this magazine. "I think it would be intelligence-based. We would vet passengers in various ways [in order to] essentially get these passengers to have a different experience through the checkpoint than the passengers who haven't been vetted."

Airports Council International-North America VP-Security and Facilitation Christopher Bidwell seconds, "We've always advocated a risk-based approach to security, whether it's screening passengers, baggage or other security applications, so we're very encouraged by what the administrator is saying now."

What would a "risk-based" checkpoint look like? Pistole has declined to be specific, saying "more details" will be coming later this year. But he has said the agency wants "to focus our limited resources on higher-risk passengers, while speeding and enhancing the passenger experience at the airport."

IATA late last year stepped forward to provide some specifics of what airlines would like to see in future checkpoints, outlining a paradigm shift that calls for pre-screening passengers prior to issuing a boarding pass to divide them into three levels of risk classification. DG and CEO Giovanni Bisignani has characterized current airport security as "an incredible mess . . . The hassle factor is absolutely unacceptable at many, many airports around the world."

Data Pre-Screening

The organization's future passenger security concept calls for "electronic data pre-screening by governments before flight" to create a "picture" of each passenger. They then would be divided into three categories upon issuance of a boarding pass: Known traveler, regular and enhanced. Checkpoints would be divided into three lanes, with IATA estimating that 30% would go through the "high-speed" known traveler lane, 60% though the regular lane and 10% through the most intensive enhanced security line. It declined to comment on passenger security for this article.

Hendricks says ATA is not willing to provide specifics of a desired alternative checkpoint but comments, "We can use technology to validate the identity of our passengers and in the future we can use that information to make an assessment on the risk-factor of the passenger based on what the information reveals . . . We absolutely wouldn't subscribe to anything that makes race, gender, national origin, those kinds of things [part of the assessment]. It's against the law."

Poole says the key to any new system will be establishment of a trusted traveler program. "As much as half of daily air travelers appear to be frequent flyers who would be eligible and potentially interested [in a trusted traveler program]," he explains. "Let's say two-thirds of those applied and got accepted, that would be 30%–40% of the daily inflow of passengers and that would make a big, big difference in how the checkpoints are configured and in the processing time. The savings could be reallocated to beef up security in other aspects of the airport."

He envisions a system in which trusted-traveler program members would "check in at a kiosk and verify biometrically that they're the person who was cleared. Then they would probably walk through a metal detector . . . [which would] probably reassure the security-theater public that we're not letting them in without something.

"In principle I don't think even that's necessary, but I would say fine, I don't object . . . And you would also need a random element. Every hundredth person or two-hundredth person . . . would be taken aside for secondary screening as another check so it's not a free pass for someone who gets in the trusted traveler program that shouldn't be."

For many longtime critics of TSA, there is enthusiasm for the agency's apparent change in strategy, though it remains to be seen how effectively and quickly it and its counterparts around the world can transition from the current approach of treating every passenger as a potential threat.

"It struck me as odd that the TSA up until now has so strongly resisted [moving to a risk-based system] and it always struck me as a double standard," says Poole. "Number one, they are applying a risk-based standard to airport employees who are cleared for access to secure areas of the airport including onto the airfield. Those people are given a criminal-history background check and, assuming they pass it, they are given a badge that gives them un-escorted access. They don't have to go through security every time they pass from the unsecured area to the secure area of the airport . . . So the TSA has had this double standard all along . . . It seems to me that if a criminal-history background check is sufficient for airport workers to have access to planes, it ought to be sufficient for frequent travelers that you know a lot about."

In fact, as Riley pointed out in his report, TSA often exempts the massive security workforce from any kind of routine screening as well. "At many airports, TSA employees are screened neither the first time nor subsequent times that they enter the secure area of an airport, in part because they are trusted employees who have undergone a background check."

Making all passengers go through the same checkpoints means they all must adhere to a series of rules and procedures—often layered on top of one another in response to terrorist incidents—that add time and complexity. "When you travel, your coat is one item, your shoes are one item, your laptop is one item, your bag is one item," Bidwell says. "Those all have to be screened separately . . . That is something in and of itself that needs to be assessed. If there is some adjustment in that area, it would significantly enhance and streamline the screening process."

Pilot Program

Clues to how security might change in the near future could come from a new crewmember screening system being tested by TSA at seven US airports to determine if pilots, and potentially flight attendants, can be allowed to bypass traditional security checkpoints. ATA, the Air Line Pilots Assn., the

Southwest Airlines Pilots' Assn. and the Coalition of Airline Pilots are involved in the effort.

Hendricks says the system, which will rely on verifying crewmembers' identities and employment status rather than physical screening, is similar to the screening method called the Crew Personnel Advanced Screening System, or Crew-PASS, developed by AIRINC and used at three US East Coast airports for about three years. Pilots at test program airports will present picture IDs and other information to TSA personnel, who will use electronic databases to verify the flight crewmember's identity. The pilot then would be allowed access to the airside area of the airport without going through security checkpoint lanes.

Pistole says the test program, started this spring and slated to last for about 90 days, "is a step in the right direction as TSA continues to explore more risk-based, intelligence-driven security solutions. We want to focus our limited resources on passenger screening."

Hendricks says, "There are similar constructs between what the known crewmember program might provide and some sort of trusted traveler program in the future."

Walking the Talk

While Pistole's remarks, the program for screening pilots and the EC's stated goal of sticking with the 2013 deadline for eliminating liquids restrictions portend change, how fast the security apparatus evolves is an open question. "I did a study comparing the US, Canada and European security . . . and what I found surprising and disappointing is that there's much talk about moving toward a risk-based approach in all of those jurisdictions but very little actually being done to implement it," Poole says. "And I think some of the same political dynamics are at work . . . Politicians have this fantasy that if they just layer on more and more things that we can have 100% assurance that no explosion, no terrorist attack can ever happen again. So you have a situation where politicians fear that any [system] where you're spending less money, using less equipment, potentially opens them up to blame if you have an incident, and that I think has driven the policymaking."

Hendricks comments, "I think [moving to a risk-based approach is] going to be a relatively slow process. We're going to have to take a very good look at technology, processes, procedures, training . . . and then we're going to have to prove that it provides the same level of security for the system. So I think it's going to be an evolutionary approach."

International coordination will be critical. "Whether it's liquids, gels and aerosols or other types of screening, we can't look at in an insular fashion," Bidwell says. "This is a global challenge that needs to be addressed across borders and that's one reason we've said for a long time that there needs to be mutual recognition of standards."

Critical Thinking

1. Is the current security system at U.S airports reactive or proactive?

2. How will innovations in airport security change the way people travel?

3. How are other countries responding to the U.S. approach to increased airport security?

4. How can technology be used to increase airport security?

Create Central

www.mhhe.com/createcentral

Internet References

European Commission Transport
   http://ec.europa.eu/transport/index_en.htm

Rand Corporation Congress Resources
   www.rand.org/congress.html

U.S. Transportation Security Administration
   www.tsa.gov

International Air Transport Association
   www.iata.org/Pages/default.aspx

CrewPASS
   www.arinc.com/products/security/crewpass.html

U.S. Air Transport Association Special Topics
   www.airlines.org/Pages/Econ_Special_Topics.aspx

New ID Technology's Role in Pinpointing Potential Threats

What good is a Federal government-issued "no-fly" list, critics rightfully ask, if it fails to keep those on the list from boarding planes?

SEBASTIAN THALER

Learning Outcomes

After reading this article, you will be able to:

- Describe some of the attempted terrorist attacks since 9/11.

- Explain which areas in the U.S. are the most vulnerable to future attacks

- Explain the importance of innovative technology in preventing terrorist attacks.

In the wake of the Sept. 11, 2001, attacks, the U.S. began instituting a wide array of security measures intended to minimize the occurrence of future terrorist acts on American soil. However, a slew of headlines since 9/11—and a careful analysis of measures now in place at the nation's seaports, Federal and state secure facilities, international borders, and airports—reveals that much work remains to be done. Put bluntly, the security level at these locations nationwide is unacceptably lax: Would-be terrorists still are capable, to an uncomfortable degree, of gaining access to U.S. critical infrastructure.

The extent of the problem becomes clearer by spotlighting certain key details of high-profile terrorism cases. First consider the ease with which the 9/11 hijackers were able to gain access to planes on that fateful morning: The box-cutter knives carried by them were permitted onboard because, at the time, any knife with a blade up to four inches long was allowed on domestic flights. Just as important, some hijackers lacked a valid, U.S. government-issued identification card. These Al Qaeda members were allowed to board their planes anyway.

Next, there is Richard Reid, the so-called "shoe bomber," who was permitted to get on an American Airlines flight in Paris on Dec. 22, 2001, wearing plastic explosives in his shoes. He was allowed to obtain a seat despite his having been prevented from flying the previous day due to his unwillingness to answer all of the passenger screeners' questions, and despite the fact that he did not check any luggage.

Almost eight years later, in September 2009, Najibullah Zazi was arrested as part of the U.S. Al Qaeda group accused of planning suicide bombings in the New York City subway system. Although good police work on the part of Scotland Yard and the FBI prevented Zazi from detonating any explosives, he had flown freely to and from Pakistan in 2008 to undergo weapons and explosives training at an Al Qaeda camp.

Two months after Zazi's planned subway attack, Maj. Nidal Malik Hassan, stationed at Ft. Hood, a U.S. Army base near Killeen, Tex., went on a shooting rampage, killing 13 people and wounding 30 others. The FBI and his superiors were privy to Hassan's extremist views for years prior to the shooting, and he was known to have corresponded with Anwar al-Awlaki, a lecturer who reportedly has inspired Islamic terrorists. Hassan also had been disciplined for proselytizing about his extreme religious views with patients and colleagues.

A few weeks after Hassan's November 2009 rampage, Umar Farouk Abdulmutallab attempted to detonate plastic explosives in his underwear while aboard a Northwest Airlines fright en route from Amsterdam to Detroit on Christmas Eve. A month prior to this attempt, Abdulmutallab's father had expressed concerns to CIA officers at the U.S. Embassy in Abuja, Nigeria, over his son's rapid drift toward religious extremism. Although Abdulmutallab's name was added to one watch list—the Terrorist Identities Datamart Environment—it was not added to the U.S. no-fly list, nor was his visa revoked.

Most recently, Faisal Shahzad, accused of planting a car bomb in New York City's Times Square on May 1, 2010, was allowed to board an Emirates flight at Kennedy Airport bound for Dubai before being detained shortly prior to takeoff. He had been placed on the no-fly list earlier in the day, but the airline checked an outdated list when Shahzad made a reservation and apparently were not suspicious when he purchased his ticket with cash. A routine post-boarding check finally identified him as being on the list, leading to his arrest.

Despite the widely varying circumstances involved in these incidents, most or all might never have occurred if certain security measures involving new technology had been in place and worked in concert with officials. Before pursuing this point in greater detail, let us review some existing measures, instituted at secure locations, that have been designed to identify individuals who might pose a security risk.

First, consider the nation's seaports, a prime target for potential terrorism. The U.S. maritime system consists of more than 300 sea and river ports with over 3,700 cargo and passenger terminals. The American economy depends on commercial shipping as the most reliable, cost-efficient method of transporting goods, with its ports handling approximately 20% of the maritime trade worldwide. This sort of volume creates a desirable target for terrorists who might seek to gain access to U.S. ports.

Securing Federal Facilities

Two other prime targets are the nation's more than 16,000 airports and 400-plus military installations, both of which have adopted heightened security measures as well. Yet, there is cause for unease. For example, a report from the Government Accountability Office presents stark findings regarding security features in Federal facilities, noting that undercover investigators were able to sneak hidden liquid explosives and detonators past security guards and checkpoints in high-risk or security Level IV Federal buildings occupied by the Homeland Security, Justice, and State departments.

A key tool in keeping such facilities safe is the use of ID cards issued to all who seek entry. For seaports, the Transportation Worker Identification Credential (TWIC) program offers a tamper-resistant biometric card to maritime employees who require unescorted access to secure areas of port and outer continental shelf facilities. It also is intended for those aboard Coast Guard merchant mariners and vessels that are regulated under the Maritime Transportation Security Act. To obtain a TWIC, an individual must provide biographic and biometric information such as fingerprints, sit for a digital photograph, and pass a security threat assessment conducted by the Transportation Security Administration.

Jointly run by the Transportation Security Administration and the Coast Guard under the aegis of the Department of Homeland Security, the TWIC program set a national compliance deadline of April 15, 2009. As of September 2009, more than 1,300,000 maritime transportation workers had been enrolled and over 1,100,000 TWICs had been activated, accounting for more than 93% of the estimated total number of eligible cardholders. Yet, this measure of success is tempered by the fact that the TWICs have yet to be utilized fully. Currently, they are serving primarily as ID cards being checked visually at checkpoints; due to the gradual and ongoing rollout of TWIC readers, the biometric information on the cards largely is going unread at the present time.

What information is encoded on TWICs? The credential is designed to hold a digital photograph, the bearer's name,

TWIC expiration data, fingerprint templates of two fingers, finger pattern templates of two fingers, a personal identification number, and a so-called Federal Agency Smart Credential number. An electronic reader is capable of extracting this data via several methods including 1D or 2D barcodes, magnetic stripes, smart chip, proximity or radio-frequency identification, and biometrics—then comparing it to information stored in a database. Card-reading technology has been designed in two varieties: fixed physical access control and portable verification readers. The former is installed in a wall or turnstile and communicates, with an external access control system; the latter may be used for portable, spot-check identity verification.

A number of companies have been contracted by the government to provide readers to ports around the country. For instance, Sagem Morpho and Veridt have specialized in fixed readers, while Intellicheck Mobilisa, Core-Street, Cross Match, and TransCore are among those who have designed handheld readers.

Steps also have been taken by the military and the Transportation Security Administration to deter terrorists from entering secure facilities. The military has adopted a number of measures, including the issuing of FiXs (Federation for Identity and Cross-Credentialing Systems) cards and Common Access Cards. FiXS authorize certified issuers of credentials that fully are compliant with the Federal Information Processing Standard 201 and the Personal Identity Verification Part 1 Standard. The Federation includes more than 20 members, including systems integrators, financial institutions, and organizations focused on promoting improved workforce protection and systems security for critical infrastructure. The Department of Defense and General Services Administration are participating government organizations.

Far better known to the general public is the "no-fly" list, created and maintained by the Federal government, consisting of names of individuals who are not permitted to board a commercial aircraft for travel into or out of the country. Created soon after 9/11, its use has stirred controversy for reported incidences of false positives, in which law-abiding citizens, including young children, mistakenly have been detained by security. Additionally, the list played a prominent role in the incidents involving Abdulmutallab and Shahzad; what good is such a list, critics rightfully ask, if it fails to keep such people from boarding planes?

One important point needs to be stressed. Although the officials charged with checking the no-fly list may be lax in their duties, technology currently exists to perform such checks quickly and efficiently. Electronic devices have been developed that can scan a passenger's ID card (*e.g.,* a driver's license or military identification card) at the boarding gate, validate its authenticity, determine whether it is lost or stolen, and check if the bearer's identity is on a watch or terrorist list. The Defense ID System developed by Intellicheck Mobilisa Inc., for example, is designed for just this purpose. Defense ID is being used at Andrews Air Force Base, West Point Military Academy, Quantico Marine Corps Base, and many other military installations. It consists of a handheld device that reads barcodes and magnetic stripes on current forms of ID cards. By scanning and comparing the information to more than 140 "bad guy" and FBI Watch databases, Defense ID can determine in the space of a few seconds if an ID is fake, if it has been reported lost or stolen, if the person presenting it has any outstanding wants and warrants, and if the individual is on an authorized roster of previously cleared personnel. In addition, Defense ID has photo-capture, incident recording, and manual search capabilities. It easily could be adapted to check the Federal no-fly list.

More Oversight Needed

Of course, the existence of cutting-edge verification technology alone will not guarantee the safeguarding of seaports, military bases, and airports against potential terrorist attack unless the technology is implemented wisely. Any endeavor as ambitious in scope as keeping potential terrorists away from secure areas or aircraft requires an equally ambitious level of oversight. A few modest proposals are offered here:

Regarding seaports, first and foremost, security personnel must ensure that TWIC readers not only are available for use at each and every port checkpoint, but that their biometric capabilities are being utilized fully. Using the cards as just mother form of ID on top of those already possessed by personnel seeking access to port facilities defeats the entire purpose of the program.

Second, it is necessary to ensure that TWIC readers from different manufacturers are uniform in performance. The government has published performance specifications to which all readers must adhere; yet it is important that each reader be tested thoroughly prior to implementation. Readers not only must be up to the tasks at hand, but proven to provide an identical level of result.

Third, TWICs should be checked as individuals gain entry to, and exit from, a port facility. This way, the authorities can keep tabs on precisely who is present on the premises at any given moment. Unauthorized personnel who may have gained access to a secure area will be apprehended as they attempt to leave through an official checkpoint.

Finally, it is vital that TWICs only be distributed to individuals who fulfill all of the eligibility requirements and who have not been convicted of any specific felonies on the disqualification list compiled by the Transportation Security Administration. Should an individual who has engaged in any of these activities—ranging from espionage to improper transportation of a hazardous material—manage to evade detection by authorities during his or her security threat assessment, the worth of the TWIC he or she is issued dearly is eliminated.

A tool is only as effective as its users. The TWIC program can play a vital role in ensuring the safety and security of U.S. ports, but this goal is contingent on the complete deployment of TWIC readers at every point of entry and the proper analysis of the information the cards contain. In addition, a more rigorous implementation of visitor cards issued by FiXs would go far toward heightening security at military bases across the country. When fully roiled out, the system will verify and authenticate all contractors and private sector employees at participating Department of Defense, government, and government-affiliated facilities. Likewise, contractor and private sector employees will be able to verify and authenticate other industry, Federal, DoD, and government employees participating in FiXs and the Defense Cross-Credentialing Identification System.

At airports, security will be maximized only when the implementation of ID readers is complete. John F. Kennedy International Airport, out of which Shahzad nearly managed to fly, has eight terminals and 14 security checkpoints. Yet, the expense of fully implementing ID scanning technology at those checkpoints, such as that manufactured by Intellicheck, has been estimated to cost as little as $1,500,000. For the price of a few full-body scanning machines, New York could put technology into place that would screen people against the "no fly" list before they ever take a seat.

Critical Thinking

1. How is the government striving to create better systems for preventing terrorism?

2. How is technology playing a role in preventing terrorism?

3. What can the government do to encourage innovation in this area?

4. Why is more oversight needed?

Create Central

www.mhhe.com/createcentral

Internet References

Transportation Worker Identification Credential (TWIC)
    https://twicprogram.tsa.dhs.gov/TWICWebApp/
DoD CAC/PIV Card Information
    www.winmagic.com/solutions/vertical/government/united-states-government#-dod-cac-piv-card
U.S. Department of Defense
    www.defense.gov/
U.S. General Services Administration
    http://gsa.gov/
Homeport TWIC Homeland Security and U.S. Coast Guard
    https://homeport.uscg.mil/mycg/portal/ep/browse.do?channelId=-24886-&channelPage=%2Fep%2Fchannel%2Fdefault.jsp&pageTypeId=13489

Sebastian Thaler is a staff writer at The Investor Relations Group, New York, which counts among its clients Intellicheck Mobilisa Inc.

Article   Prepared by: Thomas J. Badey, *Randolph-Macon College*

Robocop Drones at Home

JOSEPH NEVINS

Learning Outcomes

After reading this article, you will be able to:

- Identify the primary purpose for the development of UAVs.

- Explain how UAVs are being used today.

- Describe the potential benefits of the use of UAVs in homeland security.

- Understand potential costs and consequences of the increased use of UAVs inside the United States.

In September 2010 the House Unmanned Aerial Vehicles (UAV) Caucus held a technology fair. In the foyer of the Rayburn House Office Building, dozens of people hovered around tables covered with literature, video screens showing images of the earth's surface, and models of UAVs—popularly known as "drones." The crowd was almost exclusively male. Most were conservatively dressed in the dark suits and ties that dominate Capitol Hill, though a handful wore the desert-brown jumpsuits of UAV pilots.

In his opening remarks to the gathering, Congressman Howard "Buck" McKeon, the California Republican who co-chairs and cofounded the bipartisan caucus, spoke of its mission: "To advocate for unmanned systems and ensure we continue to invest in the future. During these tough economic times, unmanned technology is one of the few consistent and dynamic areas of growth in American industry." Indeed, one observer at an industry fair the previous month asserted that UAVs are expected to be a $15 billion-a-year industry by 2015. (More conservative estimates peg that figure anywhere from $4.5 billion to $11.5 billion.)

McKeon, the ranking member of the House Armed Services Committee and its likely chair in the upcoming Congress, has been a beneficiary of this striking growth. His district includes California's Antelope Valley, about 50 miles northeast of downtown Los Angeles, where the aerospace and military industries employ more than 20,000 people. The top four contributors to his campaign in the last election cycle were all military contractors—Lockheed Martin, Northrop Grumman, Boeing, and General Dynamics.

McKeon's remarks at the fair focused on non-lethal use of UAVs, which effectively distanced the technology from the weapons his sponsors routinely manufacture. "Reports of 'drone strikes' in our fight against terrorists regularly fill the news," he declaimed, "but less well known is how our scientists are using unmanned systems to track and predict weather patterns, how Customs and Border Protection are using unmanned systems to protect our borders, or how local law enforcement uses drones to keep our neighborhoods and police officers safe."

McKeon was echoing comments made in August 2010 at the annual show of the Association for Unmanned Vehicle Systems International (AUVSI), the world's largest nonprofit UAV-advocacy organization. At the opening plenary of the four-day event in Denver, AUVSI Chairman John Lambert took pains to emphasize the benign aspect of UAVs: "Think of the number of lives that can be saved by unmanned systems," he said.

Although that gathering featured numerous panel discussions, workshops, and technical presentations devoted to the civilian uses of unmanned systems, the emphasis in the 453 exhibitions covering the huge convention-center floor was on military applications. Many of the displays viewed by the more than 6,500 attendees showed images of stern-looking soldiers with weapons, or of unmanned vehicles accompanied by slogans such as "combat proven," "superior visual intelligence," and "mission ready."

Back at the Washington fair, Vaughn Fulton, program manager for unmanned aerial systems (UAS) at Honeywell Aerospace in Albuquerque, introduced his company's T-Hawk, an "eye in the sky" named after New Mexico's state insect, the tarantula hawk. The bug's sting is one of the most painful in the insect world, Fulton reported with a laugh. Small enough to fit in a backpack, the T-Hawk has the capacity to "hover and stare"—it can inspect from very close range—as well as to pursue. According to Fulton, about 260 are already deployed with the U.S. military in Iraq and Afghanistan.

Honeywell is also marketing the T-Hawk domestically. The Miami-Dade Police Department now has at least two of them. Its T-Hawks will reportedly be used for "tactical" operations or SWAT team situations that involve potentially dangerous individuals, though both are currently grounded pending approval from the Federal Aviation Administration (FAA). Honeywell and the many other companies producing micro UAVs hope that other local police departments as well as state cops and the U.S. Border Patrol will soon be their customers—well-founded hopes, given that both U.S. Customs and Border Protection and the Sheriff's Office of Queen Anne's County, Maryland were represented at the fair.

At this point, domestic UAV operations are extremely limited. But with the astonishing growth of the industry and the efforts of AUVSI, the UAV Caucus, and others to loosen FAA restrictions, we can expect an explosion of use by local and federal policing agencies in the near future. Some of those uses—from fighting fires to locating missing persons—will have nothing to do with killing, border surveillance, or crime control. Still, given the nature of the technology, we need to be giving close scrutiny to how and where UAVs will be put to work. There is every reason to be concerned about how the law enforcement and "homeland security" establishments will take advantage of their new tools.

Creating Risks?

Like McKeon's and Lambert's speeches, Honeywell's promotional literature emphasizes that the T-Hawk "protects lives"—namely those of the soldiers using them to clear roads, secure perimeters, and search for roadside bombs. Moreover, proponents say, because of their accurate targeting and because of the precise information that unmanned systems provide, the technology not only protects soldiers, but also civilians living near those targeted for assassination.

Such claims serve to obscure the "collateral damage" caused by UAV strikes: a New America Foundation report suggests that hundreds of Pakistani civilians have been killed by U.S. UAV activity since 2004.

Indeed, the very availability of UAVs can increase the likelihood of warfare. At a sparsely attended session on ethics at the Denver show, Noel Sharkey, a professor of artificial intelligence and robotics at the University of Sheffield in England, spoke to this matter. Sharkey agreed that UAVs are more precise. Using one for a targeted killing, he pointed out, is a lot better than carpet-bombing an area. At the same time, Sharkey noted, their accuracy is somewhat illusory—targets are often in buildings, and targeting relies on frequently faulty intelligence. And the weight placed on precision obfuscates international legal concerns: UAV strikes don't allow for due process or surrender.

UAVs permit Washington to do things it otherwise wouldn't. A recently retired CIA operative told Sharkey that, without UAVs, the military wouldn't be able to attack targets in countries such as Pakistan, Somalia, and Yemen. For Sharkey, this shows that robots are not simply an innovation in weapons. Rather, they create totally new ways to wage war. Robots lead to such asymmetry that war becomes increasingly like terrorism. In the case of the United States, the reduced risk to American soldiers means that public opposition to war will also decrease. In this regard, UAVs are in the long run war-enabling—hardly a recipe for saving lives.

Sharkey's voice was a rare dissent from the dominant view in Denver and Washington, which holds that UAVs are "just another tool in the toolbox." From this perspective, any technology has multiple uses—you can drive a nail with a hammer, or break a skull—and is thus inherently neutral in a politico-ethical sense. But as Sharkey implies, technologies can also be transformational.

The domestic concern is similar: will UAVs prove to be just another tool, or will they be transformative? Will they fundamentally alter the way ostensibly free societies are policed?

We may not know the real risks of domestic applications until more UAVs are in use, but that time also may not be far off. Six police departments in Canada and numerous departments in Europe already use the devices. In Canada their deployment is limited to sparsely populated areas for purposes ranging from video recording of crime scenes to patrolling suspected smuggling corridors along the U.S. boundary. In the United Kingdom, local police agencies have used micro UAVs for the past few years to conduct search-and-rescue activities, assist in drug-related arrests, and monitor "anti-social behavior," such as protests at a gathering of the racist British National Party in August 2009.

U.K. authorities expect to begin using much bigger and more powerful UAVs, and in a significantly expanded fashion, in the near future. According to documents obtained by *The Guardian,* Britain's Home Office plans to use military-style UAVs to police the 2012 summer Olympics. In addition, six local U.K. police agencies have joined together for a pilot project to use UAVs for "surveillance, monitoring and evidence gathering." Officials hope UAVs will be installed in "the routine work of the police, border authorities and other government agencies" across the United Kingdom.

Thus far, the Civil Aviation Authority, the United Kingdom's equivalent of the FAA, has resisted the licensing of such aircraft in "normal" airspace due to fears of collisions, but the rapid development of "sense and avoid" technology may lay these worries to rest within a few years. Despite the implications of everyday reliance on UAVs, says Stephen Graham, Professor of Cities and Society at Newcastle University, "broader concern about the regulation and control of drone surveillance of British civilian life has been notable by its absence." Graham worries that the needed regulatory mechanisms are not in place in the United Kingdom to "prevent law enforcement agencies from abusing radical extensions in their powers to vertically and covertly spy on all aspects of civilian life 24 hours a day."

In the United States, strong FAA restrictions regarding access to airspace have led a number of departments, such as the Los Angeles County Sheriff's, to put their UAV plans on hold. But other federal offices are pushing for expanded use. In 2006 the National Institute of Justice (NIJ), the research and development arm of the Department of Justice, began helping local law enforcement acquire low-cost aviation devices. Tim Adelman, a lawyer who specializes in aviation matters, was hired to spearhead the program. While manned helicopters are prohibitively expensive for most departments, UASs, Adelman points out, can cost as little as $20,000 to purchase and just pennies an hour to operate.

The Sheriff's Office of Colorado's largely rural Mesa County is one of a handful of beneficiaries of the NIJ initiative. Ben Miller, the Sheriff's quartermaster, began looking into an unmanned system in June 2008; he thought inexpensive air-borne surveillance in Mesa County could help find lost persons and keep police officers out of harm's way.

With guidance from the NIJ and support from colleagues, Miller gained approval from the FAA to use a Draganflyer X6 Helicopter, a mini helicopter weighing less than four pounds, with four spindly legs and two narrow skids for feet.

The county anticipated popular fears of "mission creep," whereby police powers expand beyond those required to meet stated aims. The Sheriff's Office reminded locals that "eyes in the sky are not new," as Miller says—satellites, manned aircraft, and surveillance cameras all have greater surveillance capacity than most micro UAVs. In any case, Miller has assured the public that his office is not using its UAV to spy randomly on the community, but to respond to crime and threats to public safety.

In the worst-case scenario—the device dropping from the sky and striking a dwelling or an individual—its light weight, Miller says, would prevent serious harm. And as for possible collisions with other aircraft, the low altitude at which micro UAVs fly makes concern unwarranted, he contends.

Since August 2009, the department has flown its UAV in a small, approved area of county-owned property, largely for training and testing purposes. To deploy the UAV outside the prescribed area, the department must apply for an emergency Certificate of Operation. Approval takes anywhere from 45 minutes to two hours, making the UAV effectively useless when the Department most wants to deploy it. Such cases occur regularly, according to Miller.

Miller says the Sheriff's Office had its "greatest success" when it conducted eight UAV flights in search of a missing man who was feared lost in a remote part of the county. Although officers did not locate the man—nor was he ever found—they concluded that he was not in the area. Miller praised the valuable experience he and his colleagues gained from the operation.

Both Adelman and Miller are hopeful that the FAA will loosen restrictions on small UAVs soon. "Predators, everyone can agree, need to be regulated," Miller says, referring to the several-ton UAVs regularly deployed for bombing runs in Pakistan and Afghanistan. "A two-pounder is another thing." Currently the FAA does not make a distinction between the two. Miller believes that part of the problem is a lack of data upon which the FAA can base its decisions—it simply does not have sufficient evidence of micro UAVs being used safely for police purposes. In this regard, Miller says, every time his department gets approval, they obtain new data, which, in turn, provides evidence to the FAA of the technology's safety and efficacy. Miller predicts that when the restrictions inevitably change, small UAVs will become a must-have tool for U.S. law enforcement agencies: "It's the next taser."

Slippery Slope

Miller's taser comparison is, perhaps, less reassuring than he thinks.

Tasers first emerged in the 1970s, but their widespread adoption by police agencies in the United States is more recent, with new, more powerful models introduced in 1999 and 2003. Taser manufacturers and thousands of U.S. law enforcement agencies hail them as safer than many conventional weapons for subduing dangerous or combative individuals and claim that they have reduced fatalities by providing officers with an effective non-lethal tool.

But skeptics have raised serious doubts. According to the Amnesty International report *Less Than Lethal?,* 334 people—about 90 percent unarmed, and many who did not appear to pose any serious threat—died in the United States after being shocked with tasers or similar conducted-energy weapons between June 2001 and August 2008. The report points out that tasers are "inherently open to abuse as they are easy to carry and easy to use and they can inflict severe pain at the push of a button without leaving substantial marks."

The taser experience speaks to two key issues concerning technologies. First, the outcomes of use are not always apparent at the outset. And, second, as Langdon Winner shows in his classic 1986 book, *The Whale and the Reactor: A Search for Limits in an Age of High Technology,* technologies are inherently political, tied to relations of power and authority. Because technologies don't exist in a social vacuum, they are not mere tools. They become integrated in social systems and everyday life, "part of our very humanity." As such, their uses tend to reflect the priorities of a society's dominant forces.

It is thus hardly surprising that the NIJ sells local police on UAVs not only by touting their value in search-and-rescue operations, but also in marijuana eradication and narcotics interception. What they don't talk about—so as not to scare off the public—are speeding tickets, Adelman says.

So while Miller hopes to use UAVs in Mesa County for rescuing lost children, much of law enforcement UAV deployment most likely will dovetail with Washington's interlocking wars on drugs, terrorism, and "illegal" immigrants, with all of the disturbing implications for civil and human rights those projects entail. The inevitable coupling of UAVs to these "wars," combined with insufficient accountability mechanisms, is a recipe both for the normalization of previously unacceptable levels of policing and for official abuse. This past September, for instance, Pennsylvania governor Ed Rendell was forced to apologize after revelations that a private "counter-terrorism" corporation contracted by the state's Office of Homeland Security had been spying on antiwar and pro-immigrant activists and environmentalists organizing against natural gas drilling.

Training for the Future

A slew of unmanned systems and related technologies are on the research and development table. New projects include insect-sized surveillance vehicles that can fly through open windows, a machine gun or grenade launcher mounted on a treaded robot, a flying humvee, and a solar-powered UAV that can remain airborne for at least five years without having to land. And then there's the "snake-bot"—a snake-like electronic robot with sensors that see and hear. *Wired* reports that this robo-snake can "slither undetected through grass and raise its head to look around, or even climb a tree for a better view. It could be the perfect robot spy."

Many unmanned surveillance and weapon technologies begin in military labs. DARPA (the Defense Advanced Research Projects Agency), the Pentagon's research and development office, is a principal incubator. There's also the Air Force Research Lab, which, according to a *Popular Science* report, released a video about micro UAVs that could carry "incapacitating chemicals, combustible payloads, or even explosives for precision targeting capability." Because the project—named after Anubis, the ancient Egyptian god of the dead—is now complete, Sharon Weinberger, the report's author, speculates that lethal micro UAVs might already be in the field. There are also efforts to capture "thermal fingerprints" from the air and projects aimed at tagging targets with invisible biological paints or micromechanical sensors dropped by UAVs, thus enabling tracking from afar.

If the priorities of the military-industrial complex shape the development and use of UAVs, so too do they shape the pool of future researchers. The military starts young: Navy Admiral Gary Roughead stated in Denver at one of the daily plenary sessions that he could "not stress enough . . . how important it is to get science, technology, engineering, and math in the elementary and middle schools."

Among those responding to such calls is DARPA. According to the September 28, 2010 edition of the Pentagon's *Armed With Science* Webcast, DARPA is investing $10 million in a four-year program called MENTOR (Manufacturing Experimentation and Outreach) that seeks to "develop and motivate a next generation cadre of system designers and manufacturing innovators," and "to reignite a passion for exploration among our nation's youth." It hopes to reach a thousand high schools.

An allied effort called Robotour is now a regular feature of AUVSI shows. At the 2010 conference, scores of middle and high school youths were welcomed to their guided tour of the exhibition hall by a video screen reading, "Robots are WAY Cool (And So Are the Humans Who Create Them)."

Daryl Davidson—the head of the AUVSI Foundation, AUVSI's educational arm, whose mission is "to provide hands-on robotic activities that will interest and challenge students of all levels, and will entice them to pursue a career in the field of robotics"—opened the event. After explaining the foundation's vision of "a world where human lives are protected by and enhanced by the regular use of robotic technologies," Davidson introduced an eight-minute video that showed images of unmanned vehicles on the move across land, sea, and air. There were no scenes of combat, and many of the vehicles performed activities that did not appear to be military-related. But images of uniformed soldiers, vehicles painted in military style—some with U.S. insignia on them—and UAVs fixing crosshairs on people and vehicles, along with the adrenaline-pumping background music, seemed to undercut Davidson's utopian vision.

Far more telling were the words of many of AUVSI's heavyweight attendees. In a plenary session, Army Brigadier General Jake Polumbo asserted the need "to take the bad guys out." Similarly, Dyke Weatherington, Deputy Director of Unmanned Warfare at the Pentagon, told the assembled, "The bad guys are not going away." And Roughead declared, "Our interests in the Navy will remain global." Military readiness, he said, was critical in a world that is both "dangerous" and "unpredictable." With calls to support "our warfighters" invoked repeatedly, research and development for UAVs will most certainly help sustain Washington's global military footprint and profligate defense spending—roughly equal to all the rest of the world's combined—far into the next decade.

The manufacturers of unmanned systems have benefited handsomely from that spending. The *Los Angeles Times* reports that in the last ten years the Pentagon has spent $20 billion on unmanned aerial systems, and the CIA and Congress have invested billions more. The AUVSI show itself has grown five-fold in the last decade. In Southern California alone, the UAV industry employs an estimated 10,000 people.

Costs and Consequences

At present there is no reason to fear that flying humvees and grenade launchers mounted on treaded robots will soon end up in local police department arsenals, or even along the U.S.-Mexico boundary. Yet because it is impossible to separate the domestic use of unmanned vehicles from the military-industrial complex that has given rise to them (especially in the post-9/11 era), it is highly likely that a number of the military instruments that emerge from the burgeoning unmanned-systems industry will end up deployed within the United States.

Should we worry? What was perhaps most striking about AUVSI 2010 and the UAV Caucus technology fair was the almost total absence among attendees and participants of the sense that there might be a downside—human, financial, or otherwise—to the embrace of unmanned systems and the larger national-security complex which they are a part of. Those downsides are inextricably related to the profound social inequalities and injustices that plague American and global society. They are real and growing, and that is unlikely to change without a shift in national priorities.

International relations scholar and retired Army Colonel Andrew Bacevich argues in *Washington Rules: America's Path to Permanent War* that what the United States currently defines as national-security priorities are the basis of endless militarism and a political-economic shipwreck. In addition to facilitating an American policy of global interventionism—with all its violence—these priorities have "allowed Washington to postpone or ignore problems demanding attention here at home."

So even if UAVs were mere tools, such outcomes would still raise an essential question: for whom and for what ends does the toolbox exist?

Critical Thinking

1. What are the benefits of using UAVs for military airstrikes?
2. Should micro UAVs be used in civilian law enforcement?
3. Do the benefits of the use of drones outweigh the costs? Explain.
4. What role should the federal government play in regulating the use of drones?

Create Central

www.mhhe.com/createcentral

Internet References

Unmanned Aerial Vehicle (UAV)
www.theuav.com

UAV Association
www.auvsi.org/Home

Honeywell Defense and Space
www.missionready.com

Civil Aviation Authority
www.caa.co.uk

Defense Advanced Research Projects Agency
www.darpa.mil

Article

Prepared by: Thomas J. Badey, *Randolph-Macon College*

Imaging Cargo's Inner Secrets

CARYN MEISSNER

Learning Outcomes

After reading this article, you will be able to:

- Describe traditional methods of cargo inspection.
- Describe how photon-based technology could be applied to cargo screening.
- Discuss the potential benefits and drawbacks of this new technology.

Each year, millions of cargo containers from around the world are shipped to U.S. ports, holding in their metal "bellies" a variety of essential goods such as food and textiles. While this method of importing freight is necessary for the nation's livelihood, monitoring the contents in such a vast volume of containers poses a challenge to homeland security experts. The events of September 11, 2001, brought transportation security issues into the limelight, including the need to ensure that cargo containers coming into U.S. ports are not carrying clandestine fissile materials.

One of the difficulties scientists face in developing detection technologies for homeland security is how to accurately and efficiently identify hidden nuclear materials without significantly slowing commerce or, worse, bringing it to a halt. With funding from a grant through the University of California (UC) Office of the President, Livermore physicist Marie-Anne Descalle and UC Berkeley collaborators are studying the effectiveness of a radiographic imaging technique for use as a primary screening tool to rapidly scan cargo shipments. "To be effective," says Descalle, "the technology must be able to identify high-atomic-number elements [high-Z, where Z is greater than 72] within a minute or less."

In previous modeling studies performed by the UC Berkeley collaborators, Monte Carlo simulations showed that the proposed radiographic method has the potential to identify small quantities—0.1 kilograms—of uranium and plutonium within containers filled with homogeneous cargo. The method, which measures high-energy photons transmitted through a material, could potentially detect other high-Z materials used as shielding for particular objects. Screening authorities applying the technique could greatly minimize the number of suspect containers, identify possible materials of interest, and then permit definitive searches as warranted.

Narrowing Down the Suspects

Current cargo screening methods typically take one of two forms. In the first method, a truck carrying radiographic equipment scans a row of containers using gamma or x rays. Similar to the way medical x-ray machines capture internal images of people's teeth and bones, this process produces a two-dimensional image of the insides of a container. Inspectors then compare these radiographs to information in the shipping manifests to determine whether additional searches are necessary. Another screening method involves reviewing the manifest, opening the container, and performing a visual inspection. In either case, the process can be quite time-consuming and is not practical for checking millions of containers.

A more efficient approach for identifying illicit materials is being studied by the Livermore-UC Berkeley team. This method uses a new photon-based radiographic technique to rapidly scan each container, which would allow port authorities to narrow the number of suspect containers in a short time and thus facilitate the flow of commerce. Stanley Prussin, a professor of nuclear engineering who leads the UC Berkeley work, says, "Our proposed primary screening process has the potential to rapidly scan containers with a high probability that 99.9 percent of the containers will not require further inspection." Containers that warrant closer examination would undergo a secondary screening during which authorities would either physically inspect the container or use other radiation detection techniques to definitively analyze the contents.

The team's research builds on a previous Livermore–UC Berkeley collaborative project known as the "nuclear car wash." (See *Science and Technology Review*, May 2004, pp. 12–15.) In this detection scheme, a container-laden truck passes over an underground generator that propagates neutrons through the cargo. Similar to driving through a car wash, the truck then proceeds through an array of large plastic scintillators that detect high-energy delayed gamma rays emitted when neutrons interact with fissile material. One concern surrounding this method is that the neutron irradiation would induce some radioactivity. According to Prussin, "Our new approach uses photons that are unlikely to produce radioactivity or would induce such low-intensity radioactivity that it would be negligible."

Small Target, Big Container

Intermodal cargo containers are typically 2.5 meters in height and width, 6 or 12 meters in length, and carry up to 27 metric tons of freight. Thus, finding a small amount (less than 1 kilogram) of hidden fissile material among a container's contents is akin to finding the proverbial needle in a haystack. Prussin says, "Our method is unique because we can in principle detect very small amounts of material, exceeding the Department of Homeland Security's sensitivity requirement for the Cargo Advanced Automated Radiography System." This system is currently being developed as a general screening method for all cargo containers entering U.S. ports.

The team's detection method uses a photon source to direct a beam of high-energy bremsstrahlung photons (x rays) through the side of a container. Depending on the cargo, the photons will either pass through the container relatively unchanged, be completely absorbed by the material inside, or undergo Compton scattering. In the last scenario, lower energy photons are produced when high-energy photons collide with atoms and then lose energy as they "bounce" off the atoms in various directions from their original trajectory.

On the opposite side of the container is a detector with an array of pixelated scintillators that measure all photons emerging from the container. "The intensity, and to some extent the energy spectrum, of the detected photons will be quite different if a material of interest is present in a container," says Prussin. "Those measurements will show us whether a container holds something of concern."

Each photon that reaches the detector produces a signal on an individual pixel. The spatial distribution of the material inside the container as well as the energies of the photons are determined from these signals. Ultimately, researchers plan to place two pixelated detectors at different angles to the container, one at the side and the other at the top, to create a more detailed radiograph that will allow them to see an object of interest and determine its dimensions. They will then use the dimensions and the estimated intensity of the source photons that have passed through the container without any interaction to derive the object's linear attenuation coefficient (a function of material density and atomic number). "The challenge is how to distinguish these photons from photons of the same energy that arrive at the detector after having been scattered one or more times," says Prussin.

Proving the Theory

Descalle, a Monte Carlo simulation expert, leads the modeling effort. The simulations support the experimental campaign and allow the team to explore spaces with larger parameters than would be possible experimentally. Initial simulations determined the requirements for the detector and proved the overall efficacy of the method. Descalle began by modeling various

well-characterized materials that could be used for building the detector to establish which ones would provide the best spatial resolution and highest efficiency. Perhaps one day soon, new materials . . . will provide even greater resolution and efficiency.

Simulations helped the team troubleshoot issues related to detector design. For example, they assessed the effectiveness of materials that could be used to shield each pixel within the detector array. Without shielding, photons coming into the detector would bounce between pixels, which would affect the team's ability to distinguish where the photons originated. "The simulations helped us identify which materials would provide the best shielding and how much shielding would be necessary," says Descalle. "We determined 1 millimeter of tungsten between each pixel would provide the most effective shielding." A prototype detector is now being built that consists of 64 pixels with individual pixel sizes of 0.6 square centimeters.

With the detector design complete, the team is focused on simulating how the method will perform under less than ideal conditions. "We are now modeling the physics of the photons interacting with the cargo and the detector material." says Descalle. "Using simulations, we can model spectra that resemble the energy spectra we expect to see in an actual detector." Additional simulations will verify whether obtaining more images of the container at different angles would improve accuracy. The set of images could be combined using reconstruction algorithms to better identify high-Z materials in three dimensions and approximate linear attenuation coefficients.

The Best of Both Worlds

The Livermore-UC Berkeley team, which also includes professor of nuclear engineering Kai Vetter and two student researchers, began the project in May and will continue perfecting its method over the next three years. Once the researchers demonstrate through simulations that the detection scheme can work under a variety of conditions, they will focus on building a second prototype. "Ultimately, we want to test the detector with surrogate and real materials to assess if it will perform as expected," says Prussin.

The success of the project thus far is very much a team effort. "We are making the best use of the expertise inside the Laboratory and the flexibility of academia to pursue an idea that is important to the public interest," says Prussin. With a little time, hard work, and high-performance computing power, the nation may soon have a more effective mechanism for revealing what is hidden inside the dark recesses of cargo containers.

Critical Thinking

1. What are some of the problems associated with screening cargo containers?
2. How is this process better than previous cargo screening?
3. What are the potential benefits and drawbacks of this new technology?

Create Central

www.mhhe.com/createcentral

Internet References

UC Berkley Lawrence Livermore National Laboratory
www.llnl.gov/

Cargo Advanced Automated Radiography System (CAARS)
www.fbo.gov/index?s=opportunity&mode=form&tab=core&id=5a58e49-735ddaac5a38ba7e15e4e63c6&_cview=1

DHS Cargo Screening
www.dhs.gov/cargo-screening

Customs and Border Patrol (CBP) Cargo Screening
www.dhs.gov/cargo-screening

Smith Detection Customs and Border Protection
www.smithsdetection.com/ports_borders.php

From *Science and Technology Review*, January/February 2010, pp. 17–19.

Article

Prepared by: Thomas J. Badey, *Randolph-Macon College*

Deception Detection

AUSTIN WRIGHT

Learning Outcomes

After reading this article, you will be able to:

- Describe how technology may be used to predict terrorists' intent.

- Discuss problems associated with the testing and refinement of this technology.

- Discuss the potential benefits and drawbacks of this technology.

Metal detectors screen for the means to commit a crime. The Department of Homeland Security is developing technology that screens for the intent to do so.

The department's Future Attribute Screening Technology, or FAST, uses body scanners to sense the fear in your eyes—and in your skin, your heartbeat and even your movements. The system places these and other variables into an algorithm that may be able to determine whether the sum of certain bodily signals is the result of hostile intent, or just someone having a bad day.

Robert P. Burns, deputy director of the Homeland Security Advanced Research Projects Agency, says the technology could help security officers at checkpoints decide which travelers should be called aside for secondary questioning. The technology is still years from completion, he adds.

About 5 percent of Homeland Security's science and technology budget goes toward these reach-for-the-sky endeavors that could have game-changing effects on national security if they succeed. The agency also is developing technologies that would detect drug-trafficking tunnels from above ground, reduce the likelihood of massive power outages and strengthen levees. "We go after the projects or ideas that other people don't want to go after because they are incredibly high-risk and could fail," says Burns, a 1981 Naval Academy graduate who spent 21 years in the private sector. "We're really pushing the envelope in terms of science and technology."

The FAST project, which began in 2006, involves 40 to 50 developers from several organizations and so far has cost the agency $20 million. It combines research from a number of academic fields into a futuristic model for stopping crime before it happens. Project collaborators from Draper Laboratory, a

Massachusetts-based not-for-profit research company, have been working with the agency to translate decades' worth of physiological studies into algorithms that gauge people's involuntary bodily signals.

"We look at a series of physical cues or behavioral cues that you give off that are a direct relation to your physical and emotional thought processes," Burns says. "You can't base anything on any one of these signals. It's the compilation that we look at and that come together."

The technology could be described as a more comprehensive, less intrusive polygraph exam. Already, privacy advocates are expressing concern. The Electronic Privacy Information Center, a Washington-based think tank, plans to push for laws that would ensure that the federal government doesn't keep records of the FAST system's measurements, and the American Civil Liberties Union is exploring its legal options for trying to halt the project.

"We think that it's an invasion of privacy to read someone's physiological bodily functions without their permission," says Jay Stanley, a spokesman for the ACLU. "It's nobody's business what my pulse rate is. It's a profound invasion of human dignity."

Burns counters that the system was designed as a way to help checkpoint security guards make better-informed decisions about which travelers to call aside for further questioning—and not as an Orwellian device for keeping medical tabs on unassuming citizens. He says he worked with Homeland Security's privacy office to make sure the program adheres to all federal laws. "The system does not record or maintain your information," Burns says. "Once any issues are resolved, the information is dumped."

The program's long-term goal is to allow the public to move with greater freedom through airports, border checkpoints and government buildings, he adds. But in its current form, the FAST system can scan only one traveler at a time, and it requires that each person answers a series of questions. Computer software compares physiological measurements taken during questioning to measurements taken before questioning.

"This is a case where technology has finally caught up to the theory, and each of our sensors has a specific theory behind it," Burns says. The system relies mainly on low-cost, widely available equipment. "We should have something that's reasonably cheap."

In 2007, Burns left his job as an executive at American Systems, a technology consulting and engineering firm, to become manager of the FAST program. In mid-2009, he was tapped to become deputy director of Homeland Security's entire advanced-projects agency. The former submarine officer is loud and animated as he describes what he says have been the most fulfilling two years of his professional life. "I was raised to value duty, honor and country," he says. "Being a public servant works really well for me."

In addition to FAST, he oversees several cutting-edge, often-secretive projects. Department researchers are developing contact-less fingerprint scanners, liquid-explosive detection devices and software to help public-safety officials make snap judgments during disasters. Another project, the resilient tunnel, aims to seal leaks and smother fires in commuter tunnels that run under rivers and other bodies of water.

University and private researchers collaborated on the tunnel project in an effort to develop gigantic deployable airbags capable of withstanding extreme water pressure. If the project succeeds, airbags would be able to keep cracking tunnels temporarily intact, giving rescue workers more time to search for trapped survivors. And in the event of a tunnel fire, airbags would be able to seal off the entrances and deprive the fire of oxygen.

"We needed to find a way to protect tunnels, because today's safeguards are super expensive," Burns says. "If we're able to bring some of these projects forward, they could truly change the game."

The FAST system has the potential to catch terrorists and their accomplices before they ever get the chance to launch their attacks, he says. Agency researchers showcased FAST at a September technology exhibition in Cambridge, Mass. They tested the system's ability to identify study participants who planned to commit a crime.

Some of the participants were given items that, if smuggled into the exhibition, would have been capable of causing a major disruption. Others were told to enter the exhibition hall, locate a hidden device and set it off. In both cases the items were inert, a fact that was unknown to the participants. Burns declines to discuss the items, the hidden device or the study's findings. Such information, he says, could compromise future experiments.

"We're doing amazingly well, but this is not ready for prime time," he says. "We would like, in fiscal year 2011, to have a single prototype that we can take to an operational location and perhaps test and do further data collection in a real-world environment."

At the exhibition, study participants, including some who were part of a control group, walked single-file through a security checkpoint. A guard asked them a series of questions. Meanwhile, a laser measured their heart and respiratory rates, an eye tracker measured their blink rates and pupil dilation, a thermal camera measured the heat on their skin and a reconfigured Nintendo Wii Balance Board measured their fidgeting. Nearby computers processed the data, and the system's software recommended to the security guard which participants should be taken aside for follow-up questioning.

"We're looking at the combination of those factors," Burns says. "We've got to make sure that whatever system is developed doesn't cause false readings. I want to make sure that if you're running late to catch your mass transit and you're carrying a large backpack, that I don't pull you over for secondary questioning because you're hot and sweaty. If you've had a bad day and are a little terse, I don't want to pull you over because you're grumpy."

So far, the results show that "we've made great progress," he says. Paul Ekman, a prominent psychologist and a consultant on the FAST project, says he's skeptical of the technology. Over the past 40 years, Ekman has pioneered the study of human emotions and their effects on facial expressions. He is ranked 59th on the Review of General Psychology's list of the 100 most eminent psychologists of the 20th Century.

Ekman was glad to offer recommendations to project researchers, but he says he doubts the system will ever outperform human observers. "I'm a little dubious, but data could convince me," he says. Ekman runs a company that trains security workers to detect signs of malicious intent in people's behaviors, such as body posture and facial twitches that last a quarter of a second. The premise of the Fox television show "Lie to Me" is based on his research.

"Whether the FAST project will succeed in being practically useful is unknown at this point," he says. "Also, testing the technology is very difficult. You can't get the stakes high enough, because of ethical constraints."

People's physiological behaviors change in measurable ways only when the cost of failure is high, and the agency's experiments lack strong negative consequences for the mock criminals, he says. Also, he adds, innocent people sometimes display physiological behaviors that would make them appear malicious, while criminals might be able to train themselves not to display those behaviors.

DHS' New Acquisition Model Shifts Risk to the Private Sector

Thomas A. Cellucci is asking the private sector, rather than taxpayers, to fund new technology that could make Americans safer. Some companies are happy to oblige.

Cellucci, the Department of Homeland Security's chief commercialization officer, has championed a new acquisition model that takes advantage of the growing demand for products that are both innovative and can be marketed to an array of public-safety agencies. His program shifts the government's investment costs to the private sector, which may also reap the potential rewards.

The Defense Department and other federal agencies should follow suit, he says.

"Why on earth would we be spending money and time developing products that private companies would be ready, willing and able to use their own resources to develop?" Cellucci says as he paces around his 10th-story Washington office. His arms flail as he talks passionately about free-market principles and the federal government's tendency to be overly bureaucratic.

"This method, to me, is as clear as the big nose on my face," he says.

But Cellucci acknowledges that the method will never replace traditional acquisition. He sees it as a more efficient way to obtain certain technologies—ones that have potentially huge payoffs for the companies able to develop them. He also emphasizes that this new way of doing business represents only a small part of the department's total acquisition program.

Two years ago, Cellucci left his technology-consulting firm to accept a five-year appointment as Homeland Security's first chief commercialization officer. The position was created to improve relations between the private sector and a then four-year-old department that had already wasted millions of dollars in failed contracts, according to congressional testimony.

After two days on the job, Cellucci had a sudden realization: "Too many companies come to the department with solutions, looking for problems."

He felt that department officials should consult with first responders and law-enforcement officers to find out what technologies and products were needed in the field. Then department officials could post those requirements online. Private companies, Cellucci believed, would invest their own money finding solutions.

The program, which launched in July 2008, is called System Efficacy Through Commercialization, Utilization, Relevance and Evaluation, or SECURE.

Today, its first product, a blast-resistant camera, is ready to hit the market.

The department has posted on its website eight documents outlining technological challenges it hopes to overcome, and an additional 40 are being drafted. These range from the ability to purify vast quantities of water during disasters to the ability to protect restricted areas from intruders.

The department is in discussions with more than 45 companies that say they can develop technology to meet those needs. If they do, they would also be required under the SECURE-program to have third-party testing agencies verify that their products work. Department officials will review test results to decide whether to issue the companies SECURE certificates, which are seals of approval that can be used as marketing tools.

"The hardest part has been convincing people that the program works," says John S. Verrico, a department spokesman. "Folks are used to the traditional acquisition model, where you go to the government, get a big fat check, do the research and development, and sell the product back to the government."

SECURE, though, has gained considerable attention in the private sector. Steve Dennis, technical director for the Homeland Security Advanced Research Projects Agency, oversaw the program's pilot project, the blast-resistant cameras. He wanted low-cost forensic cameras that could withstand explosions and firs. Transit agencies, he believed, would install these cameras in buses and trains, just like airlines install black boxes in planes. Dennis says he originally planned to pay a private company nearly a million dollars to develop the cameras, but wasn't able to obtain government funds.

"This was about the same time the SECURE program started. I said, 'Well, I've got to try it,'" he says.

But Dennis, who has been involved in government research for more than 20 years, says initially he was skeptical of the new acquisition method.

"To get companies to respond to the government's needs usually requires money—there's no way around it," he says. "I didn't think it would work, but I was faced with a problem I really needed to solve, and I had run out of options."

In June 2008, the department posted a nine-page document on its website that outlined the technological problem: "The majority of mass transit systems are not able to reliably collect, store and protect video surveillance of potential future terrorist attacks," the document states.

Dennis was intentionally vague on details, as he hoped companies would come forward with creative solutions. The document also included an estimate of how much transit agencies would be willing to pay for the technology.

In the first two weeks, 26 companies called the department to pitch ideas. Many of them asked how much government money was available. "A lot of them didn't understand," Dennis says. "After we explained, some of them said there was nothing they could do, and others said they would go talk to their executive boards to see if they could get the money themselves."

After a month, he settled on two companies that offered solid proposals and had money on hand to invest: Rhode Island-based Videology and Ontario-based Visual Defence. The companies signed agreements with the department, and they began building prototypes.

Vicki Vey Looney, Visual Defence's vice president for business development and general manager, says her company spent about $200,000 creating its product, SecurEye. "We're a small company with no clout, no high-level access," she says. "But we knew there was not a low-cost, blast-resistant camera module in existence today, and that intrigued us."

She adds, however, that some small startup companies might not have enough money on hand to participate in SECURE.

By October 2008, Visual Defence unveiled a working model.

Dennis says he was shocked by how quickly both companies moved through the process. But Verrico says it makes sense that companies would move faster when their own money is at stake. In traditional acquisition, companies sometimes draw out the process.

"When companies are using government funds or are contracted, there's no incentive for them to make the research and development go fast," he says. "They're going to continue to get the money while the project is ongoing."

Three months later, in January 2009, Homeland Security researchers began testing both companies' products. Typically, the SECURE program would require that they spend their own money having third-party agencies verify that the products work and meet the government's stated needs. But Dennis decided to make an exception in this case. He didn't think it would be fair to ask the private sector to bear the cost of blowing up a bus.

In February 2009, at Maryland's Aberdeen Proving Ground, department scientists set off an explosion that left shards of metal hanging from nearby trees. Fourteen of 16 video cameras that had been placed inside the bus survived, and their video footage was unharmed.

Over the next nine months, testing continued. Today, the two companies are pitching their products to transit agencies in the United States and abroad. Looney says she wishes Visual Defence could have rolled out its camera sooner.

"From the business side of managing the process, DHS has been exceptionally responsive to the private-sector viewpoint," she says. "But it was never fast enough. In the private sector, there's a sense of urgency, and we didn't always feel that same sense of urgency in the federal process."

Cellucci says the department isn't used to working at such a fast pace but that he's evaluating options for streamlining the process. In June, he released a report that says other federal agencies should adopt an acquisition process similar to SECURE.

Homeland Security has already launched a second program, called FutureTECH, which is for laboratories. They can partner with the department to develop technology—at their own expense.

The department has posted on its website 10 documents that detail its FutureTECH needs. All 10 focus on technologies that detect or prevent the detonations of improvised explosive devices. Cellucci says 10 to 15 university and national laboratories have applied to participate in the program.

"We're trying to give to the private sector a golden platter. We're giving them what they spend so much time and money trying to understand: What are the requirements and how many people would want it?" Cellucci says. "And nobody's better at commercializing products than the private sector."

In September, Cellucci flew to California to talk to firefighters and first responders who were battling forest fires. He hoped to identify operational requirements that could be met through the SECURE program.

"So much junk has been sold to first responders that they need assurance that products and services work," he says. "And it's hard to write detailed requirements. You have to observe. You have to question. It's one thing for them to tell you about all the smoke, and it's another thing to be choking in it."

Cellucci returned to Washington with ideas for five operational needs. Documents are being drafted and soon will be posted online.

Critical Thinking

1. Should homeland security funds be used to finance "reach-for-the-sky-endeavors?" Why or why not?
2. Is reading someone's physiological body functions an invasion of privacy? Explain your answer.
3. What are the potential benefits and drawbacks of the use of this new technology?

Create Central

www.mhhe.com/createcentral

Internet References

Electronic Privacy Information Center
   www.epic.org/

Future Attribute Screening Technology
   http://epic.org/privacy/fastproject/

Homeland Security Advanced Research Projects Agency
   www.dhs.gov/st-hsarpa

System Efficacy through Commercialization, Utilization, Relevance and Evaluation (SECURE Program)
   www.dhs.gov/secure-system-efficacy-through-commercialization-utilization-relevance-and-evaluation-program

U.S. Department of Homeland Security FutureTECH
   www.dhs.gov/futuretech

Unit VIII

UNIT

Prepared by: Thomas J. Badey, *Randolph-Macon College*

Intelligence and Homeland Security

The U.S. intelligence community has received much of the blame for the failure to prevent the attacks that occurred on 9/11. Critics argue that the intelligence community failed in its primary task: to protect the United States from foreign threats. After numerous inquiries and commission reports into the intelligence failures of 9/11, in December of 2004, President George W. Bush signed into law the Intelligence Reform and Terrorism Prevention Act. The centerpiece of the legislation was the appointment of a new Director of National Intelligence (DNI) to oversee the intelligence community—a function previously carried out by the Director of the Central Intelligence Agency. While hailed as "the most sweeping intelligence reform since the National Security Act of 1947," little has changed. The agency directors talk openly about increased cooperation, but the turf wars continue. Behind the scenes, intelligence officials appear more concerned with protecting their own fiefdoms and budgets from the potential encroachment of other agencies than pursuing the reforms needed to address future threats.

The U.S. intelligence community was established by the National Security Act of 1947 to cope with the rapidly growing Soviet threat. For more than 40 years, most of its resources were targeted at the Soviet Union. Organizational structures and collection systems were developed specifically to gather intelligence from state actors. The dominant role of the military agencies in the community reflects Cold War priorities. After the fall of the Soviet Empire in 1990, despite significant debate and calls for reform, no significant structural reforms were made.

In the mid-90s, in response to changing priorities and emerging threats, the intelligence community began to shift its focus increasingly to international terrorism and nonstate actors. Rather than designing new systems to deal with these threats, the intelligence community attempted to use existing systems to spy on nonstate actors. Little effort was made to reform its huge bureaucracies, eliminate the duplication of effort, address the lack of interoperability, and improve interagency communications. Rather than rethinking its approach to intelligence collection and analysis, state-centric models of threat assessment continued to prevail. The fundamental flaw of this approach was reflected in the belief that the best way to protect the homeland and prevent terrorism was to attack or invade a country.

The articles in this unit examine the role of the intelligence community in homeland security. The first focuses on the evolving intelligence mission of the Department of Homeland Security. It suggests that rather than focusing on a particular adversary or threat, the post-9/11 security architecture must adopt a multifaceted approach in its intelligence mission. It argues that the DHS is uniquely situated to work with state, local, and private sector partners and thus, rather than competing with traditional intelligence agencies, should focus its intelligence capabilities on its core strengths. It suggests that a smaller, more focused program would be more efficient and effective. The second reading maintains that despite a historic reluctance to establish a domestic intelligence agency, the United States has created a vast domestic intelligence establishment. It states that a "better-informed national discussion about domestic intelligence" is needed. The last article in this unit examines the new emphasis among law-enforcement and intelligence agencies to analyze social media as a means of predicting potential crises. This type of predictive analysis collects large amounts of public data in order to forecast potential future threats.

Article   Prepared by: Thomas J. Badey, *Randolph-Macon College*

"Homeland Security and Intelligence: Next Steps in Evolving the Mission"

Hearing before the House Permanent Select Committee on Intelligence.

Learning Outcomes

After reading this article, you will be able to:

- Describe the focus of the "new domestic security architecture."

- Discuss how DHS intelligence differs from traditional intelligence agencies.

- Identify key elements of a separate DHS intelligence mission.

- Discuss the role of state and local agencies and private sector entities.

American expectations of how their government secures the United States have evolved substantially, especially during the post-9/11 decade. From the post-World War II, 20th-century evolution of the national security architecture in the United States, focused on countering overseas nation-states with conventional forces, we now face requirements to protect at home. And not only to protect, but to prevent: the new, domestic security architecture is targeted more at securing borders, infrastructure, and cyberspace with defensive measures as it is at pursuing any single adversary with offensive measures.

The growth of our expectations of domestic security, and the evolution of threats away from traditional state actors toward non-state entities—drug cartels, organized crime, and terrorism are prominent examples—suggest that the DHS intelligence mission should be threat agnostic. Though the impetus for creating this new agency, in the wake of the 9/11 attacks, was clearly terrorism-based, the kinds of tools now deployed, from border security to cyber protection, are equally critical in fights against emerging adversaries.

The DHS enterprise is more complex than other agencies responsible for America's security, and its intelligence mission is correspondingly multifaceted. Its intelligence missions range from providing homeland security-specific intelligence at the federal level; integrating intelligence vertically through DHS elements; and working with state/local/private sector partners to draw their intelligence capabilities into a national picture and provide them with information. DHS, as it works to sharpen these missions, benefits from both a legislative mandate and a competitive advantage in a few areas that are unique within the federal intelligence community:

- Securing borders and analyzing travel—from threats such as terrorists, drug cartels, and alien smugglers—including integrating travel data with other federal information;
- Protecting critical infrastructure, from advising transportation partners on how to secure new transport nodes to providing sectors with after-action analysis of the infrastructure vulnerabilities exposed by overseas attacks; and
- Preventing cyber intrusions, from red-teaming vulnerabilities in the US private sector to sharing best practices among corporate entities.

Many agencies conduct all-source analysis of threat based on more traditional models of intelligence. As DHS grows its intelligence mission, though, we should understand that its development will benefit from unique data and responsibilities that other agencies do not share. The foundation for a separate DHS intelligence mission includes a few key elements:

- Access to unique, homeland-relevant data, such as CPB and ICE information;
- Responsibility for securing the border and critical infrastructure;
- Access to personnel who have intimate tactical knowledge of current issues and trends in these areas; and
- Responsibility for serving state/local partners as well as private sector partners in key infrastructure sectors.

In an age of budget constraints, pressure on DHS to focus on core areas of responsibility and capability—and to avoid emphasis on areas performed by other entities—may allow for greater focus on these areas of core competency while the agency sheds intelligence functions less central to the DHS mission. Analysts and managers in Washington's sprawling intelligence architecture often speak of the value of competitive analysis—analysts at different agencies, for example, looking at similar problems to ensure that we miss no new perspective, no potentially valuable data source.

There remains room for this type of analysis, but there are enough agencies pursuing the terrorist adversary to allow DHS to build a new analytic foundation that emphasizes data, analytic questions, and customer groups that are not the focus for other agencies. Analysis that helps private-sector partners better understand how to mitigate threats to infrastructure, for example, should win more resourcing than a focus on all-source analysis of general threats, such as work on assessing the perpetrators of attacks. Conversely, all-source analysis of terrorist groups and general terrorist trends should remain the domain of other intelligence agencies.

In contrast to intelligence agencies that have responsibilities for more traditional areas of national security, DHS's mandate should allow for collection, dissemination, and analytic work that is focused on more specific homeward-focused areas. First, the intelligence mission could be directed toward areas where DHS has inherent strengths and unique value (e.g., where its personnel and data are centered) that overlap with its legislative mandate. Second, this mission direction should emphasize areas that are not served by other agencies, particularly state/local partners whose needs are not a primary focus for any other federal agency.

In all these domains, public and private, DHS customers will require information with limited classification; in contrast to most other federal intelligence entities, DHS should focus on products that start at lower classification levels, especially unclassified and FOUO, and that can be disseminated by means almost unknown in the federal intelligence community (phone trees, Blackberries, etc.).

Partnerships and collaboration will be a determining factor in whether this refined mission succeeds. As threat grows more localized, the prospect that a state/local partner will generate the first lead to help understand a new threat, or even an emerging cell, will grow. And the federal government's need to train, and even staff, local agencies, such as major city police departments, will grow. Because major cities are the focus for threat, these urban areas also will become the sources of intelligence that will help understand these threats at the national level, DHS might move toward decentralizing more of its analytic workforce to partner with state/local agencies in the collection and dissemination of intelligence from the local level.

This new approach to intelligence—serving local partners' requirements, providing intelligence in areas (such as infrastructure) not previously served by intelligence agencies, and disseminating information by new means—reflects a transition in how Americans perceive national security. For this reason, state/local agencies, as clients for DHS intelligence, should also be involved in the development of requirements for what kinds of intelligence on emerging threats would be most helpful, from changing tactics for smuggling aliens into the United States to how to understand overseas terrorist incidents and translate them into analysis for the US.

Similarly, different private sectors in the United States, from the hospitality industry to transportation, should drive requirements for DHS, in addition to serving as sources for information about what emerging vulnerabilities these industries are seeing. DHS should utilize existing public-private partnerships to both drive requirements and aid distribution.

After the Mumbai attacks, for example, DHS intelligence might have partnered with private sector entities in the hospitality industries—and state and local police agencies responsible for major hotel centers and ports—to develop unclassified graphics and text explaining how the terrorists entered ports; how they breached perimeter security at facilities in the city; how security within facilities struggled during the ensuing battle; and how the attacks compared with other attacks in recent years against public buildings. Most or all of this information would have been available in public media, and it can be displayed in interactive, graphic format, with support from analysts who specialize not in international terrorism but instead in engineering, building security, port security, etc. The requirements for any product would have been driven by the hospitality industry and major city police chiefs. None of this bears any resemblance to what more traditional intelligence agencies have done in the post-WWII world of foreign intelligence; this type of analytic product is more closely aligned with the new, and growing, world of homeland security intelligence.

By focusing intelligence collection, dissemination, and analysis in these areas, DHS could grow an intelligence architecture that builds on its core strengths, avoid competition with agencies in other areas, such as general terrorism analysis; and provide unique product and partnerships that other agencies not only lack but will not view as their core competencies.

Because homeland security intelligence requires a new understanding of products, customers, and delivery, training managers and analysts must reflect a way of doing business that is fundamentally different than the business practices taught at agencies that have focused historically on foreign intelligence. DHS might consider the development of a homeland security training institute that develops this training—from new ways to portray information geospatially to different paths for developing requirements from state and local partners—as an entirely new enterprise. This training should include a separate element responsible for research, for bringing in American and foreign scholars who look at this issue, and for ensuring that doctrines for collecting, reporting, and analyzing knowledge in the homeland security environment is captured in one place and documented.

The creation of DHS led to a rapid growth in a workforce, and a thirst for analytic product, that required the US Government to move quickly, before the foundations of homeland security intelligence were established and before we had the luxury of a full post-9/11 decade to understand where we need to go. We have an opportunity now to step back and review how much this new enterprise differs from traditional analysis, and how we can succeed, beyond what we understood even five years ago, in delivering new, innovative product to different customers. And in how we can develop simple processes through which they deliver clear requirements to analysts in Washington and at fusion centers across the country. This review provides that opportunity.

Critical Thinking

1. Should the DHS intelligence mission be threat agnostic? Why or why not?

2. In what areas does DHS intelligence have a competitive advantage?

3. What key elements should be included in a separate DHS intelligence mission?

4. What role can state and local agencies and private sector entities play in the DHS intelligence mission?

Create Central

www.mhhe.com/createcentral

Internet References

The Aspen Institute Homeland Security Program
www.aspeninstitute.org/policy-work/homeland-security

DHS National Infrastructure Protection Plan
www.dhs.gov/national-infrastructure-protection-plan

DHS Homeland Infrastructure Threat and Risk Analysis Center (HITRAC)
www.dhs.gov/about-hitrac

U.S. House of Representatives, January 18, 2012.

Article Prepared by: Thomas J. Badey, *Randolph-Macon College*

Domestic Intelligence Today: More Security but Less Liberty?

Erik J. Dahl

Learning Outcomes

After reading this article, you will be able to:

- Describe the current domestic intelligence organizations.

- Explain the arguments for creating a new domestic intelligence agency.

- Discuss the tension between the need for security and civil liberties.

One of the most important questions about intelligence reform after the 9/11 attacks was whether the United States should establish a new domestic intelligence agency—an American equivalent of the British MI-5, some suggested. Supporters of the idea argued that only a completely new organization would be able to provide the fresh thinking and strength of focus that was needed, and they pointed out that the US was the only Western country without such an organization. Critics said the Federal Bureau of Investigation (FBI) was already well on its way to reinventing itself as just the sort of intelligence-driven agency the country needed and that establishing a new domestic intelligence agency would require the creation of a costly new bureaucracy to duplicate capabilities that already existed.

That debate was eventually settled in the negative. Although a number of major reforms were made to American intelligence—including, most notably, the establishment of the position of the Director of National Intelligence (DNI)—no central domestic intelligence agency has been created. Instead, the intelligence functions of the FBI have been beefed up and several new organizations have been created, including the National Counterterrorism Center (NCTC). Although occasionally the argument is still heard that the US needs a domestic intelligence service,[1] in general most intelligence professionals and outside observers appear to agree that no new domestic intelligence organization is necessary.

But this essay argues that even though we as a nation decided not to establish a domestic intelligence organization, we have in recent years done just that: we have created a vast domestic intelligence establishment, one which few Americans understand and which does not receive the oversight and scrutiny it deserves. There is good news here: this domestic intelligence system appears to have been successful in increasing security within the US, as demonstrated by numerous foiled terrorist plots and the lack of another major successful attack on American soil since 9/11. But there is also bad news: these gains are coming at the cost of increasing domestic surveillance and at the risk of civil liberties.

This essay begins by reviewing the debate over whether a domestic intelligence agency was needed after 9/11. It then describes the current system of homeland security intelligence within the US, including the growth of new intelligence organizations at the state and local level, and argues that this constitutes a de facto domestic intelligence organization. Next it demonstrates that the development of this domestic intelligence structure has moved the balance between security and liberty quite firmly in the direction of more security, but less liberty. The essay concludes by arguing that even though these developments might very well be acceptable to the American people, we cannot know whether they are acceptable or not without a better-informed national discussion about domestic intelligence.[2]

The Debate Over a Domestic Intelligence Agency

One aspect of the debate over intelligence reform following the 9/11 attacks was the question of whether the United States should establish a new domestic intelligence agency. Although the question was often framed in terms of whether the US should create an organization modeled on the British MI-5, several options were widely discussed.

The change supported by many experts was to form an independent intelligence service within the FBI. The FBI already had the lead on most domestic intelligence issues and since 9/11 had been increasing its focus on intelligence, so forming such an organization within the FBI appeared to be the simplest option, involving few changes to the rest of the intelligence community. A group of six experienced intelligence and national security experts, writing in *The Economist,* argued for this approach.[3] The *WMD Commission Report* also supported such a change, proposing that the counter-terrorism, counter-intelligence, and intelligence services of the FBI be combined to create a new National Security Service.[4]

Critics, however, argued either that such a change was unnecessary because the FBI was already transforming itself into an intelligence-driven agency, or that it would be a danger-ous move because the FBI was likely to remain primarily a law enforcement organization, unsuited to the intelligence mission and inclined to use its increasing intelligence and surveillance powers at the risk of civil liberties.

Another idea was to create a new intelligence agency under the newly created Department of Homeland Security (DHS). Federal Judge Richard Posner, for example, argued for such an organization, to be called the Security Intelligence Service, with the head of this agency to be dual-hatted as the DNI's dep-uty for domestic intelligence.[5]

The idea that was most often talked about was to create a wholly new, independent organization, possibly modeled on the British MI-5 (which is officially known as the Security Ser-vice). Supporters of the idea noted that most Western countries have some sort of domestic intelligence agency. In Britain MI-5 collects and analyzes domestic intelligence, but it has no police power or arrest authority; foreign intelligence in the British sys-tem is handled by MI-6, the Secret Intelligence Service.[6] Critics argued that the MI-5 model was unlikely to be applicable to the US because Britain is a much smaller, more centralized coun-try with fewer local police forces and a powerful Home Office, while the US is much larger and decentralized, with thousands of independent local police and sheriff's departments.

Experts also examined domestic intelligence models from other countries, including Australia, India, France, and Germany.[7] Other than MI-5, the model most often pointed to as appropri-ate for the US was the Canadian Security Intelligence Service (CSIS). The CSIS was established relatively recently (1984), after the Canadian national police force (the Royal Canadian Mounted Police) was found to have broken the law and violated civil liberties in dealing with Quebec separatist groups and other internal threats.[8]

Support for a new domestic intelligence agency was never as strong as it had been for other major reforms such as the estab-lishment of a Director of National Intelligence. The 9/11 Com-mission recommended against creating such a new agency, and although discussion continues about whether or not the nation's domestic intelligence structure is adequately organized, there seems to be little impetus for setting up a US version of MI-5.[9]

The most extensive study of the question was conducted by RAND, at the request of the Department of Homeland Secu-rity, and resulted in three volumes of reports.[10] RAND was specifically not asked by DHS to offer recommendations, but these reports can hardly be seen as ringing endorsements for the idea of a new domestic agency. When the RAND researchers surveyed a group of experts, most expressed the view that the current organization for domestic intelligence wasn't very good; but they also said they did not think that any reorganization was

likely to improve the situation.[11] Gregory Treverton summed up the study this way: "Caution and deliberations are the watch-words for this study's conclusions."[12]

Current Domestic Intelligence Organization

In its analysis for DHS, RAND outlined what it called the "domestic intelligence enterprise."[13] This enterprise encom-passes a complex system that includes counterterrorism organi-zations led by the NCTC; other federal-level organizations and efforts, including those within the FBI, DHS, and Department of Defense; and state, local, and private sector activities. Some of the experts consulted by RAND saw this domestic intelli-gence enterprise as problematic because it was uncoordinated and thus potentially ineffective; one described domestic intel-ligence as "a pickup ballgame without a real structure, leader-ship, management, or output."[14] But even though our domestic intelligence system may not have a centralized structure, it is more coordinated and also more effective than most Americans realize, and constitutes a de facto—but little understood—domestic intelligence system.

It is difficult, if not impossible, for the American public to accurately gauge the size of the country's domestic intelligence effort. Much of that effort is deservedly kept secret, as is the overall scope of America's intelligence activities at home and abroad. The size of the national intelligence community is not precisely known, but in 2009 then-Director of National Intel-ligence Dennis Blair described it as a 200,000-person, $75 billion per year enterprise.[15] By the next year the intelligence budget had grown to $80.1 billion. That number is believed to be twice what it was in 2001, and it is considerably more than the $53 billion spent on the Department of Homeland Security in 2010.[16]

An investigation into the country's intelligence and coun-terterrorism structure by *The Washington Post* described what it called "a Top Secret America hidden from public view and lacking in thorough oversight."[17] The *Post* found that some 854,000 people hold top secret security clearances, and that at least 263 government agencies and organizations had been cre-ated or reorganized as a response to 9/11.

The office of the DNI is itself a large entity, with some 1,800 employees as of 2010, and has come to be considered one of the seventeen top-level agencies of the intelligence commu-nity.[18] Within the Department of Homeland Security there are at least nine separate intelligence elements, including the Office of Intelligence and Analysis and intelligence organizations of six separate DHS components: Customs and Border Protection, Immigration and Customs Enforcement, Citizenship and Immi-gration Services, Transportation Security Administration, the Coast Guard, and the Secret Service.[19]

Since 9/11 the FBI has greatly increased the priority it gives to intelligence and counter-terrorism, setting up a new National Security Branch, increasing the number and status of its intel-ligence analysts, and establishing Field Intelligence Groups in each of its fifty-six field offices. The FBI has also been busy developing new networks of informants within the United States: its 2008 budget request said that it "recruits new CHS [confidential human sources] every day," and needed more money to do it, with apparently 15,000 sources needing to be validated.[20]

Some elements of national and military intelligence have become more involved in domestic surveillance since 9/11. The National Security Agency (NSA), for example, which was revealed in 2005 to have been involved in what was called the Terrorist Surveillance Program, reportedly continues to conduct a significant amount of domestic intelligence collection.[21] As an indication of the growth in the NSA's business—although presumably much of the growth is in foreign intelligence—the agency is building a new data storage center in Utah that will reportedly cost $1.7 billion and occupy as much as one million square feet of space, larger than the US Capitol building.

Some domestic counterintelligence activities of the Department of Defense have drawn criticism since 9/11, in particular the now-defunct Counterintelligence Field Activity (CIFA). But in general, military and other national security intelligence capabilities have not been utilized domestically to any great degree, because of civil liberties concerns as well as Posse Comitatus restrictions on the use of military personnel for law enforcement. For example, an effort to establish a National Applications Office (NAO) to coordinate the domestic use of reconnaissance satellites failed after members of Congress opposed it.[22] And the US Northern Command, established after the 9/11 attacks to coordinate US military support for homeland defense and security, has been careful to focus most of its intelligence efforts toward homeland defense—focusing on threats from outside the US—and takes a very limited role in domestic intelligence and surveillance (such as helping to coordinate reconnaissance assets when needed to support state and federal authorities following emergencies such as the Gulf oil spill and Hurricane Katrina).

Another area where military capabilities have not seen widespread domestic use is with unmanned aerial vehicles, or UAV. Although UAV have become a mainstay of US military operations overseas, they are little used within the US, even by civilian authorities. United States Customs and Border Protection does operate small numbers of UAV along the country's northern and southern borders, and a few local law enforcement agencies have experimented with the technology, but they remain an underutilized capability.[23]

A growth area for intelligence since 9/11 has been in the development of national intelligence centers, combining and coordinating efforts of a wide variety of organizations on specific problems. In some cases these centers are new, such as the National Counterterrorism Center and the National Counterproliferation Center. In other cases already existing intelligence organizations have been redesignated as national centers, such as the National Maritime Intelligence Center at Suitland, Maryland, and the National Center for Medical Intelligence at Fort Detrick, Maryland.

There are a number of other new or growing federal intelligence agencies and organizations, including the El Paso Intelligence Center (EPIC), a multi-agency counter drug center run jointly by the DEA and DHS, and the interagency National Gang Intelligence Center. There are also operational organizations that are significant users of intelligence, including the 106 FBI-led Joint Terrorism Task Forces that are critical tools in combating domestic terrorism, and High Intensity Drug Trafficking Area (HIDTA) Intelligence and Investigative Support Centers, which are counter-drug efforts sponsored by the Office of National Drug Control Policy.[24] There are also two Joint Interagency Task Forces (JIATFs), one in Hawaii and the other in Key West, Florida, which are interagency counter-drug organizations nominally under Department of Defense control.

At the next level down from the federal level of intelligence is a network of seventy-two state and local intelligence fusion centers. These centers receive DHS funding and support, and many of them have a DHS intelligence liaison officer assigned to them full time, providing analytical support and reach-back capability to DHS headquarters. These fusion centers are not widely known, but they have had some notable successes in helping to prevent terrorist attacks and assisting law enforcement agencies in capturing criminals.[25]

These fusion centers, however, have also generated controversy.[26] The American Civil Liberties Union argues that:

> The federal government's increasing efforts to formalize, standardize, and network these state, local, and regional intelligence centers—and plug them directly into the intelligence community's Information Sharing Environment—are the functional equivalent of creating a new national domestic intelligence agency that deputizes a broad range of personnel from all levels of government, the private sector, and the military to spy on their fellow Americans.[27]

Bruce Fein, a lawyer and former federal official who is a frequent government critic, testified before the House Homeland Security Committee that the US "should abandon fusion centers that engage 800,000 state and local law enforcement officers in the business of gathering and sharing allegedly domestic or international terrorism intelligence."[28]

The best known of these state and local organizations is actually not part of the national fusion center network: the New York Police Department's intelligence division.[29] The NYPD intelligence effort includes liaison officers in some eleven countries overseas, analysts who reportedly speak more languages than can be found in the New York office of the FBI, and even a program that takes police recruits out of the police academy and places them in undercover positions, in some cases conducting investigations inside mosques in the New York City area.[30]

Balancing Security and Liberty

The 9/11 Commission argued that we should not have to trade security for liberty, calling the choice between the two a "false choice."[31] But it seems that the balance and the tradeoff are very real today. There is nothing new in this: as a RAND study notes, "Throughout US history, in times of national security crisis, civil liberties have been curtailed in exchange for perceived greater security, the balance between liberties and security generally being restored after each crisis."[32] What is new today, ten years after the 9/11 attacks, is that the balance has not yet been restored, and in some ways the balance continues to shift toward greater governmental power.

In some cases, this increased government authority is obvious: more intrusive screening at airports, for example, continues the tilt toward greater security at the expense of liberty (and occasionally, dignity). In other cases, the greater powers of government are less evident. As an example, there is a great deal of attention paid today to the previously little-known Foreign Intelligence Surveillance Court (FISC), which is empowered to issue warrants for domestic searches and surveillance under the Foreign Intelligence and Surveillance Act (FISA). But while fewer than fifty FISA orders were issued in 2006, during that same year the FBI issued more than 28,000 of what are called National Security Letters (NSLs), which can authorize search or surveillance of US persons but do not require review by a court or judge.[33] In 2010 the FBI made 24,287 NSL requests pertaining to US persons, but only 1,579 applications to the FISC for surveillance and search authority.[34]

The FBI is expanding its domestic intelligence and surveillance operations in other ways, as well. It is changing its own internal rules to give its agents more leeway to conduct investigations and surveillance, such as by searching databases or sorting through a person's trash.[35] And it appears to be making greater use of undercover informants in intelligence investigations, leading in some cases to successful arrests and prosecutions, but in others to controversy.[36]

One of the most controversial aspects of domestic intelligence after 9/11 was the Patriot Act, which significantly expanded the ability of government authorities to collect information within the US and lowered the "wall" separating criminal investigation from foreign intelligence gathering. In the years since it was first passed several of the Patriot Act's provisions have been renewed, adding tighter controls of government activity. But in general the government has retained its increased authorities. Several of these provisions, which had been scheduled to "sunset," or expire, were renewed in May 2011, with the renewal receiving as much attention for the way it happened—President Obama, who was in Europe, authorized the use of an autopen machine to sign the bill into law—as for the fact that it occurred at all.[37]

Because so much of intelligence work—including domestic intelligence—needs to be hidden from view, a considerable amount of secrecy might be acceptable as long as the American public could be confident that its legislators or others were watching out for the public. As Gregory Treverton writes, "The public doesn't need to know the details of what is being done in its name. It does need to know that some body independent of an administration does know and does approve."[38] The problem is that Congressional oversight of intelligence matters is widely regarded as weak, and much of the day-to-day supervision of intelligence agencies is conducted by organizations such as the National Security Council, the Office of Management and Budget, and agency inspectors general. Such oversight is often useful, but it still means the Executive Branch is supervising itself.

Concerns over oversight of the national intelligence community are heightened when the focus shifts to state and local intelligence efforts. Although most local fusion centers receive federal funds and receive operating guidelines from DHS and the Department of Justice, they are under state or local control and as such are not subject to any strong, centralized oversight. And programs such as the Nationwide Suspicious Activity Reporting Initiative, which is being implemented in cities and states around the country, show great potential for helping to prevent terrorist attacks and detect other criminal activity, but they also raise questions about civil liberties.[39]

Critics argue that in the past ten years the balance between security and liberty has shifted far too much toward security, leading to a great increase in government power. In the words of Laura Murphy of the ACLU, "It feels as though scissors have cut out whole portions of our liberties in the name of fighting the war on terrorism."[40] This may be an overstatement, but it does seem clear that the development of a vast domestic intelligence structure since 9/11 has moved the balance quite firmly in the direction of more security, and less liberty.

Conclusion: Where to From Here?

By its very nature, domestic and homeland security intelligence is intrusive and risks infringing on civil liberties. As then-Secretary of Homeland Security Michael Chertoff put it:

> Intelligence, as you know, is not only about spies and satellites. Intelligence is about the thousands and thousands of routine, everyday observations and activities. Surveillances, interactions—each of which may be taken in isolation as not a particularly meaningful piece of information, but when fused together, gives us a sense of the patterns and the flow that really is at the core of what intelligence analysis is really about.[41]

These thousands and thousands of observations are largely observations about people and events in America, and in the years since 9/11 America has created a domestic intelligence system to collect them. In some cases the people are terrorists or other types of criminals, and the intelligence collected has helped to prevent bad events from happening. But in many cases these observations, this intelligence, is about routine activities undertaken by ordinary Americans and others who do not intend to cause harm.

Unless the threat situation changes dramatically, we are not likely to see a new American domestic intelligence agency anytime soon. In the place of an "American MI-5," however, a huge and expensive domestic intelligence system has been constructed. This system has thus far succeeded in keeping America safer than most experts would have predicted ten years ago, but it has also reduced civil liberties in ways that many Americans fail to understand. Precisely because it was unplanned and is decentralized, this domestic intelligence system has not received the oversight it deserves. In the long run, American liberty as well as security will gain from a fuller discussion of the benefits and risks of homeland security intelligence.

Notes

1. See for example James Burch, "Intelligence and Homeland Security," in *Intelligence: The Secret World of Spies, An Anthology,* 3rd ed., Loch K. Johnson and James J. Wirtz, eds. (NY: Oxford University Press, 2011), 499–516.

2. Although this essay focuses on domestic intelligence, the debate over the balance between security and liberty touches on many other issues including the proper handling and treatment of terrorism suspects, enhanced interrogation and torture, and overseas military operations such as targeted killings. For discussion of some of these broader issues, see the hearing on "Civil Liberties and National Security" before the House Judiciary Committee Subcommittee on the Constitution, Civil Rights, and Civil Liberties, December 9, 2010, http://judiciary .house.gov/hearings/hear_101209.html.

3. "America Needs More Spies," *The Economist,* July 12, 2003.

4. Commission on the Intelligence Capabilities of the United States Regarding Weapons of Mass Destruction (the Silberman-Robb Commission), *Report to the President of the United States* (March 31, 2005), 465, www.fas.org/irp/offdocs/wmd_ chapter10.pdf.

5. Posner is a prolific writer on intelligence (and other topics). See for example his "Remaking Domestic Intelligence," American Enterprise Institute working paper #111, June 20, 2005, www.aei.org/docLib/20050621_DomesticIntelligence3.pdf.

6. For background on MI-5 see Todd Masse, *Domestic Intelligence in the United Kingdom: Applicability of the MI-5 Model to the United States* (Washington, DC: Congressional Research Service, May 19, 2003).

7. Burch, "Intelligence and Homeland Security"; Brian A. Jackson, ed., *Considering the Creation of a Domestic Intelligence Agency in the United States: Lessons from the Experiences of Australia, Canada, France, Germany, and the United Kingdom* (Santa Monica, CA: RAND, 2009).

8. Gregory F. Treverton, *Intelligence for an Age of Terror* (NY: Cambridge University Press, 2009), 127. Richard Posner also sees value in the CSIS model; see his "Remaking Domestic Intelligence," cited above.

9. An example of the continuing discussion about domestic intelligence is Eric Rosenbach and Aki Peritz, "Domestic Intelligence," Belfer Center for Science and International Affairs Memorandum, Harvard Kennedy School, July 2009, at http://belfercenter.ksg.harvard.edu/publication/19152/ domestic_intelligence.html.

10. Brian A. Jackson, ed., *The Challenge of Domestic Intelligence in a Free Society* (Santa Monica, CA: RAND, 2009); Jackson, *Considering the Creation of a Domestic Intelligence Agency in the United States;* and Gregory F. Treverton, *Reorganizing U.S. Domestic Intelligence: Assessing the Options* (Santa Monica, CA: RAND, 2008).

11. Treverton, *Reorganizing U.S. Domestic Intelligence,* chap. 5.

12. Treverton, *Reorganizing U.S. Domestic Intelligence,* 101.

13. Jackson, *The Challenge of Domestic Intelligence,* Figure 3.1, p. 52.

14. Ibid., note 14, p. 72.

15. Siobhan Gorman, "Spy Chief Says U.S. Hunting al Qaeda More Effectively," *The Wall Street Journal,* September 17, 2009.

16. Ken Dilanian, "U.S. Reveals Skyrocketing Cost of Intelligence Gathering Since 9/11 Attacks," *Los Angeles Times,* October 28, 2010.

17. Dana Priest and William M. Arkin, "A Hidden World, Growing Beyond Control," *The Washington Post,* July 19, 2010.

18. The personnel figures were noted in a speech by David R. Shedd, the Deputy Director of National Intelligence for Policy, Plans, and Requirements, in April 2010: www.dni.gov/ speeches/20100406_2_speech.pdf. It should be noted that the current DNI, James Clapper, has said he intends to streamline the office.

19. Mark A. Randol, "The Department of Homeland Security Intelligence Enterprise: Operational Overview and Oversight Challenges for Congress," Congressional Research Service, March 19, 2010.

20. Federal Bureau of Investigation, *FY 2008 Authorization and Budget Request to Congress,* 4–23 and 4–24, at www.justice .gov/jmd/2008justification/pdf/33_fbi_se.pdf. See also the Federation of American Scientists Secrecy News Blog, "The FBI as an Intelligence Organization," August 27, 2007, www .fas.org/blog/secrecy/2007/08/the_fbi_as_an_intelligence_org .html.

21. Siobhan Gorman, "NSA's Domestic Spying Grows as Agency Sweeps Up Data," *Wall Street Journal,* March 10, 2008.

22. Jeffrey T. Richelson, "The Office That Never Was: The Failed Creation of the National Applications Office," *International Journal of Intelligence and Counterintelligence* 24, no. 1 (2011): 68–118.

23. Chad C. Haddal and Jeremiah Gertler, *Homeland Security: Unmanned Aerial Vehicles and Border Surveillance* (Washington, DC; Congressional Research Service, July 8, 2010); Peter Finn, "Domestic Use of Aerial Drones by Law Enforcement Likely to Prompt Privacy Debate," *The Washington Post,* January 23, 2011.

24. The HIDTA program is a combined effort of federal, state, and local law enforcement authorities covering at least part of forty-five states. As of 2010, there were thirty-two Intelligence and Investigative Support Centers in the program. See Office of National Drug Control Policy, *High Intensity Drug Trafficking Areas Program Report to Congress* (June 2010), www.whitehousedrugpolicy.gov/pdf/hidta_2010.pdf.

25. The Colorado Information and Analysis Center (CIAC), for example, was recognized as the Fusion Center of the Year in February 2010 for its support to the Najibullah Zazi terrorism investigation, and more recently it provided information that helped lead to the arrest of a bombing suspect; see "Fusion Centers: Empowering State and Local Partners to Address Homeland Security Issues," DHS blog July 18, 2011, http://blog .dhs.gov/2011/07/fusion-centers-empowering-state-and.html.

26. Ken Dilanian, "Fusion Centers Gather Terrorism Intelligence— and Much More," *Los Angeles Times,* November 15, 2010.

27. Mike German and Jay Stanley, "Fusion Center Update," American Civil Liberties Union, July 2008, www.aclu.org/pdfs/ privacy/fusion_update_20080729.pdf.

28. Bruce Fein, statement before the Subcommittee on Intelligence Sharing and Terrorism Risk Assessment, House Committee on Homeland Security, hearing on "The Future of Fusion Centers: Potential Promise and Dangers," April 1, 2009, http://hsc-democrats.house.gov/hearings/index.asp?ID=186.

29. Alan Feuer, "The Terror Translators," *New York Times,* September 17, 2010.

30. Tom Hays, "FBI No-show in NYC Terror Probe Raises Questions," Associated Press, May 14, 2011.

31. The National Commission on Terrorist Attacks Upon the United States, *The 9/11 Commission Report, authorized ed.* (New York: Norton, 2004), 395.

32. Genevieve Lester, "Societal Acceptability of Domestic Intelligence," in *The Challenge of Domestic Intelligence in a Free Society,* Brain A. Jackson, ed., (Santa Monica, CA: RAND, 2009), 90.

33. U.S. Department of Justice Office of the Inspector General, *A Review of the FBI's Use of National Security Letters: Assessment of Corrective Actions and Examinations* of NSL Usage in 2006, 108, www.justice.gov/oig/special/s0803b/final .pdf). See also Edward C. Liu, *Amendments to the Foreign Intelligence Surveillance Act (FISA) Extended Until June 1, 2015* (Washington, DC: Congressional Research Service, June 16, 2011).

34. See "Domestic Intelligence Surveillance Grew in 2010," entry in the Federation of American Scientists Secrecy News blog, www.fas.org/blog/secrecy/2011/05/2010_fisa.html.

35. Charlie Savage, "F.B.I. Agents Get Leeway to Push Privacy Bounds," *New York Times,* June 13, 2011.

36. Jerry Markon, "Tension Grows Between Calif. Muslims, FBI after Informant Infiltrates Mosque," *Washington Post,* December 5, 2010.

37. The three provisions were technically amendments to the Foreign Intelligence Surveillance Act (FISA); two had been originally enacted as part of the Patriot Act, and one had been included in the Intelligence Reform and Terrorism Prevention Act of 2004. For background see Liu, *Amendments to the Foreign Intelligence Surveillance Act.*

38. Gregory Treverton, "Intelligence Test," *Democracy* 11 (Winter 2009): 65, www.democracyjournal.org/11/6667.php.

39. John Farmer, Jr., "How to Spot a Terrorist," *New York Times,* September 28, 2010.

40. Laura W. Murphy, "Stopping the Flow of Power to the Executive Branch," testimony before the Subcommittee on the Constitutions, Civil Rights and Civil Liberties, Committee on the Judiciary, U.S. House of Representatives, December 9, 2010.

41. "Remarks by the Secretary of Homeland Security Michael Chertoff," Bureau of Justice Assistance, March 14, 2006, at www.dhs.gov/xnews/speeches/speech_0273.shtm.

Critical Thinking

1. Is a new domestic intelligence agency needed? Why?
2. What are some of the underlying problems with the current intelligence?
3. Is the need for domestic security more important than protecting civil liberties? Explain.

Create Central

www.mhhe.com/createcentral

Internet References

Federal Bureau of Investigation
www.fbi.gov/

National Counterterrorism Center
www.nctc.gov/

High Intensity Drug Trafficking Areas (HIDTA) Program
www.whitehouse.gov/ondcp/high-intensity-drug-trafficking-areas -program

Foreign Intelligence Surveillance Court (FISC)
http://epic.org/privacy/terrorism/fisa/fisc.html

El Paso Intelligence Center (EPIC)
www.justice.gov/dea/ops/intel.shtml#EPIC

ERIK J. DAHL is assistant professor of national security affairs at the Naval Postgraduate School in Monterey, California, and a faculty member of the Center for Homeland Defense and Security. His research focuses on intelligence, terrorism, and international and homeland security, and he is currently writing a book titled *Preventing Surprise Attack: Intelligence Failure and Success from Pearl Harbor to the Present.*

Dahl, Erik J. From *Homeland Security Affairs,* vol. 7, The 9/11 Essays, September 2011, pp. 1–9. Copyright © 2011 by Eric Dahl. Reprinted by permission of the author.

Article   Prepared by: Thomas J. Badey, *Randolph-Macon College*

Mining the Masses

SHARON WEINBERGER

Learning Outcomes

After reading this article, you will be able to:

- Explain how Twitter and other types of social media can be used as warning indicators.

- Describe the potential benefits of large-scale data mining for domestic intelligence.

- Discuss potential drawbacks associated with social media monitoring by the government.

Building the Magic Eight Ball

Officials eye exploitation of Twitter, microblogs for intelligence

Last August, a magnitude-5.9 earthquake shook Washington, toppling chimneys, cracking masonry and even damaging the National Cathedral and Washington Monument. In less than a minute, that same earthquake could be felt up the East Coast and in New York.

But for many there and elsewhere, the first tipoff that something had hit the nation's capital was not the shockwave, but the massive outpouring on Twitter.

"The D.C. earthquake marked a new high watermark, which was 7,500 tweets per second," says Sean Love, the geospatial business development director for Northrop Grumman. "The people in New York actually knew about the earthquake via Twitter before they felt the vibration; so the news passed faster than the tremors through the ground."

For many working in the U.S. military and the intelligence community (IC), this realization—that Twitter and other forms of social media can help provide an early warning indicator, like radar spotting an aircraft—is spurring a sudden interest in research to help harness this new information revolution. The departments of Homeland Security and Defense, and the IC, have all started projects designed to harness social media to provide early alerts of potential crises, the next Arab Spring or military conflict.

Mining information from microblogs—like Twitter and other forms of social media ranging from Facebook posts to Wikipedia entries, is not entirely new. Commercial companies have been moving swiftly into social media monitoring for several years, generating algorithms to predict everything from fast-moving clothing trends to movie ticket sales. The field,

often referred to as predictive analytics, involves mining large volumes of public data to make forecasts.

For the past two years, Northrop has been working on its own proprietary technology that it describes as an "open source ingest engine," which collects publicly available data, such as Twitter posts. "One of the nastiest data problems that we have is open-source data," says Northrop's Love, pointing to the deluge of data available on the Web, ranging from simple Google searches to the so-called "deep web."

The company's open-source exploitation system crawls through all the available online data on a particular subject, and then performs an automated triage, sorting and narrowing data. One test case used by Northrop to demonstrate its technology concerns the Zetas drug cartel in Mexico. The company collected data from 300 websites, ranging from those of the U.S. and Mexican governments to social media. "We're able to extract out people, organizations, places, etc., and start to make some sense and curate the data as it's being ingested," says Steve Relitz, principal investigator for the Northrop project.

The goal is to whittle down the amount of relevant data that analysts have to work through to glean important information about the cartel's activities. "That starts to neck down the information flow problem from two billion people on the web down to 34 or 100 documents that an analyst can get their brain wrapped around," says Relitz. "Then you can take this data and export it out to other tools, like link analysis or categorization, to understand what is in the data that you've now constrained."

So far, Northrop has funded the work internally, but it recently applied for the Open Source Indicators program sponsored by the Intelligence Advanced Research Projects Activity (IARPA), a research and development arm of the IC. IARPA is looking for approaches to combining open-source data, from Twitter to public webcams, to help make specific predictions about future events, such as political protests.

Companies are also looking to combine social media and other open-source data with imagery to help the military and IC forecast events geospatially. Herndon, Va.-based GeoEye, for example, has a proprietary program called Signature Analyst that blends the company's experience with imagery and geospatial data with software that makes predictions about human activity, be it refugee movements or roadside bomb attacks.

One example the company is using focuses on the Lord's Resistance Army, a militant group plaguing several African countries. "We were curious if we could figure out the patterns of some of the activities, whether it was hostile activities or recruiting, and we wanted to see if we could predict where that may go into the future," says Will Albers, a senior geospatial analyst at GeoEye. "We also wanted to look at internally displaced persons; we wanted to find out if we could predict where they may go in the future."

Using open-source data from the United Nations, alongside environmental and geospatial data, Signature Analyst generates predictions about where refugees and militants will go. Those predictions are then correlated to specific geographic locations. "It's an area-reduction tool," says Albers. "Instead of putting all my resources in one large area, I can focus on a smaller set and have a higher probability of finding what we're looking for."

As more companies move into predictive analytics, the challenge is both collecting the data and then finding models that can help mine that data to make predictions. One approach taken by Aptima of Woburn, Mass., is to look at the spread of ideas as something akin to the spread of disease. Aptima recently received a contract from the U.S. Office of Naval Research for E-MEME, a tool designed to demonstrate the natural language processing algorithms needed to identify and characterize memes, as in ideas that spread from person to person. The goal is to provide governments with the ability to better prepare for everything from social protests to political crises, according to Robert McCormack, Aptima's principal investigator for the project.

Like diseases, memes can start with a seemingly isolated outbreak and then unexpectedly grow into a proverbial epidemic. "At a fundamental level, there are similar dynamics between the spread of disease and the spread of ideas," McCormack says, pointing to the way pathogens spread by personal contact, whether through shaking hands or kissing.

Aptima is focusing heavily on the Arab Spring that swept across the Middle East and North Africa starting in December 2010. The hope is that E-MEME can provide intel analysts with a way of quickly identifying brewing social or political ideas based on data culled from social media and online news. It could also be used to model the susceptibility of a population to the spread of particular ideas or beliefs.

This work is not without its challenges, McCormack acknowledges. For now, Aptima is looking only at English-language data, and although it plans to expand into foreign languages, automated translation tools are still imperfect. Another challenge that Aptima and other companies face is making sense of the truncated style of Twitter writing. People writing online often misspell words, or they use new or previously unknown abbreviations and style.

Finally, though the company hopes that much can be learned from the spread of disease, McCormack is quick to point out that there are important differences in how diseases, versus ideas, travel. "Multiple exposures to a pathogen monotonically increase the probability of infection," he says of diseases. "But, in the realm of ideas, this is not necessarily the case; multiple encounters with an idea can actually decrease the likelihood of adoption."

It is understanding those differences that is key to making the idea-based models work and be useful.

While companies involved in tracking social media tend to emphasize the applications for humanitarian relief, it is also clear that governments, whether in the U.S. or abroad, will be interested in monitoring social media to help shape military and even law enforcement responses to a crisis or event.

In fact, in January, the U.S. Federal Bureau of Investigation released a call for market information on social media monitoring tools. The agency, according to the announcement, was interested in tools that would allow it to monitor social media and help predict potential "bad actors."

While the defense, intelligence and law enforcement communities clearly are embracing many elements of predictive analytics and social media, at least some senior officials are voicing skepticism. Speaking late last year in San Antonio, James Clapper, director of national intelligence, pointed to the growing importance of social media in events like the Arab Spring. But he also warned that it was no "silver bullet" for understanding the world. Such open-source intel was merely a tool for understanding the underlying dynamics taking place, he said, and not a crystal ball.

"[It] isn't going to predict for you when the tipping point is reached, and some autocrat decides his time's up," Clapper said. "Until we develop more of a mind-reading capability, I don't think that's in the cards."

The first word of a U.S. raid that killed Osama bin Laden came via Twitter from a resident of Abbottabad, Pakistan.

Darpa hosted Network Challenge in 2009, an exercise with teams using social networking to spot 10 red weather balloons across the U.S.

Critical Thinking

1. What are the limits of predictive analytics?
2. How can large scale data mining be used to increase domestic security?
3. Is government monitoring of social media an invasion of privacy? Explain your answer.

Create Central

www.mhhe.com/createcentral

Internet References

Northrop Grumman Geospatial Intelligence
www.is.northropgrumman.com/products/geospatial_intelligence/index.html

The Intelligence Advanced Research Projects Activity (IARPA)
www.iarpa.gov/index.html

GeoEye Enabling Technology
www.geoeye.com/CorpSite/products/enabling-technology/

Aptima's Epidemiological Modeling of the Evolution of MEssages (E-MEME)
www.aptima.com/news/2012/aptima-develops-e-meme-track-infectiousness-ideas-across-groups-and-geography

Unit IX

UNIT

Prepared by: Thomas J. Badey, *Randolph-Macon College*

Homeland Security and Civil Liberties

There is an inherent tension between the need for security and the need to ensure the protection of our civil liberties. Terrorism exploits this tension. Although terrorists may have different objectives, one of the main purposes of terrorism is to provoke government overreaction. As governments indiscriminately target communities and groups that may pose, or are perceived to pose, a potential threat, the rights of innocent people are violated. Terrorists gain support. Violence escalates.

Democratic governments are in a difficult position. If governments fail to protect their citizens from terrorist attacks, they fail to fulfill one of their fundamental obligations and will inevitably lose the support of the public. If governments, in order to prevent terrorism, violate the civil rights of their citizens and threaten civil liberties, they undermine the very principles on which they were founded. There is little room to maneuver between the two; there is little room for error.

Critics of the Bush Administration and its legislative initiatives after 9/11 claim that the U.S. government has violated civil rights and jeopardized civil liberties in its war on terrorism. They accused the Attorney General and the Bush Administration of using "McCarthy-like" tactics in the persecution of minorities. Censurers feared that new powers, derived from legislation like the U.S. Patriot Act, would be used against U.S. citizens. They were concerned about the increased access of government agencies to personal information. And they argued that the indefinite detention of terrorist suspects without charges, justified by the creation of special categories of prisoner, undermined basic constitutional protections.

Supporters of the U.S. Patriot Act claim that it has been instrumental in creating better cooperation and more effective information exchange between the CIA and the FBI. They argue that terrorists hide behind and seek to abuse the inherent protections offered by democratic societies in order to destroy them. They also believe that in order to weed out those who would abuse our system, they need greater access to public records and personal information. Proponents claim that in order

to protect our national security and prevent the occurrence of another 9/11, they must have greater flexibility in the treatment and interrogation of terrorist suspects. They see the creation of special categories of prisoners and the use of prison camps outside of the United States as vital. They see the extraction of valuable information from terrorist suspects without legal constraints as vital to American interests. These supporters believe that our right to be free from terror is more important than a terrorist suspect's right to legal representation and due process. They think that the use of special military courts is essential, as it will allow for the use of classified information by the prosecution while being able to limit the access of the accused.

The articles in this unit reflect the tenor of the ongoing civil rights debate in homeland security. Most are openly critical of the continuing excesses and warn of increased government intrusion into our private lives; few, however, offer viable alternatives to the existing policies.

In the first article of this unit, Donna Lieberman warns that in the wake of 9/11, restrictions on political protest, hyper-aggressive policing and surveillance, and even torture have become the "new normal." She argues that although increased security may be necessary, civil liberties must not be sacrificed. Next, Jacqueline Smith-Mason asserts that modern security and surveillance technologies "blur the line between privacy rights and public safety in the post 9-11 era." She uses the example of airport body scanners to describe the infringement on privacy. The third article focuses on what the ACLU describes as a "widespread abuse of travelers" by Customs and Border Protection (CBP) officers. It examines the case of Anastasio Hernandez Rojas, who died while in the custody of CBP. Finally, Meher Ahmad offers a firsthand account of her experiences with racial profiling at U.S. airports. The article highlights the impact the climate of fear and suspicion has on the certain ethnic groups in the United States and certainly gives us cause for pause and reflection.

Article   Prepared by: Thomas J. Badey, *Randolph-Macon College*

Privacy Rights . . .
Versus Public Safety after 9/11

Jacqueline Smith-Mason

Learning Outcomes

After reading this article, you will be able to:

- Explain the legal foundation for the right to privacy.

- Discuss why full-body scans and pat-downs by the TSA have caused public concern.

- Describe the tension between the need for increased security and the right to privacy.

The increase of global positioning system satellite tracking devices, combined with the ease of data mining, and other technological advances, such as airport security scanners, blur the line between privacy rights and public safety in the post-9/11 era. On the one hand, video surveillance can aid in capturing criminals in the act or on the run and airport magnetometers help prevent terrorists from sneaking a bomb onto a plane. But while most Americans have grown accustomed to surveillance cameras in banks, grocery stores and even their local gym, some travelers began complaining in November 2010 when the Transportation Security Administration (TSA)—building on the Aviation and Transportation Security Act signed into law on Nov. 19, 2001,. in the wake of 9/11—implemented pat-down searches and body-scanning technology at airports as part of the effort to increase homeland security in the war on terror. Americans appreciate the intent of the heightened precautionary measures, of course, but there are those who feel physically violated and publicly humiliated in what they consider an invasion of privacy.

> **History teaches us that grave threats to liberty often come in times of urgency, when constitutional rights seem too extravagant to endure.**
>
> —U.S. Supreme Court Associate Justice Thurgood Marshall, 1989

The U.S. Constitution does not specifically mention the right to privacy. However, the right to privacy seems to fall alongside the freedom of speech (First Amendment), prevention of unreasonable search and seizure (Fourth Amendment), upholding freedom of non-enumerated rights (Ninth Amendment), and entitlement of citizenship (Fourteenth Amendment) cited in certain U.S. Supreme Court decisions including how a state's ban on contraception violated the right to marital privacy (Griswold v. Connecticut, 1965) and how a woman's right to abortion falls within the general right of privacy (Roe v. Wade, 1973). Additionally, Congress passed the Privacy Act in 1974 to protect citizens from unauthorized use of data collected by the federal government, such as by the Social Security Administration or Internal Revenue Service. Over time, the right to privacy has grown to be a core value of U.S. democracy and iconic as baseball and apple pie in American culture.

The underlying premise is that the right to privacy provides Americans with a certain level of comfort and assurance that individuals will not be abused by those in seats of governmental power, for instance, the TSA or the Federal Bureau of Investigation. Yet the American Civil Liberties Union and other watchdog/advocacy groups such as Privacy International and the Center for Democracy and Technology, examining privacy issues on multiple fronts ranging from national security to electronic communications to video surveillance, argue that the potential for abuse exists.

Although the TSA says that digital body images will not be stored and that the possibility of these images ending up on the Internet is nonexistent, it is not being truthful, objectors contend, because it is reasonable to assume that the images might be needed for litigation and, therefore, retained in the event that someone is found to have an explosive. Other self-conscious travelers consider the digital body images embarrassing. And passengers and airline crews have raised questions about exposure to radiation. The TSA, not to mention the White House, counters that these security procedures protect the greater good, even if they make a few people uncomfortable; that even repeated exposure to the radiation is not harmful, citing, as recently as March. experts from the Food and Drug Administration and third-party scientists; and that those leery of full-body scans have an alternative: a full-body pat-down. Some travelers, however, report that the full-body pat-down is invasive and that having a stranger touching them is disconcerting. (In April, an eight-year-old Oregon boy was subject to one on his way to Disneyland; so was a 6-year-old girl in New Orleans. And last November, John Tyner, a 31-year-old software programmer, called the pat-down he received at San Diego International Airport "groping" and "sexual assault.") Thus, these disgruntled travelers must choose between the lesser of two evils if they want to fly, if singled out by security.

Complicating matters is the media hype that focuses on these disgruntled travelers. (For example, the parents of the 6-year-old girl appeared on *Good Morning America,* and ABC News and CNN were only two of many major outlets to report on Tyner.) Yet a *USA Today*/Gallup poll from November 2010 found that 71 percent of travelers who had flown at least twice during that year said the loss of privacy from full-body scans and pat-downs was worth it if it meant preventing an act of terrorism. However, 62 percent of those surveyed said they had not flown in the past 12 months. Yet, in a further twist, 79 percent said they're just as likely to fly now; with all these changes in protocols, as in the past. Meanwhile, "The Department of Homeland Security said that of the estimated 28 million people who flew during the first two weeks of the new security measures, TSA received fewer than 700 complaints," according to Michael A. Memoli and Brian Bennett in *The Los Angeles Times* on Nov. 22, 2010. "Of all the passengers who were asked to submit to a full-body scan," they wrote, "only one percent have chosen to opt out and instead undergo a pat-down."

Another perspective is that flying is a privilege, not a right, and the TSA's first priority must be safety. If someone does not want to be subjected to a pat-down or full-body scan, another mode of transportation should be considered, when feasible. It's not possible to return to pre-9/11 business as usual when it comes to national security and air travel. The enemy and warfare have changed. In order to fight back, adaptation is necessary, and part of that adjustment means giving up a certain level of privacy.

Context and Priorities

Interestingly, while there has been a lot of concern about airport safety versus privacy rights, many people freely post information, photographs and videos, sometimes quite personal, about themselves on social media sites and other components of the Internet and never give this a second thought. Until, that is, they're suspended from school for cyberbullying; fired for criticizing an employer in a blog; threatened by data breaches such as the 77 million user accounts of Sony's video game online network that were hacked into in April; or victimized outright by identity theft, which occurs to more than nine million Americans each year, estimates the Federal Trade Commission. (President George W. Bush issued an executive order in 2006 establishing a task force on identity theft. The

earlier Identity Theft and Assumption Deterrence Act of 1998 made identity theft a federal crime.) Whether we realize it or not, we leave a trail of information for marketing strategists and data mining companies to peruse and exploit. In many ways, that sounds more alarming than intrusive airport security measures. No wonder there's even a National Data Privacy Day, on Jan. 28.

For most people, swiping a discount card at a local grocery store or using an E-Z Pass to move through a tollbooth a few seconds faster than a person paying with currency does not feel like an invasion of privacy. On the other hand, the store can track what, where and when you buy and create a permanent electronic record of your spending habits, and the government knows the make and model of your vehicle and the time and day when you travel through the tollbooth. Certainly, the media and blogosphere devote much attention to airport horror stories. Absolutely, invasive pat-downs are a problem and full-body scans might be worrisome. However, consumers should not ignore how they erode their privacy for the sake of convenience or saving money. In some ways, complaints about the TSA and about how the mechanisms of daily lives leave a data trail to be mined by others are an oxymoron.

Addressing national security in the post-9/11 era requires educating the public and weighing alternatives. Americans can never underestimate the enemy. Who would have thought that terrorists would conceal explosives in their underwear or fly hijacked planes into the World Trade Center? Prior to 9/11, these scenarios would have been viewed as ridiculous. Today, as people commemorate those who perished in the terrorist attacks and in the war on terror, and reflect on the sacrifices made by so many in the spirit of protecting life, liberty and the pursuit of happiness, all levels of government face the difficult challenge of balancing privacy rights with public safety. Likewise, Americans must also ask: What am I willing to give up so that there is never a repeat of 9/11?

Critical Thinking

1. What are the advantages and disadvantages of the use of increasingly invasive technologies used in airport security?
2. Is the use data mining by private industry more acceptable than by governments? Why or why not?
3. What rights are you willing to give up in order to prevent another 9/11?

Create Central

www.mhhe.com/createcentral

Internet References

Transportation Security Administration
   www.tsa.gov
Federal Bureau of Investigations
   www.fbi.gov/

Department of Homeland Security
www.dhs.gov/

Aviation and Transportation Security Act
www.govtrack.us/congress/bills/107/s1447

JACQUELINE SMITH-MASON (Virginia Commonwealth University), a specialist in public policy as well as criminal justice, is Assistant Dean and Director of Undergraduate Research of the Honors College at Virginia Commonwealth University (VCU). She previously taught political science and criminal justice at the VCU L. Douglas Wilder School of Government and Public Affairs. Earlier in her career, Smith-Mason was a policy analyst for the Virginia Criminal Sentencing Commission and assistant director of institutional research at the State Council of Higher Education for Virginia. She serves on the board of directors of Assisting Families of Inmates and the Institutional Review Board at the Virginia Department of Corrections. Smith-Mason earned a B.A. in sociology from George Mason University and an M.S. in criminal justice and a Ph.D. in public policy and administration from VCU. Email her at jsmithmason@vcu.edu.

Article

Prepared by: Thomas J. Badey, *Randolph-Macon College*

On the Boundary of Abuse and Accountability

JOSEPH NEVINS

Learning Outcomes

After reading this article, you will be able to:

- Explain how 9/11 has affected security along the U.S.-Mexican border.

- Describe the events leading to death of Hernández Rojas.

- Identify potential reason for the increases in reports of abuse by CBP officers.

On May 10, the American Civil Liberties Union filed a complaint with the U.S. Department of Homeland Security (DHS), the cabinet-level department that includes U.S. Customs and Border Protection (CBP), the target of the grievance. The 17-page complaint focuses on what the ACLU characterizes as "widespread abuse of travelers" by CBP officers at ports of entry along the U.S.-Mexico boundary.[1]

The alleged abuses—a number of which are graphically detailed in the complaint—include "excessive force; unwarranted, invasive and humiliating personal searches; unjustified and repeated detentions based on misidentification; and the use of coercion to force individuals to surrender their legal rights, citizenship documents, and property."

Because the victims of these abuses typically "find themselves without effective means of seeking redress," asserts the ACLU, the cases are not thoroughly and independently investigated—despite "repeated bilateral commitments between the governments of the United States and Mexico throughout the past three administrations to treat all migrants in a manner that respects their human rights and dignity."

For such reasons, the ACLU takes DHS to task for its lack of "commitment to investigating abuse of power, and the resulting civil and human rights abuses, by CBP officers." The ACLU calls for immediate investigations of the cases detailed in the complaint and demands "a comprehensive investigation of whether CBP Office of Field Operations officers are complying with their obligations under the U.S. Constitution, international law, and agency guidelines." The ACLU hopes the investigation will generate recommendations for institutional changes to border officer training, as well as oversight and accountability mechanisms with the goal of preventing further abuses.

What does accountability mean in such a case, and what should the parameters of the process be—that is, if a key goal is to prevent future instances of brutality? These are among the questions raised by the ACLU's intervention.

Instructive in this regard is one of the most atrocious, high-profile cases highlighted by the ACLU complaint—the killing of Anastasio Hernández Rojas. The complaint comes on the heels of the PBS documentary *Crossing the Line at the Border,* which provides shocking evidence, including witness accounts and new video footage, that U.S. federal agents brutally beat, tased, and ultimately killed Hernández Rojas in May 2010—while he lay on the ground with his arms handcuffed behind his back.[2] The revelations provide a compelling counter to the official tale of what transpired.[3]

Born in Mexico, Hernández Rojas arrived in the United States at the age of 16. For more than 27 years, he lived and labored in el norte, where he married and had five children. In May 2010, after losing his construction job, he was arrested for shoplifting. When a background check showed that he was in the country without official sanction, the police turned him over to federal authorities, who deported him to Mexico. Not willing to accept exile from his wife and children, Hernández Rojas quickly crossed back into the United States, but Border Patrol agents intercepted him in a remote area in southern California as he tried to head home.

At the detention facility, an agent allegedly assaulted and injured Hernández Rojas, which led him to express a desire to file a complaint. That same agent reportedly was one of two who drove him back—alone—to the official port of entry in San Ysidro (the southernmost portion of San Diego) to deport him again. It was there, just a few feet from the actual boundary with Mexico, where the nighttime, deadly assault took place, involving over a dozen agents.

A San Diego County Medical Examiner's report concluded that Hernández Rojas died of a heart attack triggered by the Taser and ruled his death a homicide. (According to an

Amnesty International report, 334 people died in the United States between June 2001 and August 2008 after being shocked with a conducted-energy weapon, such as a Taser—a supposedly nonlethal device.[4]) Hernández Rojas also had broken ribs, several loosened teeth, bruises all over his body and head, and an injury to his spine.

What allowed the beating and electrocution to go legally unchallenged was the uncritical acceptance of the CBP account of events by authorities at various levels. According to the agency's official story, agents did what they did because an unhandcuffed Hernández Rojas "became combative," and the use of batons and the Taser was necessary to "subdue the individual and maintain officer safety."[5]

The blatant nature of the brutality, the cover-up, and what appear to be clear violations of the law have helped to provoke widespread outcry From press conferences, to an online petition, demonstrations, and myriad news reports, a national campaign has emerged, with pressure mounting on federal authorities to conduct a far-reaching investigation into Hernández Rojas's death.[6]

More broadly, advocates—such as John Carlos Frey, a documentary filmmaker and an investigative reporter involved with the making of *Crossing the Line at the Border*—point to an institutional culture of impunity that allows killings by Border Patrol agents to go virtually unexamined outside the agency. In an op-ed in the *Los Angeles Times,* Frey emphasizes that at least eight cases have been documented since May 2010 in which the Border Patrol's extreme use of force has resulted in the death of unarmed and non-combative migrants. He points to the rush to recruit ever more agents in the aftermath of 9/11 and the lower standards of recruitment and training as contributing to the fatal violence.[7]

The CBP has refused to release the names of the agents involved, so it is not known whether relatively new agents recruited and trained under less rigorous criteria are responsible for these deaths. But his argument suggests that better-qualified agents are the answer to the problem. Rigorous applicant screening, good training, and some sort of public oversight mechanism are no doubt preferable to the lack thereof. But in privileging such factors, what gets obscured is the everyday violence—and death and suffering—that the federal boundary and immigration enforcement apparatus causes through its normal practices.

Over the last couple of decades, thousands of migrants have lost their lives trying to traverse the U.S.-Mexico borderlands and enter the United States in order to find work or rejoin loved ones. U.S. authorities have also sent millions into exile abroad, many of them long-standing U.S. residents with almost nonexistent ties to their countries of birth. In the process they have separated hundreds of thousands of children from their parents.[8] They have also reduced the life spans of many deportees: In a particularly egregious case, one of the first people "removed" to Haiti after the Obama administration resumed deportations to the earthquake-ravaged country in 2011 contracted and died of cholera soon after arriving.[9]

The law and the institutionalized nature of the practices that produce these outcomes help to obscure the violence they embody and the related death and suffering. But just because many do not see the violence for what it is—death-producing—does not mean it is anything less.

Since the establishment of the U.S.-Mexico boundary, killing people and denying life has been central to the international divide. Its very foundation necessitated a war of conquest and the dispossession of the Native and Mexican populations in the borderlands. In the face of so many who refuse to accept the original injustice, the maintenance of the U.S.-Mexico border has required various forms of violence on a regular basis ever since. In a world of profound inequality—one predicated on the production of differences such as race, class, and nationality—the boundary reflects and reproduces who gets what rights and resources. It illustrates and shapes the very nature of life and death, and the various states in between.

Anastasio Hernández Rojas was born on the wrong side of the boundary dividing people and places of privilege from those of disadvantage. Like countless others in the eyes of the U.S. ruling class, he thus became disposable. When U.S. authorities deported Hernández Rojas to Mexico and deprived him of his right to be with his family, they effectively denied his right to live. And when they beat and tased him to death, they did so as well.

There is no question that even within the parameters of DHS/CBP policing something is dreadfully wrong—not only at the U.S.-Mexico boundary but throughout the territory in which the CBP is active. As the ACLU asserts, the cases it discusses are "consistent with a pattern of CBP abuse along the border, in detention facilities, and in other parts of the interior."

It is important to bring to light the parties responsible for these abuses and hold them accountable. This will hopefully go a long way to minimizing the reoccurrence of such injustices. But achieving true justice and accountability in cases such as Hernández Rojas's killing requires that we go far beyond the parameters of this particular incident.

It necessitates that we contest the very socio-territorial arrangement that made him—and makes countless others—disposable in the first place. If we fail to do so, we will end up affirming and strengthening a boundary that grants life to some, and consigns so many others to death.

Notes

1. ACLU, "Customs and Border Protection—Complaint," May 10, 2012, available at aclu.org.

2. Elizabeth Aguilera, "New Video in 2010 Taser Border Death," *San Diego Union-Tribune,* April 19, 2012.

3. Brian Epstein, *Crossing the Line at the Border,* PBS, April 20, 2012, available at pbs.org.

4. Amnesty International, *"Less Than Lethal"? The Use of Stun Weapons in US Law Enforcement* (Amnesty International Publications, December 16, 2008).

5. Randal C. Archibold, "San Diego Police Investigate the Death of a Mexican Man Resisting Deportation," *The New York Times,* June 1, 2010.

6. Elizabeth Aguilera, "Border-Death Documentary Helps Launch National Campaign," *San Diego Union-Tribune,* April 24, 2012.

7. John Carlos Frey, "What's Going On With the Border Patrol?" *Los Angeles Times,* April 20, 2012.

8. See Seth Freed Wessler, "U.S. Deports 46K Parents With Citizen Kids in Just Six Months," Colorlines.com, November 3, 2011.

9. Jamilah King, "Haitian Deportee Dies After Cholera Symptoms," Colorlines.com, February 7, 2011.

Critical Thinking

1. What role does the CBP play in homeland security?
2. How has 9/11 changed security along the U.S.-Mexican border?
3. Is the use of force against unarmed and non-combative migrants justified? Support your answer.
4. What factors have led to increased violence against illegal migrants?

Create Central

www.mhhe.com/createcentral

Internet References

American Civil Liberties Union
www.aclu.org/

U.S. Customs and Border Patrol
www.cbp.gov/

Crossing the Line at the Border PBS Video
www.pbs.org/wnet/need-to-know/security/video-first-look-crossing-the-line/13597/

Department of Homeland Security
www.dhs.gov/

North American Congress on Latin America
www.nacla.org/

JOSEPH NEVINS teaches geography at Vasar College in Poughkeepsie. New York. Among his books are *Dy.ng to Live: A Story of U.S. Immigration in an Age of Global Apartheid* (City Lights/Open Media, 2008) and Operation Gatekeeper and Beyond: The War on "Illegals" and the Remaking of the U.S.-Mexico Boundary (Routledge, 2010).

Nevins, Joseph. From *NACLA*, vol. 45, no. 2, Summer 2012, pp. 64–66. Copyright © 2012 by NACLA Report on the Americas. Reprinted by permission.

Article   Prepared by: Thomas J. Badey, *Randolph-Macon College*

My Homeland Security Journey

I grew up in a suburb of Indianapolis called Carmel and never found myself to be any different from my predominantly white friends, except for the odd unibrow joke and clarifying the pronunciation of my name during roll call.

MEHER AHMAD

Learning Outcomes

After reading this article, you will be able to:

- Describe the personal experiences of Meher Ahmad after 9/11.

- Explain how airport security has changed post 9/11

- Discuss the impact of racial profiling on U.S. citizens of foreign descent.

On 9/11, hours after our teacher choked back tears to tell our fourth grade class the Twin Towers had been attacked, we all sat watching the news on the television. Some of us were crying, but we didn't quite comprehend why. A clip came on of people cheering around the world. First there was a reel of young Palestinians clamoring for the camera's attention. Someone in class pointed to the TV and said, "They did it!" I thought, "Why would they be celebrating when all these people are covered in ash and my teacher is crying?"

Then the newscast cut to a similar crowd of Pakistani boys jumping on cars in the street. Whoever pointed at the Palestinians was still pointing at the TV, this time suggesting that Pakistanis had done it. I could not even begin to grasp why Pakistanis would be happy about the attack, let alone what they had to do with all of the people running from a collapsing building in New York. Even if no one turned to me after the clip ended, I was acutely aware of the fact that I was Pakistani and not American.

Nearly eleven years after 9/11, virtually every Pakistani family in the area has a Homeland Security tale to tell. My Homeland Security journey began in the summer of 2002, the first time I flew since 9/11 for a family vacation to Hawaii. I was eleven years old. At the airport waiting to check in, I was playing Game Boy with my kid brother on the floor, ignoring the exchange the airline official was having with my parents.

But when I looked up, the attendant was flustered and scared, I could tell. A feeling of panic reached my stomach, which only worsened when a police officer showed up. My brother and I wondered, "Why are we under arrest?" "What's happening?" "What's wrong?" We tugged at our parents' pant legs, and they told us sweetly in Urdu that we weren't under arrest and to please stop bothering them, be quiet, and sit over there, for God's sake.

My parents tell me now that the FBI was crosschecking our names, and while we waited for hours at the check-in desk, an agent in the Washington, D.C., office verified our identities. After a while, a friendly looking man in a white shirt and blue jeans escorted us to our newly booked flight, as our original one had taken off long ago. He told us it was most likely my name that had set off the security flag.

The man we sat next to on the flight wasn't an ordinary passenger. My mom murmured to me as we squeezed past him that it figures she would be the one person next to such a big man on the long flight. He answered in perfect Urdu, our secret language for making fun of strangers in public. With a visage not unlike Brad Pitt's, he was the last person I would think to speak Urdu fluently, but after describing to us his time in Islamabad as a former CIA agent, I could see why he did. Strange as it was, we arrived in Hawaii, and I shelved the journey in the back of my mind.

Suspicion greeted us every time we traveled, and in my teenage years I responded with sarcasm. I'd ask the TSA agent why I was being stopped, just so I could roll my eyes when they repeated it was a random search.

A few years of that bratty attitude didn't bring me any satisfaction, and now as an experienced navigator of airport security, I remain as polite and cooperative as possible. After all, it isn't the fault of the TSA agent, who probably just wants to go home, that I'm being stopped. Instead of a smirk, I sport a smile. I know the drill, so let's get this over with.

As I approached the row of agents in Chicago O'Hare this winter, I made bets with my father and brother about my chances of getting stopped. We reached the desk and slipped our passports through the glass. A few minutes after looking through my family's passports, the immigration officer finally picked mine up. He glanced up at me; I was staring intently back at him so as to signal complete confidence, a cover for the self-consciousness seasoned with a hint of doubt that creeps into my head every time I hand my passport over to American immigration. It's like slowing down when you see a cop car in the rearview mirror even if you're driving five below.

I ran a reel of situations through my head that the agent might misconstrue. What if my interviews with women in the Islamic Action Front in Jordan could be used against me? What if the fact that I was in Cairo after the Coptic riots was misconstrued? I went to the West Bank; could that be it?

The immigration officer made a brief phone call to a shadowy figure that I liken to the Wizard of Oz. I won the bet. We were escorted to the cubicle-like office of O'Hare's Homeland Security.

I tried to make myself comfortable on the impossibly narrow benches in the waiting room and glanced at a few posters with waving American flags that reminded me of my rights within that space. I was a suspect yet again.

A month before I landed in O'Hare, I found myself in a similarly tiny cordoned-off area where unsightly travelers like myself were corralled at the Allenby Bridge into Israel from Jordan. Surrounded by Arabs, mostly Palestinians who had likely been waiting for more than an hour before I joined them, I noticed the crowd wasn't frustrated or defeated. They were playing games on their cell phones, reading the newspaper, conversing with their neighbors. It didn't seem to bother them that they had been waiting for so long; it was the norm.

I had known that I was going to join them in their wait when the Israeli immigration officer opened my passport. I'm used to the disappointed look on security personnel's faces when I hand them my passport because before 2004, I carried a Pakistani one. Pakistani passports are notoriously easy to forge. On my old passport, my name was misspelled (written in ballpoint pen), crossed out, and rewritten with an arrow pointing to the correct spelling. I could understand why its validity was always in question.

But now, with a fresh American passport and citizenship, I expected to be presumed innocent. This thing has holograms and chips in it: What more could you want? But my passport isn't the kind an immigration officer likes to see:

Name: Ahmad, Noor Meher

Birthplace: Islamabad, Pakistan

Places Traveled: Pakistan, Jordan, Egypt, Turkey, Lebanon, Israel, United Kingdom

In Israel, they didn't pretend that the thorough and condescending questioning of my identity was random, as I'm always assured in the United States. It was blatantly discriminatory,

and as I waved to my Caucasian American friends, who told me before they would wait in solidarity outside of the terminal, I was strangely comforted by the openly racist security policy of the IDF.

Back in O'Hare, the scene was tenser. My flight had come from Istanbul and it was full of people that ended up in the same waiting room as us. Though nobody told us not to talk, everyone kept quiet and spoke only in hushed tones. After an hour of anxiously watching the clock get closer to the time our connecting flight departed, I saw the Homeland Security agent come toward me to give me my passport back. He was smiling as if he just handed me a steaming apple pie.

After sprinting through the terminal, we ended up missing our flight, and that's when the helplessness of our situation hit me. There was nothing I could have done to get out of that gray waiting room faster. I couldn't prove to the agent that I was an all-American girl, that I drink Coca-Cola and frequently indulge in *The Real Housewives* series. I couldn't avoid my own identity.

Eleven years after my classmate pointed his finger at Pakistanis celebrating 9/11, I've now encountered a growing mass of finger-pointers. It used to be the only place I felt uncomfortably different was at an Arby's in rural Indiana. Now, I can sense the glares on my back as agents search my bags in plain view of my fellow passengers. It doesn't feel like they'll stop pointing any time soon.

Critical Thinking

1. How effective is racial profiling as a tool in airport security?
2. Why did Ahmad feel less intimidated when questioned by Israeli than U.S. security?
3. How does racial profiling impact U.S. citizens of foreign descent?

Create Central

www.mhhe.com/createcentral

Internet References

Israel Defense Forces
www.idf.il/english/
Transportation Security Administration
www.tsa.gov
U.S. Citizenship and Immigration Services
www.uscis.gov/portal/site/uscis
The American Immigration Council
www.americanimmigrationcouncil.org/

MEHER AHMAD, an intern at The Progressive, is a junior at the University of Wisconsin-Madison majoring in International Studies and Middle East Studies.

Ahmad, Meher. Reprinted by permission from *The Progressive*, May 2012, pp. 30–32. Copyright © 2012 by The Progressive, 409 E Main St, Madison, WI 53703. www.progressive.org

Unit X

UNIT

Prepared by: Thomas J. Badey, *Randolph-Macon College*

The Future of Homeland Security

A decade after its initial conception, the Department of Homeland security has become an integral part of the U.S. national security structure. As the DHS continues to mature, questions about the long-term goals of the department continue to surface. The DHS faces monumental challenges. It must not only protect the United States from future terrorist attacks but it must also respond effectively to both natural and human-made disasters. Despite its best efforts, the DHS continues to be the focal point of public criticism. How well it will be able to accomplish its mission in the future remains to be seen.

The long-term success of U.S. homeland security policy depends on four main factors: the relative effectiveness of the Department of Homeland Security, the future developments in international terrorism, continued public support of homeland security policies, and, most importantly, its ability to convince the public and policymakers that the billions of dollars spent annually on homeland security are well spent.

The future of homeland security policy depends on the ability of the DHS to continue to mature and complete the ongoing merge into an effective organization. In this multiyear process, Janet Napolitano, like her predecessors, must continue to reform, restructure, and integrate what once were 22 different agencies into a cohesive unit capable of protecting the homeland. Organizational cultures, past interagency rivalries, and turf wars with other government agencies must be overcome in order for DHS to be effective.

The success of U.S. homeland security policy also depends on future developments in the evolution of international terrorism. While the United States has focused almost exclusively on al-Qaeda and Islamic fundamentalist-inspired terrorism around the world, significant changes have taken place in Asia and Latin America. New leaders are increasingly challenging U.S. hegemony, as popular discontent with U.S. policies is on the rise. The proliferation of nuclear technologies has given rise to increased concerns about the use of weapons of mass destruction (WMD) by international terrorists. For the DHS, changes in international terrorism pose a two-fold problem. If terrorists choose to limit their activities and focus on attacks against U.S. resources abroad, political and economic support for domestic security may eventually wane. If terrorists manage to repeatedly

attack targets in the United States, the competence and utility of the new department will soon be questioned.

The success of homeland security is also dependent on public support. After the attacks on 9/11, there was a tremendous amount of support for homeland security policy. Although some people voiced concerns about actions taken by the Bush Administration, most accepted the fact that the primary motive for these actions was to protect the American people. Most Americans trusted the U.S. government to act in their best interest. U.S. policies overseas and scandals at home have increasingly eroded this trust. Increased domestic surveillance, as well as indefinite detentions and accusations of torture and abuse of prisoners, continue to undermine public support for the administration and its homeland security policy. In the long run, homeland security will only be successful if it has the support and trust of the American people.

Last, and most important, in order for the DHS to be successful, it must convince the public and policymakers that the billions of dollars spent annually on homeland security are necessary and well spent. As the U.S. national debt continues to rise above $16 trillion, increased scrutiny of national security spending is inevitable. While in the first decade of its existence the primary focus of DHS has been on the integration of multiple agencies and their missions, much of the next decade will likely focus on streamlining its bureaucracies and increased efficiency. As the decade of almost unlimited security spending reaches its end, the DHS will inevitably have to learn how to do more with less.

The articles in this unit examine the prospects for the future of homeland security. The first article focuses on an amendment added to the Department of Homeland Security Authorization Act of 2011 designed to evaluate the DHS's analytical capabilities and to evaluate cost, effectiveness, and efficiency of the DHS's analytical corps. Last, Stephen Flynn argues that the United States "has made a mess of homeland security." He believes that the United States should recalibrate its approach to homeland security by asking its citizens to "unite in preparing for future emergencies." Both articles highlight the continuing need for a long-term strategic vision of how homeland security should be structured.

Article   Prepared by: Thomas J. Badey, *Randolph-Macon College*

A Report Card for Homeland Security

Are our intelligence analysts really keeping us safer? Or are they wasting money and providing "Google-deep" information? A new amendment promises to find out.

DAVEED GARTENSTEIN-ROSS

Learning Outcomes

After reading this article, you will be able to:

- Identify four areas of the DHS's analytical capability under review.

- Identify some of the major problems in this area.

- Discuss potential reasons for the problems with the DHS's analytical capability.

While the U.S. faces severely constrained resources, the threat posed by violent non-state actors is unlikely to disappear soon. America is shackled by an economy that's in shambles and over $14 trillion in national debt; one of al Qaeda's recent adaptations has been to leverage this weakened state, executing *smaller but more frequent attacks* designed to drive up the costs of providing security, and thus grind down the U.S. economy. In this challenging environment, the agencies charged with safeguarding our national security will be forced to do more with less. An amendment to the Department of Homeland Security Authorization Act of 2011 that Sen. Tom Coburn (R.-Okla.) notified the Senate's Homeland Security and Governmental Affairs Committee of on Tuesday provides a laudable first step.

Co-sponsored by Senators Scott Brown (R.-Mass.) and Ron Johnson (R.-Wisc.), the amendment calls for the Government Accountability Office, within a year of enactment of the Act, to submit an unclassified report on DHS's analytic capabilities. The four major areas that the report would analyze are DHS's reliance on contractors for its intelligence analysis, whether DHS's analysts are developed with an adequate level of specialization, whether parts of DHS's intelligence analysis organization overlap or are duplicative, and the accuracy and usefulness of DHS's analytic products. All four of these areas are important, and worthy of the GAO's examination.

A key question about the massive expansion of the intelligence community that occurred after 9/11 is whether we are truly better off because of it. Is our raw intelligence better? Has our analysis improved? Is it having a significant operational impact? These subjects must be explored with diligence and humility in the age of austerity that we're entering.

All four questions that Sen. Coburn's amendment would have the GAO explore constitute important subjects. Contractors are increasingly looking like a permanent part of the national security apparatus. In February of last year, Senators Joseph Lieberman and Susan Collins, the chairman and ranking member of the Homeland Security and Governmental Affairs Committee, *were "astounded" to learn* that there were more contractors than civilian employees working for DHS.

One problem is that contractors are simply more expensive, on average, than are federal employees. A report submitted by the Senate Select Committee on Intelligence *noted* in 2007 that "the average annual cost of a U.S. government civilian employee is $126,500, while the average annual cost of a 'fully loaded' (including overhead) core contractor is $250,000." Thus, as of 2008, contractors comprised about 29 percent of the workforce in the Office of the Director of National Intelligence's agencies, but they received pay equal to 49 percent of the agencies' personnel budgets. Understanding the role contractors play within DHS is a critical part of trimming its budget (though I'm skeptical that the problem can be satisfactorily addressed absent civil service reform).

The second question posed by Sen. Coburn's amendment, whether DHS's analysts are adequately specializing, is similarly important. There is currently a distinct lack of specialists within the U.S. intelligence community writ large, and the tendency to produce generalists can result in "Google-deep" conclusions that analysts with a bit more background and context would recognize as flawed.

Governmental analysts I've spoken with tell me that they see few professional incentives to develop into specialists. This can drive up costs when the intelligence community has to hire contractors as specialists, particularly if those doing the hiring have difficulty telling the difference between a good and a bad specialist. When this is the case, more outside experts are hired than are needed. Thus there is dead weight. Are professional incentives for specialization better within DHS than in other analytic shops, or can they be improved?

The third question that Sen. Coburn's amendment poses is whether parts of DHS's intelligence analysis organization overlap, or are redundant. One U.S. intelligence analyst told me that within the overall apparatus, there is "a massive amount of very general, duplicative work that could be streamlined just through proper coordination."

In addition to the inefficiencies associated with this situation, analytical shortcomings are produced—and Sen. Coburn's amendment also seeks to assess the overall usefulness of DHS's analytic products. In a culture of non-specialists, analysts may be dissuaded from drawing controversial conclusions. According to insiders, platitudes are often used in lieu of actual analysis when analysts lack the confidence and experience to take positions that some might regard as controversial. This can lead to errors.

It goes without saying that not all analysts fall into this trap. There are many astute intelligence analysts within government. But the current culture of intelligence analysis has often produced suboptimal work product, something that should give rise to questions about systemic fixes.

DHS's analytic corps is not the only part of the intelligence apparatus of which these questions should be asked, but it's necessary to start somewhere. Nor should reform of the intelligence community be undertaken lightly. But Sen. Coburn's amendment offers a solid first step toward obtaining the detailed knowledge of the intelligence apparatus necessary to move toward a more skilled corps of analysts with deeper knowledge of the areas they're studying. Ultimately, doing so won't just improve our intelligence, but will also allow us to adapt better to al Qaeda and other foes engaged in asymmetric warfare. It will save us money in the long run.

Critical Thinking

1. How can homeland security costs be reduced without increasing vulnerability?
2. Has the Department of Homeland Security made us better equip to identify potential threats? Why or why not?
3. Why does the DHS really need its own analytical capability?

Create Central

www.mhhe.com/createcentral

Internet References

Department of Homeland Security Authorization Act of 2011
www.opencongress.org/bill/112-s1546/show

U.S. Senate Committee on Homeland Security and Governmental Affairs
www.hsgac.senate.gov/

U.S. Senate Select Committee on Intelligence
www.intelligence.senate.gov/

Department Homeland Security
www.dhs.gov

Office of the Director of National Intelligence
www.dni.gov/index.php/about/organization

Article

Prepared by: Thomas J. Badey, *Randolph-Macon College*

Recalibrating Homeland Security
Mobilizing American Society to Prepare for Disaster

Stephen Flynn

Learning Outcomes

After reading this article, you will be able to:

- Identify Flynn's main criticisms of homeland security.

- List the changes Flynn suggests to improve homeland security.

- Discuss why or why not Flynn's suggestion will be followed.

The United States has made a mess of homeland security. This is hardly surprising. The policymakers responsible for developing homeland security policy in the wake of September 11, 2001, did so under extraordinary conditions and with few guideposts. The Bush administration's emphasis on combating terrorism overseas meant that it devoted limited strategic attention to the top-down law enforcement and border-focused efforts of the federal departments and agencies assigned new homeland security responsibilities. President Barack Obama has largely continued his predecessor's policies, and congressional oversight has been haphazard. As a result, nearly a decade after al Qaeda struck the World Trade Center and the Pentagon, Washington still lacks a coherent strategy for harnessing the nation's best assets for managing risks to the homeland—civil society and the private sector.

For much of its history, the United States drew on the strength of its citizens in times of crisis, with volunteers joining fire brigades and civilians enlisting or being drafted to fight the nation's wars. But during the Cold War, keeping the threat of a nuclear holocaust at bay required career military and intelligence professionals operating within a large, complex, and highly secretive national security establishment. The sheer size and lethality of U.S. and Soviet nuclear arsenals rendered civil defense measures largely futile. By the time the Berlin Wall came down and the Soviet Union collapsed, two generations of Americans had grown accustomed to sitting on the sidelines and the national security community had become used to operating in a world of its own.

To an extraordinary extent, this same self-contained Cold War–era national security apparatus is what Washington is using today to confront the far different challenge presented by terrorism. U.S. federal law enforcement agencies, the border agencies, and the Transportation Security Administration (TSA) are subsumed in a world of security clearances and classified documents. Prohibited from sharing information on threats and vulnerabilities with the general public, these departments' officials have become increasingly isolated from the people that they serve.

This is the wrong approach to protecting the homeland. Even with the help of their state and local counterparts, these federal agencies cannot detect and intercept every act of terrorism. Police, firefighters, and other emergency responders will not always be immediately at hand to protect and rescue those in harm's way. Professionals are usually not the first responders to terrorist attacks and other disasters. A sidewalk T-shirt vendor, not a police patrol officer, sounded the alarm about Faisal Shahzad's SUV in his May 2010 car-bombing attempt on New York's Times Square. Courageous passengers and flight-crew members, not a federal air marshal, helped disrupt the suicide-bombing attempt by Umar Farouk Abdulmutallab aboard Northwest Airlines Flight 253 on Christmas Day 2009. It often falls to ordinary citizens—family, friends, neighbors, and bystanders—to lend a hand in times of crisis.

Coping with terrorism requires localized, open, and inclusive engagement of civil society. But the U.S. government has neither adequately informed nor empowered civilians to play a meaningful role in defending the country. To better involve civilians in homeland security, the United States must remove the inadvertent obstacles it has placed in their way. Citizens, in turn, must be willing to grapple with the risks they and their communities are likely to face and embrace a more active role in preparing for disasters.

Developing Trust

To improve the nation's capacity to manage dangers, federal agencies must avoid alienating the very people they are responsible for protecting. Regrettably, Washington's growing homeland security bureaucracy has largely overlooked the need to garner support from the public. New security measures are advanced without spelling out the vulnerability that they are designed to address. The American public has generally tolerated this thus far, but presuming the public's submissiveness risks breeding resentment and lack of cooperation over time. Alternatively, when citizens understand the appropriateness of a given security measure, they will be more willing to collaborate to achieve its goal.

When the TSA introduced full-body x-ray scanners and enhanced pat-downs at U.S. airports last fall, it prioritized public compliance over public acceptance. Given the coercive tools at its disposal, the TSA correctly presumed that it could force civilian acquiescence to this more intrusive passenger screening process. But the marginal additional capabilities provided by the scanners and pat-downs came at a heavy cost. Public confusion and anger over the new program, expressed by the Thanksgiving holiday travel opt-out campaign, spawned a vocal minority that has sown general public skepticism and may impede future U.S. government efforts to improve homeland security.

In explaining its security measures to the public, the government should not promise more than it can deliver. U.S. officials should avoid making the kind of statements issued frequently after September 11 to the effect that terrorists have to be right only once, whereas U.S. officials have to be right 100 percent of the time. Such declarations might demonstrate firm resolve, but they set an impossible standard; no security regime is foolproof. Common drug-smuggling techniques can evade the new scanning technology at U.S. airports. Radiation portal monitors, deployed with much fanfare at U.S. seaports, are unlikely to detect shielded nuclear material, raising the possibility that a nuclear weapon or dirty bomb encased in lead could pass through undetected. Public officials should acknowledge the potential limits of these technologies and other security protocols in deterring terrorists. Creating unrealistic expectations guarantees anger, disappointment, and mistrust should a terrorist attack succeed.

U.S. policymakers should also refrain from measures that provide the optics of security rather than real security. For example, the presence of cement barriers outside a train station may reassure daily commuters. But if those barriers are not anchored to the ground, an explosive-laden truck could ram them aside and make it to the station's entrance. The ensuing tragedy would leave commuters feeling rightfully deceived and the families of victims outraged. Security protocols must survive a "morning-after test"; that is, they should be able to withstand a postmortem by the public about their adequacy, even if they failed to thwart an attack. If the post-incident assessment deems the security measures to be lacking credibility, there will be hell to pay.

Open Up

National Security officials should also resist the secrecy reflex. U.S. intelligence and federal law enforcement agencies perform too much homeland security work behind closed doors. Their proclivity to operate in a world of restricted documents and windowless rooms often leaves both the private sector and the general public out of the loop.

On the surface, it seems sensible to avoid releasing information about vulnerabilities or security measures that potential adversaries could exploit. But this insularity often undermines the defense of critical infrastructure, such as seaports, dams, and waterworks. In determining the best way to protect a suspension bridge, for example, the bridge's chief engineer is likely to have ideas that would not occur to a law enforcement or military professional working in the Department of Homeland Security. But government officials frequently fail to consult that engineer. They will share security information only with vetted company security officers, who in turn are barred from passing this information on to senior executives and managers who do not hold active security clearances. As a result, investment and operational decisions are often made with scant attention paid to the potential security stakes.

The U.S. government should increase its transparency with the broader public as well. Many policymakers believe that candor about potential dangers may generate excessive public fear. Yet the secrecy reflex often contributes to public anxiety. People are most frightened when they sense their vulnerability to threats but feel powerless to address them. U.S. officials have stated for nearly a decade that terrorism is a clear and present danger, but they have given citizens little information about how to cope with that hazard. Instead, citizens are told to proceed with their daily routines because the government is hard at work protecting them. The psychological effect of this is similar to that of a doctor telling a patient that she is suffering from a potentially life-threatening illness but providing only vague guidance about how to combat it. No one wants to receive disturbing news from his physician, but a prognosis becomes less stressful when doctors provide patients with all the details, a clear description of the available treatments, and the opportunity to make decisions that allow the patient to assert some personal control over the outcome. In the same way, the U.S. government can decrease fears of terrorism by giving the American public the information it needs to better withstand, rapidly recover from, and adapt to the next major terrorist attack.

Flight attendants routinely tell passengers that they may need to use their seat cushions to stay afloat in the event of an emergency water landing. Although escaping a plane in the water is a frightening scenario, this safety instruction does not generate panic among passengers. Similarly, there is no reason why civilians should not be told what bombs and detonators look like, on the very remote chance that someone like the "Christmas Day bomber" ends up seated next to one of them on a plane. Having better-informed airport workers, flight crews, and passengers could prove a far more effective safeguard than deploying hundreds of new body scanners at airports.

Avoid Overreacting

Washington must also avoid overstating the threat of terrorism. Terrorist attacks are not all the same. Small-scale attacks of limited destructiveness pose the most likely terrorist danger to the United States today. Aligned groups or other terrorist organizations may still organize catastrophic attacks, but such ambitious terrorist operations require groups of operatives with capable leaders, communications with those overseeing the planning, and time to conduct surveillance and to rehearse. Money, identity documents, and safe houses for operatives must be secured, and other logistical needs must be met. All this effort creates multiple opportunities for intelligence and law enforcement agents to disrupt plots before they come to fruition.

In the face of these challenges, terrorists have adapted their tactics. Now, attacks on U.S. soil are likely to be perpetrated by homegrown operatives who act alone or with one or two accomplices. Such operations are difficult to detect and intercept. Yet lone gunmen and suicide bombers can inflict only limited damage. Tragically, such attacks will destroy property and take innocent lives. But Mother Nature generates far more frequent and disastrous incidents. Virtually no terrorist scenario could equal the devastation caused by the March 2011 earthquake and tsunami that hit northern Japan. Similarly, it is hard to imagine that a terrorist armed with a weapon of mass destruction could produce more casualties than a global outbreak of a virulent strain of the flu virus: epidemiologists estimate that as many as 100 million people died of the Spanish flu in 1918. Even when terrorism is measured against other national security challenges, some perspective is warranted. During the height of the Cold War, a nuclear exchange with the Soviet Union would have left two-thirds of the American people dead and much of the world in ruins. That was a true existential danger, and one that the most ambitious terrorists cannot hope to match.

Similarly, U.S. policymakers must avoid overreacting to terrorist incidents when they do occur. In the aftermath of the bombing attempt aboard Northwest Airlines Flight 253, congressional leaders on both the left and the right declared it better to overreact than underreact to the risk of terrorism. This rare bipartisan consensus was unfortunately entirely wrong. Terrorism is fueled by the confidence that Americans will react to it by embracing draconian measures that damage the U.S. economy. Al Qaeda's October 2010 attempt to bomb airplanes by hiding explosives in ink cartridges shipped from Yemen was consistent with this strategy. The terrorists hoped that the mid-air destruction of any plane—cargo or civilian—would spur U.S. officials to respond with costly and disruptive methods that would undermine the movement of global cargo. In other words, their strategy depends on how Americans react—or, more precisely, overreact—to acts of terrorism.

Yet such smaller-scale, less destructive, and less lethal operations, even if unsuccessful, can produce this overreaction only when overwrought media coverage and political recriminations generate a rush to deploy expensive and often counterproductive new defenses. Conversely, a response of confident resilience to acts of terrorism would provide a real measure of deterrence by demonstrating that such attacks will not achieve their desired ends. Although the United States cannot prevent every act of terrorism, it can control how it responds to them.

The Way Forward

The U.S. Government can avoid hindering its own actions to protect the homeland by building trust and setting proper expectations with civilians. To develop a comprehensive homeland security strategy, however, Washington should place greater emphasis on developing adequate societal resilience. Resilience is the capacity of individuals, communities, companies, and the government to withstand, respond to, adapt to, and recover from disasters. Since disruptions can come not just from terrorism but also from natural and accidental sources as well, advancing resilience translates into building a general level of preparedness. Ideally, a program of resilience would address the most likely risks that people, cities, or enterprises may face. This would minimize the potential for complacency while assuring a level of basic skills, such as first aid and effective emergency communications, which are useful no matter the hazard.

Building societal resilience requires a bottom-up, open, and participatory process—that is, the exact inverse of the way U.S. policymakers have approached homeland security to date. A program of resilience mandates individuals, communities, and companies to take precautions within their respective areas of control. Success is measured by the continuity or rapid restoration of important systems, infrastructure, and societal values in the face of an attack or other danger.

Resilience begins on the level of individuals. A program of resilience would promote self-reliance in the face of unexpected events, encouraging civilians to remain calm when the normal rhythms of life get interrupted. It would also teach individuals to make themselves aware of the risks that may confront them and to be resourceful by learning how to react to crises. And it would make preparedness a civic virtue by instructing civilians to refrain from requesting professional assistance unless absolutely necessary, thus freeing up manpower for those in the greatest need.

Promoting individual resilience involves acknowledging that many Americans have become increasingly complacent and helpless in the face of large-scale danger. Reversing this trend demands a special emphasis on educating young people. Students should learn to embrace preparedness as both a practical necessity and an opportunity to serve others. These students, in turn, can teach their parents information-age survival skills, such as texting, which may offer the only means to communicate when cellular networks are overloaded (800 text messages consume the same bandwidth as a one-minute call). As demonstrated in the aftermath of the 2010 Haitian earthquake and the Deepwater Horizon oil spill that same year, social media are transforming the way rescuers and survivors respond to crises. These new tools have the power to turn traditional, top-down emergency management on its head.

Resilience also applies to communities. The U.S. government can promote resilience on the communal level by providing meaningful incentives for collaboration across the public, private, and nonprofit sectors before, during, and after disasters. Much like at the individual level of resilience, communities should aspire to cope with disasters without outside assistance to the greatest degree possible.

Building resilient communities requires providing community leaders with tools to measure and improve their preparedness based on a widely accepted standard. The Community and Regional Resilience Institute, a government-funded research program based at Tennessee's Oak Ridge National Laboratory, has spearheaded an attempt to define the parameters of resilience, modeled on the method by which fire and building codes were created and are maintained. It has drawn on a network of former governors and former and current mayors, emergency planners, and academics to develop detailed guidelines and comprehensive supporting resources that will allow communities to devise resilience plans tailored to their needs. Other countries, including Australia, Israel, and the United Kingdom, have instituted similar programs. Federal and state governments could provide communities that implement a comprehensive risk-awareness strategy and a broad-based engagement program with tangible financial rewards, such as reduced insurance premiums and improved bond ratings.

U.S. companies compose the third tier of resilience. Resilient companies should make business continuity a top priority in the face of a disaster. They should invest in contingency planning and employee training that allow them to serve and protect their customers under any circumstance. Corporations must also study the capabilities of and partner with their suppliers and surrounding communities. Much like individuals and communities, corporations with resilience would possess the ability to sustain essential functions and quickly resume their operations at full capacity after a disaster. Resilience may also bring financial benefits to companies able to demonstrate their dependability in the wake of a major disruption. Such companies are likely to experience an increase in market share by maintaining regular customers and attracting new ones as well.

Although most large corporations invest in measures that improve resilience, smaller companies—which are the backbone of local economies and yet are constrained by limited resources—generally do not. But small businesses can rectify this in a low-cost manner by creating a buddy system between companies located in different regions. For instance, a furniture store in Gulfport, Mississippi, that may fall victim to an August hurricane could partner with a furniture store in Nashville, Tennessee, that may suffer from spring flooding. These businesses would agree to assist each other in providing backup support for data, personnel, customers, and suppliers in the event of a disaster.

Instilling Resilience

To his credit, Obama explicitly identified resilience as a national security imperative in his May 2010 National Security Strategy. Homeland Security Secretary Janet Napolitano did the same in the February 2010 Quadrennial Homeland Security Review.

Both have made frequent references to the importance of resilience in their speeches. But neither the federal bureaucracy nor the general public appears to be paying much attention.

The approaching tenth anniversary of September 11 will provide Obama with an opportunity to recalibrate the nation's approach to homeland security. While honoring the enormous sacrifice of the U.S. armed forces and those who have been working to protect the U.S. homeland, he should ask citizens to step forward and assume their own unique role. For individuals, families, neighbors, employers, and employees, the way to honor the lives so tragically lost in the Twin Towers, in the Pentagon, and aboard United Airlines Flight 93 is to unite in preparing for future emergencies. The president should ask citizens from every walk of life to embrace a personal commitment to making the United States more resilient.

When passengers enter the new body scanners at U.S. airports, they are directed by TSA screeners to hold their hands above their heads and stand still while their images are taken. The position closely resembles the universal stance for surrendering—undoubtedly why many find the process so uncomfortable. An emphasis on resilience, by contrast, is consistent with the U.S. tradition of grit, determination, and hope in the face of adversity. When tested, Americans have always bounced back better and stronger. It is long past time for Washington to stop treating civil society as a child to be sheltered and to acknowledge the limits and counterproductive consequences of relying so heavily on protective measures. In good times and bad, the greatest asset of the United States has always been its people.

Critical Thinking

1. What is the citizen's role in fighting terrorism?
2. How have government actions eroded citizens' trust?
3. Should Homeland Security be reformed? How?

Create Central

www.mhhe.com/createcentral

Internet References

Northwest Airlines Flight 253 Terror Plot Christmas Day 2009
    http://janetnapolitano.com/northwest-airlines-flight-253-terror-plot-christmas-day-2009
Oak Ridge National Labotory
    www.ornl.gov/
The National Commission on the Deepwater Horizon Oil Spill
    www.oilspillcommission.gov/
May 2010 National Security Strategy
    www.whitehouse.gov/sites/default/files/rss_viewer/national_security_strategy.pdf
February 2010 Quadrennial Homeland Security Review
    www.dhs.gov/quadrennial-homeland-security-review-qhsr